BEER-CAN CHICKEN

BEER-CAN CHICKEN

[AND 74 OTHER OFFBEAT RECIPES FOR THE GRILL]

STEVEN RAICHLEN

ILLUSTRATIONS BY JIM LAMBRENOS

WORKMAN PUBLISHING • NEW YORK

TO BARBARA,
The fire in my barbecue,
The bubbles in my beer.

Copyright © 2002 by Steven Raichlen
Illustrations © 2002 by Jim Lambrenos

This book references Web sites that may be of interest to the reader.
Every effort has been made to ensure that the information about these
Web sites is correct and up-to-date as of press time.

Library of Congress Cataloging-in-Publication Data
Raichlen, Steven.
Beer-can chicken : and 74 other offbeat recipes for the grill / Steven Raichlen.
p. cm.
Includes index.
ISBN 0-7611-2016-5
1. Barbecue cookery. 2. Cookery (Chicken). I. Title

TX840.B3 R3553 2002
641.5'784—dc21   2002016845

Cover design: Paul Hanson
Book design: Lisa Hollander with Susan Macleod
Cover photograph by Fernando Diez

Workman books are available at special discounts when purchased in bulk
for premiums and sales promotions as well as for fund-raising or educa-
tional use. Special editions or book excerpts can also be created to specifi-
cation. For details, contact the Special Sales Director at the address below.

Workman Publishing Company, Inc.
708 Broadway
New York, NY 10003-9555
www.workman.com

Printed in the U.S.A.
First printing: April 2002
10 9 8 7 6 5 4 3 2 1

ACKNOWLEDGMENTS

This may be a small book, but it took the hard work of a lot of people to bring it to fruition. The author would like to thank:

Suzanne Rafer, for her skillful editing and friendship

Lisa Hollander, for her lovely design work

Peter Workman, for his commitment to barbecue (who else would be wacky enough to publish a book on beer-can chicken?)

Barbara "Hawkeye" Mateer, for her meticulous copy editing

Jim Eber and Kate Tyler, publicists extraordinaire

Patty Bozza, Patty Berg, Kim Cox, Katherine Deitrich, Beth Doty, Jenny Mandel, Sue Macleod, Kim Newman, Pat Upton, Paul Gamarello, Paul Hanson, Bruce Harris, and all my other friends at Workman Publishing

My agent, Angela Miller

My computer guru, Allan Drezner

My recipe tester, Elida Proenza

A huge thanks to all you Bubbas and pit bosses out there who so generously shared your knowledge about smoking, grilling, and new ways to use beer!

And finally, my wife, Barbara, for surviving another book!

CONTENTS

CAN-DO GRILLING

Quiche, fajitas, carpaccio, tiramisu, and the currently unavoidable sushi and crème brûlée—every few years, a dish or two comes along that captures the fancy and taste of a generation. Typically, it's a dish that most people had never heard of one year, then couldn't seem to live without the next.

And now another dish is about to join the ranks of these gastronomic superstars—a dish that, once seen, you simply must prepare for your family and friends. A classic of the barbecue scene in the United States about to go mainstream. I'm talking about beer-can chicken.

The idea is startlingly simple: You grill a chicken upright over an open can of beer. What results is the moistest, most succulent, and most flavorful chicken you've ever tasted. And let's face it, few things have more power to pop eyes and slack jaws than the sight of a gorgeous roast chicken perched jauntily upright on that beer can.

Since the moment I encountered my first beer-can chicken at a barbecue contest, I've made this singular dish to the great delight of television audiences and cooking class students, of family members and guests in my home. I've varied the recipe, using different beers or other steaming liquids and a wide range of seasonings. For that matter, I've used the beer-can method for cooking a wide range of poultry, from quail to turkey. I've come to regard beer-can chicken not just as an offbeat cooking method but a way of life.

I offer this book as a guide to the fine points of beer-can chicken—and other surprising dishes you can grill. I hope you'll use it as a springboard for your imagination. And I look forward to hearing about your favorite beer-can chicken creations. You can reach me on my Web site: www.barbecuebible.com.

Now pop open a cold one, and get ready to have some fun.

THE OFFBEAT GRILL

The best chicken I ever tasted wasn't Paul Bocuse's truffle-and-foie-gras-stuffed *poulet de Bresse en vessie* (poached in a pig's bladder). It wasn't the chicken I once dined on in Hong Kong, wrapped in lotus leaves, baked in a mound of clay, and served with a hammer for cracking its casing. It wasn't even my Aunt Annette's plump, juicy, golden *gedempte* capon (although that last comes close). No, the best chicken I ever tasted came off a barbecue pit in Memphis, Tennessee, where it had been smoked upright in a singularly undignified position: straddling an open can of beer.

Beer-can chicken, also known as drunken chicken, dancing chicken, or chicken on a throne (and some other names not fit to print in a family cookbook) is a classic on the American competition barbecue circuit. To make it, you roast a seasoned chicken in an upright position on an open can of beer. This is usually done on a barbecue grill using the indirect method of grilling or in a smoker, but you can also roast beer-can chicken in the oven.

I first tasted beer-can chicken in 1996, at the Memphis in May World Championship Barbecue Cooking Contest on the banks of the Mississippi River. Since then I have written about it in *The New York Times,* demonstrated it on *Good Morning America,* and taught how to make it in countless cooking classes across the United States. Everywhere it has met with enthusiastic acclaim.

1

A TECHNIQUE LIKE NO OTHER

So what is it that makes beer-can chicken so irresistible? Well, first there's the flavor and texture. The rising vapors impart a delicate beer flavor, simultaneously keeping the bird juicy and tender. And because the steaming takes place inside the chicken, the meat stays moist but the skin doesn't become soggy.

Then, there's the benefit of grilling the chicken upright. A vertical position allows the fat to drain off and the skin to cook evenly, even on the back. The result is a bird that's crackling crisp on the outside, moist and tender inside, and bursting with barbecue flavors.

Next, there's the irresistible tang of wood smoke, for beer-can chicken is almost always cooked in the presence of smoldering wood or wood chips. To reinforce the beer flavor, many pit masters actually soak their wood chips in beer.

Finally, of course, there's the wow factor. Few sights are more amusing or arresting than a chicken on a can of beer on the grill, its breast thrust forward, its legs stretched out in a leisurely fashion. Some folks heighten the comic effect by inserting a stalk of celery for a head, the eyes, nose, and mouth formed by cloves stuck in the celery.

The Birth of a Legend

My initiation into the rites of beer-can chicken came from the Bryce Boar Blazers barbecue team. I happened on their site at Memphis in May one Friday afternoon just as team captain Jim Birdsong was lifting the lid off a giant smoker. Inside were a half-dozen chickens, their skins bronzed with smoke and gritty with spice rub, sitting upright on cans of one of America's favorite beers. The Blazers had injected their chickens with Cajun seasoning, using the culinary version of a hypodermic syringe, and rubbed brown sugar and onion and garlic powders under and over the skin. They seasoned the open cans of beer with more spice rub before inserting them in the cavities of the upright birds. Then the Blazers slow roasted the birds to perfection in a smoker for 4 hours over smoldering mesquite. It's easy to see how these slamming beer-can chickens won the Bryce Boar Blazers a coveted first place at the Memphis in May barbecue contest the next day.

So where did beer-can chicken originate?

Jim Birdsong says he learned it from one of his company's customers in Texas. WCBCC (World Championship Barbecue Cooking Contest) chairman Mike Cannon saw his first beer-can chicken at the Delta Jubilee Cook Off in Clarksville, Mississippi. But beer-can chicken could be found even outside the quirky world of competition barbecue. My cousin Rob Raichlen, who works for the Los Angeles Clippers and knows his way around a kettle grill, practically lived on beer-can chicken at University of Southern California cookouts. He learned how to make it from a college roommate from New Orleans. I have since been able to confirm that Louisiana connection. While I was talking barbecue on a New Orleans radio talk show, a half-dozen listeners called in to volunteer their recipes for beer-can chicken. One confided that he adds garlic and onion juice to the beer can. For another, the secret was a generous shot of crab boil.

"The birth of beer-can chicken is sort of like the domestication of animals," suggests Ardie "Remus Powers" Davis, one of the most respected judges on the barbecue circuit, recognizable by his signature bowler hat and tuxedo studs fashioned from pork ribs. "It just happened everywhere at once." (Davis barbecues his chickens on "tall boys," 16-ounce cans of beer.)

A Runaway Revolution

Beer-can chicken is just the beginning. In the five years since I first encountered this singular dish, I've experimented with every imaginable bird, brew, and seasoning. In the following pages, you'll find instructions for beer canning duck, game hen, partridge, quail, and even turkey. (The turkey is roasted on a giant 32-ounce can of ale, while the quail are cooked on diminutive 6-ounce cans of fruit juice.)

As for beverages, I've used everything from beer to wine to soda to fruit juices and nectars to lemonade, cranberry juice, and even iced tea. The seasonings alone will take you on a tour of the world's barbecue trail, from Mexican chili rubs to Mediterranean herb pastes to fiery Asian spice mixes. The great thing about beer-can chicken is once you understand the basic principle, there's no limit to where experimentation will take you.

Writing about beer-can chicken and its variations led me to think about other wacky things you could cook on the grill: Chicken breasts grilled under rocks. Steaks grilled with hay. Fish grilled on boards. Vegetables roasted in the embers. Not to mention foods you'd never dream of grilling—from eggs to seaweed to ice cream. In writing this book, I let my imagination run wild and I hope that you will, as well.

If you have any reservations about grilling a chicken with a beer can inside, rest assured that the process has been thoroughly professionally tested and is perfectly safe. You don't have cause for any qualms here— *as long as the beer can is open.* Never grill a bird on an unopened can!

Every beer-can recipe in this book calls for opening the beer or soda can and pouring out half of its contents before placing it and the bird on the grill. This avoids any risk of the can exploding. As a further safeguard, the recipes call for making additional holes in the lid of the can with a church key-style bottle opener.

To avoid spilling hot beer or soda, always use long-handled tongs or heatproof gloves to transfer the chicken from the grill or oven to a platter. If using tongs, grasp the chicken by the can and use another pair of tongs to steady the top of the chicken so it remains upright. You will want to present the chicken on its can to your guests at the table, but take it to your kitchen or work area to remove the can and carve the bird. For detailed instructions on the best way to remove the can, see page 28.

GETTING STARTED

Over the years, I've cooked a lot of beer-can chickens, and I've tried varying the methods just about every way I can think of. Competition barbecuers cook the birds on smokers at a relatively low temperature (225° to 250°F) for a long time (2½ to 4 hours). Smokers produce the richest smoke flavor, but they never really crisp the skin.

I prefer to cook beer-can chickens on a conventional charcoal or gas grill at a higher temperature (350°F), so the recipes that you'll see here don't include instructions for smokers. If you'd like to grill a beer-can chicken in a smoker, add 1 to 2 hours to the cooking times in the recipes.

By grilling using the indirect method (see below) and adding wood chips to the coals or smoker box, you still get an intense smoke flavor. A higher heat has two advantages: You don't have to wait 4 hours for dinner (the chicken cooks in 1¼ to 1½ hours). And the chicken skin always comes out crackling crisp.

Being a grill guy, I of course recommend cooking beer-can chicken and its variations on the grill. But condo and apartment dwellers, as well as indoor-only chefs, should take comfort in the knowledge that beer-can chicken can be cooked in the oven with almost equally spectacular results. You get the same eye-popping presentation, the same crackling crisp skin and succulent meat. The only thing you're missing is the flavor of wood smoke. When cooking beer-can chicken in the oven, set it at the same temperature you'd use for grilling, usually 350°F. Position the oven rack low enough to accommodate the full height of a chicken (or turkey) on a beer can, so the bird doesn't touch the roof of the oven. Place the chicken on its beer can in a roasting pan and take care when placing it in the oven or taking it out not to spill the beer from the can. The oven cooks by the indirect method, of course. To direct grill indoors, use your broiler or a grill pan on your stovetop.

GRILLS

Beer-can chicken and its variations can be cooked equally well on charcoal and gas grills. The former have two advantages: Charcoal grills are easier to smoke on, and they enable you to burn wood. The drawback is that charcoal grills are fussier and messier to use and slightly less predictable.

Gas grills offer the advantage of lighting at the push of a button and maintaining a consistent heat with the turn of a knob. Their chief disadvantage is slightly diminished flavor, for unlike charcoal, gas leaves no taste. (Actually, when it comes to gas, not tasting it is a good thing!) It's also harder to smoke using a gas grill, although many new models have smoker boxes with dedicated burners, which makes this task easier.

Gas and charcoal grills both do a great job cooking beer-can chicken, and because they're outdoors, you keep the mess out of your kitchen and you can introduce the flavor of wood smoke. Almost all the recipes in this book call for using either a charcoal or a gas grill. You will find a few dishes that are best cooked over charcoal.

Charcoal Grills

Charcoal grills come in all shapes and sizes: You'll need one that's large enough to set up for indirect grilling (see page 9)—ideally about 23 inches across. The grill should have a tightly fitting domed

lid that's high enough to accommodate a chicken
(and if you're really into it, a turkey) on a beer or
soda can. The grill
should also have
vents for adjusting
the airflow and, thus,
the heat. A hinged
grill grate makes it
easy to add wood
chips to the coals. The

common kettle grill works great
for beer canning chicken, as does the 55-gallon steel
drum grill. In fact, about the only charcoal grills
that won't work for beer canning a chicken are flat-
top table grills and hibachis.

Gas Grills

However much we may rhapsodize over charcoal
grills, the vast majority of people in the United
States grill on gas. For beer canning, you'll need a
gas grill with at least two heat zones. It, too, must
have a lid high enough to accommodate a chicken
on a can. Other desirable features for a gas grill
include a built-in thermometer, drip pan, and
smoker box with a dedicated burner;
however, you can cook
beer-can chicken without
these. Always make sure
you have enough gas in the
tank before beginning to grill
your chicken. I try to keep a full
extra tank on hand.

DIRECT GRILLING

The recipes in this book call for several grilling
methods, most often direct or indirect. Direct
grilling is what most of the world means when it
talks about grilling: The food is cooked directly over

the fire. Direct grilling is a high-heat method used to cook relatively small or thin pieces of food quickly. Typically steaks, chops, chicken breasts, fish fillets, vegetables, and bread are grilled directly.

GRILL	TEMPERATURES
High	450° to 650°F
Medium-high	400°F
Medium	325° to 350°F
Medium-low	300°F
Low	225° to 250°F

There are two ways to set up a grill for direct grilling. In the first, the glowing coals are spread in an even layer to make a **single-zone fire** over which the food will be cooked. On a gas grill, you'd simply light the appropriate burner. This method is fine for cooking a small amount of food, say a steak or chicken breasts for one or two.

You'll get better heat control if you build a **three-zone fire,** consisting of a hot zone, medium zone, and cool or safety zone. To do this using a charcoal grill, rake two thirds of the coals into a double layer over one third of the bottom of the grill. Rake the rest of the coals into a single layer in the center third. Leave the remaining third coal free. Use the hot (double-coal) zone for searing, the medium (single-coal) zone for cooking, and the cool zone for warming or letting the food cool off if it starts to burn.

To set up a gas grill for three-zone grilling, on a two-burner gas grill, set one burner on high and one burner on medium, using the warming rack as your safety zone. On a three- or four-burner gas grill, set one burner on high, one or two burners on medium, and leave the last burner off.

INDIRECT GRILLING

Larger foods, like pork shoulders and whole chickens, would burn if grilled directly. As its name suggests, in indirect grilling the food is cooked next to, not directly over, the fire. The grill lid is closed to hold in the heat, turning the grill into a sort of outdoor oven. This is also the method used to cook tough cuts of meat, like brisket and ribs, that require long, slow cooking at a low or moderate heat. Indirect grilling allows you to work over a more moderate fire (300° to 375°F) and makes it easy to introduce the flavor of wood smoke. This is the method to use to cook beer-can chicken.

To grill on a charcoal grill using the indirect method, dump or rake glowing coals in two piles at opposite sides of the grill (some grills come with special side baskets for this purpose). Place an aluminum foil drip pan in the center of the grill, between the mounds of embers. You'll grill your chicken or other food in the center of the grate over the drip pan (that is, away from the heat), while keeping the grill covered. By adjusting the top and bottom vents you can obtain the temperature you desire (usually medium, about 350°F). When grilling indirectly for more than 1 hour or so, you'll need to add twelve fresh charcoal briquettes per side or a corresponding amount of lump charcoal. You can add coals you've ignited in a chimney starter; re-cover the grill immediately afterward. Or you can add unlit charcoal—leave the grill uncovered for a few minutes until it ignites, then put the cover back on.

To grill on a gas grill using the indirect method, if you have a two-burner gas grill, light one side and put what you are cooking on the other, unlit, side. If you have a three-burner gas grill, light the front and rear or outside burners and grill in the center. If you have a four-burner gas grill, light the outside burners and again cook the food in the center. No matter which kind of gas grill you own, preheat the burner or burners you are lighting to high, and when they are hot, adjust the burner knobs to obtain the desired heat.

SMOKING

Wood smoke is essential to the flavor of beer-can chicken. Wood comes in two forms for smoking: chips and chunks. For a light wood flavor, simply toss unsoaked chips or chunks on the coals—a technique used mainly in direct grilling. For a more pronounced smoke flavor—the sort associated with traditional American barbecue— soak the chips or chunks in water (or a mixture of water and beer) for an hour, then drain them before

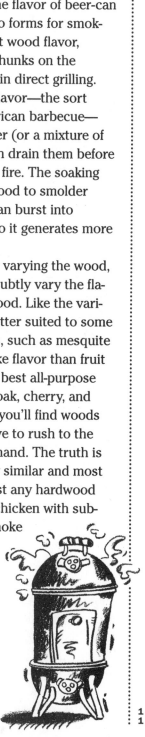

adding them to the fire. The soaking causes the wood to smolder rather than burst into flames, so it generates more smoke.

By varying the wood, you can subtly vary the flavor of the food. Like the various spices, certain woods are better suited to some meats than others. Heavy woods, such as mesquite and pecan, have a stronger smoke flavor than fruit woods, like apple or cherry. The best all-purpose woods for smoking are hickory, oak, cherry, and apple. In the recipes that follow, you'll find woods suggested, but don't feel you have to rush to the store if you don't have them on hand. The truth is that the smoke flavors are pretty similar and most chips are interchangeable. Almost any hardwood can be used to smoke beer-can chicken with sublime results. *Never* attempt to smoke with softwoods, which put out an unpleasant sooty smoke, or pressure-treated lumber, which contains noxious chemicals.

To smoke on a charcoal grill, simply toss the wood chips or chunks on the piles of glowing embers before you put the food on the grate.

To smoke on a gas grill, if your grill has a smoker box (a long, slender drawer or box into which you can put wood chips for smoking), fill it with wood chips and light the burner under or next to it on high until you see smoke. If your gas grill lacks a smoker box, you can position wood chunks (not chips) under the grill grate directly over one of the burners or pilot lights and preheat on high until you see smoke. Once you see smoke, turn the grill down to the temperature at which you plan to cook.

If you want to use wood chips in a gas grill that doesn't have a smoker box, you'll need to make a smoker pouch. Wrap the soaked chips in heavy-duty aluminum foil to make a pillow-shaped pouch. Poke a few holes in the top of the pouch with a pencil or knife tip, and place the pouch under the grate over one of the burners. The traditional drawback to gas grills is that many don't get hot enough for smoking. To overcome this, preheat the grill to high until you see smoke—lots of it— then turn the burner knobs to reduce the heat to the desired temperature and put on the food.

FUELS

For a charcoal grill, I like to use lump charcoal, made from pure wood and recognizable by its irregular-shaped chunks. This is a natural product, containing no additives or fillers. Look for it at grill shops and natural foods stores, or order it from one of the Mail-Order Sources (see page 311).

Of course, the vast majority of grillers in the United States use charcoal briquettes, which, in addition to raw wood, often contain furniture scraps, coal dust, and petroleum binders. This may sound off-putting—it *is* off-putting—and partially lit briquettes give off a strong acrid smoke flavor. But the truth is that if you let the briquettes burn down to glowing coals, these impurities burn off and the food will taste pretty much the same as if it had been cooked over lump charcoal. And even though I prefer lump charcoal, and use it whenever I can, I also want to go on record reporting that most of the competition barbecue champs use briquettes.

In other parts of the world, grill maestros grill over wood instead of charcoal. The advantage is obvious: Wood releases smoke and other flavorful components when it burns. Charcoal loses these components in the manufacturing process. It used to be that to grill on wood you needed whole logs and an industrial-strength grill. Now you can buy wood chunks at your local hardware or grill store. Simply light them in a chimney starter (see page 15). When the embers glow red, rake them out in the bottom of the grill just as you would charcoal. Remember that wood burns more quickly than charcoal, so you'll need to replenish the fuel every 30 minutes or so. (To learn how to gauge the heat of a charcoal fire, see page 14.)

When cooking beer-can chicken on a gas grill, you'll be using propane or natural gas. The only thing you need to do is make sure you have enough for a couple hours of cooking. This may seem pretty obvious, yet even the mightiest of gas grillers has been known to run out of gas.

KEEP IT CLEAN

Forget what Bubba says. All true grill masters religiously clean their grill grates before putting the food on the fire. To do so, preheat the grate (it's a lot easier to clean a hot grate than a cold one) and brush it vigorously a few times with a stiff-bristled wire brush to knock off any rust, ash, or burnt-on debris. Dislodge any really stubborn debris with the metal scraper you'll likely find at the end of the brush.

The next step is to oil the grill grate before you put on the food. Oiling the grate prevents food from sticking, obviously, but it also gives you better grill marks. And, while it isn't necessary for beer-can chicken, it's essential when you grill chicken under a stone and prepare some of the various steaks and fish dishes in this book. To oil your grate, once it's hot, fold a paper towel into a thick pad and, using tongs, dip it into a bowl of vegetable oil and rub it over the bars of the grate. Alternatively, you can rub a chunk of beef fat or bacon over the hot grate. I prefer using a paper towel, because it helps to clean the grate in addition to oiling it. Never spray oil onto the grill grate over the fire. The very tiny droplets of oil can catch fire, resulting in a flare-up.

As for follow-up maintenance, brush the grill grate again after you're done cooking. When the grill is cool, discard the fat in the drip pan. I'm not a fanatic about cleaning the fire box, which holds the coals, but do remove any visible pools of grease or large chunks of burnt-on food with a garden trowel.

GAUGING THE HEAT OF A CHARCOAL FIRE

To gauge the heat, hold your hand about 4 inches above the grate and start counting "one Mississippi, two Mississippi, three Mississippi." Soon the intensity of the heat will force you to remove your hand.

- A high fire is a two to three Mississippi fire.

- A medium-high fire is a four to five Mississippi fire.

- A medium fire is a six to eight Mississippi fire.

- A medium-low fire is a nine to ten Mississippi fire.

- A low fire is an eleven to twelve Mississippi fire.

EQUIPMENT

To get any job done properly, you need the right tools. This is the case, whether you're beer canning chickens or roasting potatoes in the coals. Here's a look at some equipment you'll want to help you make perfect beer-can chicken and other barbecue every time. You'll find mail-order sources for many of these on page 311.

Chimney starter: Used to light charcoal, the chimney starter is a vertical metal pipe 6 to 8 inches wide and 10 to 12 inches tall, with a wire partition in the center and a heat-proof handle. To use one, fill the top section with charcoal and place a crumpled newspaper or paraffin starter in the bottom. Light the paper or starter, place the starter on the bottom grill grate, and within 15 to 25 minutes, you'll have evenly lit, brightly glowing coals. Pour the coals onto the grate, rake them out, and you're ready to go. The coals are fired up evenly without resorting to lighter fluid. Buy the largest chimney starter you can find. One large chimney starter will hold enough coals for an hour of direct or indirect grilling in a standard (23-inch) kettle grill.

Paraffin starter: A nonpetroleum-based igniting agent that looks like a milky white ice cube. Simply touch a match to a paraffin starter and it will light in seconds, without the oily smoke associated with lighter fluid. I prefer this to crumpled newspaper when using a chimney starter: The coals never fail to catch fire.

Electric starter: An alternative to the chimney starter, the electric starter is a looped metal heating element you bury in the coals to light them. Simply plug it in and you'll have glowing coals in 15 to 20 minutes—again without using lighter fluid. Just be careful not to burn yourself on the metal loop.

Side baskets for the grill: Wire or flat metal baskets make indirect grilling in a charcoal grill a snap. Just place them at opposite sides of the fire-box and fill them with glowing coals. Side baskets are manufactured by Weber.

Grate with hinged side panels: Having hinged panels at either side of the grate facilitates indirect grilling even more. Lift the panels with tongs to add fresh coals or wood chips to the fire as needed. That way, you won't need to lift off the grate each time you want to restoke the fire. These, too, are manufactured by Weber.

Aluminum foil drip pans: Another essential for beer canning a chicken on a charcoal grill. Positioned under the grate between the mounds of coal, an aluminum foil drip pan will catch the drip-ping fat, which will be considerable. Note: Most gas grills have built-in drip pans. Be sure to empty them often. Aluminum foil drip pans are also useful for soaking wood chips, marinating meats, and holding root vegetables as they come off the coals. Foil pans come in many sizes. Although they are avail-able at grill and hardware stores, the ones from supermarkets work just fine—no need to double up. I always keep lots in several sizes on hand.

Grill brush: A long-handled, stiff wire brush is essential for cleaning the grill grate before putting the food on to cook.

Tongs: The one tool you don't want to be without. Get yourself a couple of pairs of long-handled, spring-loaded tongs (one good source is a restaurant supply house). They have rigid tubular arms that won't buckle. These are the kind of tongs professional chefs and pit masters use. The best commercial barbecue tongs are those made by Grilla Gear (available at housewares stores and grill shops).

Barbecue fork: Use a fork sparingly for turning meats. However, don't poke the meat as you would a pin cushion, or you'll drain out the juices.

Funnel: Many of the recipes you'll see here call for wine or another flavorful liquid to be poured into an empty beer can. A funnel allows you to do this without making a mess. Trust me—I've tried it without one.

Basting brush: For brushing melted butter and other bastes on the meat, you'll need a long-handled brush. Be sure to buy a brush with natural bristles, which won't melt when held over the fire.

Mister or spray bottle: Great for spraying a thin layer of beer, wine, fruit juice, or other flavorful liquid over a chicken, without running the risk of knocking it over with a basting brush.

Instant-read meat thermometer: Essential for testing doneness. The model favored by the pros looks like a giant straight pin. Insert the probe (the slender needle end) at least 2 inches into the meat but not so it touches a bone. When checking the temperature of thin pieces of meat, like steaks

and chops, insert the thermometer through
the side.

Disposable latex or plastic gloves:

More and more pit masters are wearing these to
handle meats and apply rubs. For one, they're more
hygienic than using your bare hands, and for two,
they keep your hands clean. You'll find them at
pharmacies.

Heavy-duty insulated rubber gloves:

The pros wear rubber gloves when pulling pork
shoulders, and they're invaluable when you are
removing the beer can from the chicken. The safest
way to handle a beer-can chicken without tipping it
is to use your hands. Insulated synthetic rubber
gloves make that possible. One good brand is the
Stanley Super Chem gloves.

Church key-style can opener: The pointed

beak on a church key can opener is perfect for making additional holes in beer cans.

PUTTING IT ALL TOGETHER

Frequently Asked Questions About Beer-Can Chicken

What sort of beer should I use? Canned beers tend to be among the mildest (some would say blandest) on the market. Even with the best of them, the actual beer flavor you get from beer canning is delicate. Thus, you can pretty much use any beer that comes in a can for beer canning. However, if you also plan to use the beer in a marinade, baste, or barbecue sauce, select a brew you wouldn't mind drinking straight. The better beers from abroad and from microbreweries in the United States only come in bottles. If you want to use one

 of these premium beers, pour it through a funnel into a clean empty beer can that hasn't already been used for cooking or into a chicken-roasting device (see page 24).

Is there any special type of can I should look for? All the beer and other beverages in cans called for in this book are available in seamless aluminum ones with pop-tops. This is what I recommend for my recipes. To eliminate even a remote risk of lead poisoning, avoid the old-fashioned soldered cans—the ones that have a seam visible at the bottom.

What size can should I use? The standard 12-ounce can is the perfect size for a 3½-pound chicken, and in a pinch you can use it to cook a game hen. The diminutive "mini" (8-ounce can) works well for game hens, while the oversize "tall boy" (16-ounce can) is ideal for large roasting chickens and ducks. Quail and squab can be cooked on 6-ounce fruit juice cans. Bring in the heavy artillery for a turkey—a jumbo 32-ounce can of Foster's ale from Australia.

Can you really taste the difference in beverages used for roasting?

A great deal of ink has been spilled over whether or not you can taste the beverage used for beer canning. I believe that beer imparts a delicate malty, hoppy flavor to chicken and that soft drinks and fruit juices add their own subtle essences as well. But remember: The advantages of beer canning lie not only in the beer flavor it imparts but also in its internal steaming and vertical roasting.

How can I boost the beer flavor?

To reinforce the flavor, I often use more of the beer or other beverage as an ingredient in the marinade, glaze, or accompanying barbecue sauce. Thus, in the following pages, you'll find recipes for barbecue sauce made with dark beer; and with root beer and black cherry soda, peach nectar, and even prune juice.

What if I or my guests don't drink alcohol?

You can use an almost endless number of soft drink and fruit juice cans for beer canning. In the following pages you'll find recipes for everything from cola and iced-tea chicken to root-beer game hens, pear-nectar partridge, and pineapple-juice quail.

When should I set up the grill?

In order to make the recipes as easy to follow as possible, I have suggested starting by preparing the rub or marinade, then the chicken, then the sauce or condiments, and finally by lighting the grill. If you're a time-starved cook (and who isn't these days?), you may want to start by lighting the charcoal and then prepare the rub and chicken while the grill is preheating. Put the chicken on and while it's cooking, you can make the sauce and side dishes. This requires a little juggling, but that's how most experienced grill masters cook.

Does it matter what sort of chicken I use?
Conventional culinary wisdom holds that the final dish can be only as good as the raw materials. This may be true in haute cuisine, but beer canning is such a flavor-boosting cooking technique that even an ordinary chicken comes out superb when cooked on a can. So imagine the results you'll get if you start with an organic, grain-fed, or kosher chicken. These birds may look anemic—they're not fed marigold petals to make them turn yellow—but

their texture is noticeably firmer, their flavor more robust.

How many people does one chicken serve?
A standard-size chicken weighs 3½ to 4 pounds and will feed two hungry people or four people when there's a lot of other food being served and if you're not counting on any leftover drumsticks. (A whole duck will serve two.)

How do I prep the chicken?
Hygiene and common sense dictate rinsing the chicken inside and out before seasoning and beer canning. Remove the bag of giblets and save them for another use. Blot the chicken dry inside and out with paper towels before using, then toss the towels directly into the garbage. When you're finished prepping raw poultry, be sure to thoroughly wash the prep area, the utensils used to prep, and your hands with hot water and plenty of soap.

Why do I need to oil the chicken? Over the years, I've found that a light coat of oil on the outside of the bird helps to hold the spices and crisp the skin.

What about rubs? Tradition calls for the chicken to be seasoned with a rub before beer canning. The basic barbecue rub calls for salt, pepper, paprika, and brown sugar. Other flavorings might include onion, garlic, or chili powders; ground cumin, cayenne, cinnamon, or dry mustard; or just about any other spice or herb found in your spice rack or garden. You can also use a wet rub—also known as a spice paste—made by blending herbs, spices, and seasonings with a small amount of liquid, like vinegar, oil, fruit juice, or water. Sprinkle or spread your rub or seasoning in the front and main cavities of the bird, then all over the outside of the bird, rubbing it onto the meat and skin with your fingers (that's why it's called a rub). Lift the flap of skin over the neck and rub some seasoning on the breast. In fact, some grill jockeys worm their fingers under the skin so they can sandwich the seasoning between the skin and meat.

When should the rub be applied? There are two ways to use a rub: as a seasoning or as a cure. For the mildest flavor, apply the rub just prior to grilling. For a more complex flavor, rub the chicken 4 to 24 hours ahead of time and let cure, covered, in the refrigerator.

What about marinades? Marinades (wet seasoning mixtures that contain a lot of liquid) are another great way to flavor chicken before beer canning. Marinate the chicken in a deep bowl just large enough to hold it or in a large, resealable plas-

tic bag. (If you use a plastic bag, placing it in a bowl
or pot to hold it upright will make it easier to fill.)
Put the bird in the refrigerator to marinate, and turn
it two or three times so it absorbs the marinade
evenly.

Are the liquids used for beer canning in this book interchangeable? Absolutely!

I've always maintained that there's no such thing as
a mistake in the kitchen, just a new recipe waiting
to be discovered. Feel free to mix and match the
beverages, rubs, sauces, and condiments from the
recipes in this book. Who knows, you may create a
new masterpiece!

Are there any tricks to preparing a can? First, wash the can all over with soapy water,

and rinse well. Next, pop the top. *Never grill a bird
on an unopened can of beer.* Using a church key-
style opener, make a couple of additional holes in
the top of the can (this helps spread out the
steam). Finally, pour out half the contents of the
can. Frequently you'll use this liquid as an ingredient in a marinade or barbecue sauce. In the case of
beer, you can use it to soak the wood chips. Of
course, you could always just drink it.

Why do you oil a fruit juice can when cooking quail? Quail contain a lot less fat than

chickens or game hens. And they also fit much
more tightly over the can. Oiling the can keeps the
meat and skin from sticking to the metal.

Do I need a vertical chicken roaster?

No. However, if you're nervous about the can tipping or if you want to use a liquid other than one
that comes in a can, like wine, a vertical chicken
roaster may be appropriate (see pages 24 to 25
for descriptions of some of the vertical roasters
available).

"BEER-CAN" CHICKEN ROASTERS

Beer canning is darn near the perfect way to cook chicken—darn near. The only hitch is the less than rock-solid stability of a bird perched on a beer can—the chance it will tip over unless perfectly balanced. This has led a number of barbecue-loving entrepreneurs to invent vertical chicken roasters that eliminate the risk of a tipping beer can. They can either support the beer can itself or serve as a receptacle for beer or other flavorful liquids. (Cookware shops also sell vertical chicken roasters that aren't specifically designed for beer canning. They're great for vertical roasting, but in order to get the full effect of beer-can chicken, you need a roaster with a liquid holder or a space for a beer can for steaming.) Of course, no vertical chicken roaster has the cool, whimsy, or, dare I say, the understated elegance of a chicken roasting on a real beer can. But if it helps prevent you from spilling precious beer, hey, why not use one? (For information on where to find vertical chicken roasters, see Mail-Order Sources, page 311.)

BRAD'S ROASTIN' POST: Developed by Brad Holland, creator of The Holland Grill, the Roastin' Post consists of a vertical metal tube mounted on a flat circular base. The narrow width of the tube (it's slender enough to fit up a quail and holds a third of a cup of liquid) allows for easy insertion in any fowl, while rows of holes on the side release the flavorful steam evenly. Available from the Holland Grill Company and from Uncle Joe's True Value.

BUSTER'S DRUNK CHICKEN ROOST: Jesse "Buster" Burgin believes beer-can chicken is so good that you won't want to make just one. So he created a device that allows you to roast four birds at a time. Shaped a little like a four-leaf clover, the Drunk Chicken Roost has four tubular supports that hold four beer or soda cans upright at once. The stainless steel device is dishwasher safe and is sturdy enough to withstand oven cleaner to remove any stubborn stains.

CAPTAIN STEVE'S BEER-CAN ROASTER: Believing that at least part of the thrill of making beer-can chicken is seeing the beer can, Floridian Steve Heide created a wire frame with a wide, stable base into which the beer can fits. Simply snap the beer can into the frame and insert it in the chicken. When not in use, the roaster folds flat to fit in a kitchen drawer.

PAPA JEABERT'S CHICKEN UP!: If you've ever fretted about the fat that drips off the chicken during roasting, this device is for you. Invented by Phil Gremillion of Lafayette, Louisiana, the Chicken Up! consists of an open, square or rectangular, polished aluminum metal box with an upright metal tube in the center. The top of the tube is cut on the diagonal to facilitate easy insertion. The box serves as a steady base and catches any drippings, eliminating flare-ups. Simply fill the tube with beer, wine, cola, or other flavored liquid and you're ready to roast. It's available in five different models, including one for a turkey.

WILLIE'S CHICKEN SITTER: This curious device looks like a large, inverted ceramic funnel with a sealed base. You pour the beer or other flavored liquid into it and place the chicken on top. Unlike the other roasting devices, the sitter is entirely ceramic, so metal never touches the chicken. There is also one for turkeys. Available from Nunez Enterprises or The Barbecue Store.

What's the easiest way to insert the beer can?

There are two ways. You can place the beer can upright in the center of a roasting pan and, holding the chicken upright with one hand and spreading the legs and opening the cavity with the other, gently lower the bird onto the can. The other way is to hold the chicken almost upright with one hand and the beer can at a slight angle with the other. Insert the beer can into the chicken, taking care not to spill the liquid. Twist as needed to get a tight fit.

How can I keep the chicken from tipping?

By forming a tripod. Pull the chicken legs forward and apart. They will form the front legs of the tripod. The can itself serves as the third leg.

What happens if the bird tips anyway?

Simply stand it up and continue cooking. A little spilled beer never hurt anyone. While it's most unlikely, if you suspect you've lost all the beer, wearing grill mitts, replace the can with a fresh open one that has been half emptied. Remember to make extra holes in the lid.

What's the ideal temperature for beer canning chicken?

I like to cook my chicken at 350°F. That's hot enough to melt out the fat and crisp the skin without burning it. A gas grill comes equipped with a burner thermostat. To learn how to gauge the temperature of a charcoal grill, see page 14.

Can I baste the chicken as it cooks?

Grill masters baste meats to keep them moist during grilling. This isn't usually a problem with beer-can chicken, as the internal steaming and vertical roasting do a fine job of basting by themselves. The one reason to baste a beer-can chicken is to add an extra layer of flavor. If you do baste, do so carefully, dabbing the brush lightly so you don't knock the bird over. I often do my basting with a spray bottle or mister, spraying a light mist of beer, soda pop, fruit juice, vinegar, or soy sauce over the bird. Using a spray bottle has two advantages over using the traditional brush: it applies a thin, even coat all over the bird and eliminates the risk of knocking it over with the brush.

What if my chicken browns too fast?

Lower the heat and/or loosely tent the bird with aluminum foil to prevent it from burning.

How do I know when the chicken is cooked?

There are three basic tests for done-ness. The most accurate is to use an instant-read meat thermometer. Steady the chicken with one hand using clean, well-insulated rubber gloves or a pair of tongs. Insert the metal probe of the thermometer into the thickest part of the thigh, but away from the bone. The temperature should be about 180°F. Alternatively, insert a slender metal skewer in the thigh and leave it there for 10 seconds. It should come out very hot to the touch and the juices that run from the hole should be clear. Another test is to wiggle one of the legs, again steadying the chicken with your other hand. The leg should move loosely and freely in the joint.

Does a trace of pink or red mean the chicken isn't done?

Pit masters look for a tinge of pink or red just below the skin of the chicken—a so-called smoke ring that's a natural part of the smoking process and a signature of master grillsmanship. However, the meat next to the bones (especially at the leg joints) should not be red. If your chicken isn't cooked through, simply put it back on the grill.

What's the best way to take a beer-can chicken off the grill?
Carefully! I use heavy-duty tongs to grasp it by the can just under the bird's bottom. Wearing a clean well-insulated rubber glove, I use my other hand to steady the bird. Alternatively, remove the bird from the heat with your hands, which again you've protected with those insulated rubber gloves.

What's the best way to remove the beer can?
Again, carefully. Wearing insulated rubber gloves, hold the chicken slightly on an angle with one hand. Carefully pull out the can with the other (you may need to twist or wiggle it back and forth a few times to loosen it). Or, you can hold the chicken upright with one set of tongs and remove the can with another set. Note: When removing the can, I always work over the sink  or a roasting pan just in case the liquid spills. Remember, there's hot liquid here. Be careful not to burn yourself.

Can I reuse the beer?
No. Throw away any beer that's left when you've finished grilling.

Can I reuse the can?
No. The can gets pretty beaten up during the grilling process. Always start with a fresh can.

What if I don't have a grill (or my condo association won't let me use one)?
Excellent beer-can chicken can be cooked in the oven. The only thing you'll be missing is the smoke flavor (see pages 6 to 7 for instructions).

Can I cook beer-can chicken on an electric grill?

With difficulty. To set up a grill for indirect grilling, you need at least two heat zones. Most electric grills have only one. However, if you want to try beer-can chicken on an electric grill, place the chicken on a metal pie pan (open side down) that's set inside an old metal cake pan (open side up). This creates a buffer under the chicken so the bottom won't burn, in effect enabling you to grill indirectly.

Can I reach you if I have a question?

Visit my Web site, barbecuebible.com, and click on the Ask the Grilling Guru section. It may take me a week or so to get back to you, but I will. By the way, I'd love to hear not only about your problems, but about your successes and new creations.

A NOTE ABOUT BASIC INGREDIENTS

Salt. Pepper. Butter. Brown sugar.

These are ingredients grill jockeys around the world reach for on a daily basis. Not all are created equal, however, and the type of seasoning, even something as simple as salt, can have a big impact on the results.

Barbecue sauce: Being the Grilling Guru and all, I usually make my own barbecue sauce. But there are many great commercial sauces out there, and if a recipe calls for barbecue sauce and you don't have time to make your own, it's fine to use one of these.

Butter: Like dark brown and light brown sugar, salted and unsalted butter are more or less interchangeable when it comes to grilling. Most competition pit masters use salted butter, which has more flavor than unsalted. You can pretty much achieve the same effect by using unsalted butter and adding an extra sprinkle of salt. If a recipe calls for two tablespoons salted butter and all you have is unsalted (or vice versa), it's not worth making a special trip to the store.

Fruit juices: The difference between fresh and frozen (or reconstituted or commercial) orange, lemon, or lime juice is enormous. I am uncompromising on this point—if a recipe calls for fresh juice, use freshly squeezed. On the other hand, commercial peach and pear nectars or cranberry juice work just fine.

Mustard: Cheap ballpark mustard is the condiment of choice among many American pit masters. But I prefer the refinement of French mustards, particularly smooth Dijon or grainy Meaux.

Oil: It adds richness to marinades, succulence to bastes, and luster to grilled fare of all sorts, not just chicken. It keeps fish and chicken breasts from sticking to the grill grate, and a drizzle applied just before serving can add a whole new dimension of flavor. I'm talking about that lifeblood of barbecue: oil. When choosing an oil, I look for ones that pay a flavor dividend: olive oil for Mediterranean or California-style grilling, sesame oil for Asian recipes. All have the fruity-nutty flavor of the ingredients they're pressed from and add extra flavor. The olive oil should be extra virgin, that is, an oil with low acidity and a pronounced fruity flavor. Sesame oil should be Asian style—pressed from roasted sesame seeds and very nutty. For a more neutral oil that adds no flavor of its own (when you don't want the taste of the oil to intrude), use canola or another vegetable oil.

Pepper: It's hard to imagine barbecue without the aromatic heat of pepper—whatever other seasonings you may add. In the best of all possible worlds, you'd grind whole black or white peppercorns whenever pepper is called for. Freshly ground pepper has a stronger, brighter, and more aromatic flavor than preground. It's the difference between VHS and DVD. That being said, most of the world's grill jockeys use preground black pepper with great success. It's certainly more convenient, and none of the recipes in this book will suffer too terribly if you use it. One good compromise is to grind a quarter cup or so of whole peppercorns in a spice mill or coffee grinder every few weeks. Store the resulting powder in a jar. That way, you get the aromatic burn of freshly ground pepper with a pinch of your fingers—without having to fuss with a pepper mill every time.

Salt: I like coarse salt—either kosher or sea—for grilling. The large crystals dissolve more slowly than table salt, so they give the food little salty bursts of flavor. Sea salt has the added advantage of containing trace elements from the ocean, so it's particularly good with seafood (it's also plenty tasty with poultry). Kosher salt also has coarse crystals. It's very pure and a little more economical than sea salt.

Sugar: Unless otherwise called for in the recipes here, use granulated white sugar. When brown sugar is called for, you can use light or dark brown—whichever you have on hand. Dark brown contains a little more molasses, so it has a richer flavor, but both will work. It's not worth running out to the grocery store to buy a tablespoon of light brown sugar when you already have dark brown on hand.

BEER-CAN CHICKEN

A barbecue without beer is like, well, a pit without smoke or a grill without fire. And the beer's not just for drinking. In this chapter, you'll find the original beer-can chicken in all its glory, not to mention delectable variations inspired by my travels on the world's barbecue trail. Chicken Carbonnade, for example, suggests what this barbecue classic would be had it been invented by a Belgian pit master, while Beer-Can Tandoori, Beijing Chicken, and Truffled Chicken reflect an Indian, Chinese, and Italian approach. You'll even learn how to make a Japanese-style sake chicken on a beer can. So, pop open a cold one, fire up the grill, and let the good times roll.

BASIC BEER-CAN CHICKEN

Okay, here it is. The master recipe for the *ur*-beer-can chicken, the showstopper that will dazzle your family and friends. If you've never made beer-can chicken before, start here, and once you've mastered the basic procedure, there's no limit to its variations.

> **TIPS:** *Use soda or fruit juice instead of beer. Substitute any of the rubs in this book to season the chicken or use your favorite commercial rub (you can vary the ethnic character of the chicken simply by the rub you use). As you can see, the possibilities are endless.*

1 can (12 ounces) beer
1 chicken (3½ to 4 pounds)
2 tablespoons All-Purpose Barbecue Rub (recipe follows) or your favorite commercial rub
2 teaspoons vegetable oil

YOU'LL ALSO NEED:
2 cups wood chips or chunks (preferably hickory or cherry), soaked for 1 hour in water and/or beer to cover, then drained
Vertical chicken roaster (optional)

1. Pop the tab off the beer can. Pour half of the beer (¾ cup) over the soaking wood chips or chunks, or reserve for another use. If cooking the chicken on the can, using a church key-style can opener, make 2 additional holes in its top. Set the can of beer aside.

2. Remove the packet of giblets from the body cavity of the chicken and set aside for another use. Remove and discard the fat just inside the body and neck cavities. Rinse the chicken, inside and out, under cold running water and then drain and blot dry, inside and out, with paper towels. Sprinkle 1 teaspoon of the rub inside the body cavity and ½ teaspoon inside the neck cavity of the chicken. Drizzle the oil over the outside of the bird and rub or brush it all over the skin. Sprinkle the outside of the bird with 1 tablespoon of rub and rub it all over the skin. Spoon the remaining 1½ teaspoons of rub into the beer through a hole in the top of the can. Don't worry if the beer foams up: This is normal.

3. If cooking on a can: Hold the bird upright, with the opening of the body cavity at the bottom, and lower it onto the beer can so the can fits into the cavity. Pull the chicken legs forward to form a sort of tripod, so the bird stands upright. The rear leg of the tripod is the beer can.

If cooking on a roaster: Fill it with the beer mixture and position the chicken on top, following the manufacturer's instructions.

4. Tuck the tips of the wings behind the chicken's back.

5. Set up the grill for indirect grilling (see page 9 for both charcoal and gas) and preheat to medium. If using a charcoal grill, place a large drip pan in the center. If using a gas grill, place all the wood chips or chunks in the smoker box or in a smoker pouch (see page 12) and preheat on high until you see smoke, then reduce the heat to medium.

6. When ready to cook, if using a charcoal grill, toss all of the wood chips or chunks on the coals. Stand the chicken up in the center of the hot grate, over the drip pan and away from the heat. Cover the grill and cook the chicken until the skin is a dark golden brown and very crisp and the meat is cooked through (about 180°F on an instant-read meat thermometer inserted in the thickest part of a thigh, but not touching the bone), 1¼ to 1½ hours (see page 27 for other tests for doneness). If using a charcoal grill, you'll need to add 12 fresh coals per side after 1 hour. If the chicken skin starts to brown too much, loosely tent the bird with aluminum foil.

7. If cooking on a can: Using tongs, hold the bird by the can and carefully transfer it in an upright position to a platter.

If cooking on a roaster: Use oven mitts or pot holders to remove the bird from the grill while it's still on the vertical roaster.

8. Present the bird to your guests. Let the chicken rest for 5 minutes, then carefully lift it off its support. Take care not to spill the hot beer or otherwise burn yourself. Halve, quarter, or carve the chicken and serve.

SERVES 2 to 4

All-Purpose Barbecue Rub

Variations on this rub have appeared in each of my barbecue books. There are four basic ingredients—salt, black pepper, paprika, and brown sugar— and by varying the proportions you can create an almost endless variety of flavors. For a spicier rub use hot paprika instead of sweet paprika. You could also substitute granulated sugar, light brown sugar, or Sucanat (powdered evaporated sugarcane juice) for the dark brown sugar. There isn't a fish that swims, a bird that flies, or a beast that walks that wouldn't benefit from a generous sprinkling of this multipurpose rub.

¼ cup coarse salt (kosher or sea)
¼ cup dark brown sugar
¼ cup sweet paprika
2 tablespoons freshly ground black pepper

1. Put the salt, brown sugar, paprika, and pepper in a small bowl and stir to mix. (Your fingers actually work better for mixing the rub than a spoon or whisk does.)

2. Store the rub in an airtight jar away from heat and light; it will keep for at least 6 months.

MAKES about ¾ cup

INDIRECT GRILLING

BREWMEISTER'S CHICKEN

Beer is more than the perfect beverage to serve with barbecue—it's the lifeblood of live-fire cooking. Of course, any chicken steamed over a beer can will pick up a mild flavor, but in this recipe the ante is upped by marinating the bird in a mixture of beer, mustard, and soy sauce. To gild the lily, as it were, serve the Brewmeister's Chicken with Dark Beer BBQ Sauce.

TIP: *Dark beers include some ales, all porters, and the darkest of all, stout. I like their sweet malty flavor for this recipe. Unfortunately, most dark beer comes in bottles, not cans, so use a dark beer for marinating and a conventional canned beer for grilling or transfer the dark beer to an empty beer can. Note: This marinade is amazing for all manner of meat, from steaks to pork loins to lamb chops.*

ADVANCE PREPARATION: **4 to 12 hours for marinating the chicken**

FOR THE CHICKEN AND MARINADE:

1 can or bottle (12 ounces) dark beer

⅓ cup Dijon mustard

⅓ cup soy sauce

2 tablespoons fresh lemon juice

1 medium-size onion, finely chopped

4 cloves garlic, crushed with the side of a cleaver

1 teaspoon of your favorite hot sauce

1 teaspoon coarse salt (kosher or sea)

½ teaspoon freshly ground black pepper

1 chicken (3½ to 4 pounds)

FOR THE RUB:

2 teaspoons paprika

2 teaspoons dry mustard

2 teaspoons coarse salt (kosher or sea)

1 teaspoon freshly ground black pepper

½ teaspoon ground cumin

½ teaspoon celery seed

¼ teaspoon ground nutmeg

1 can (12 ounces) beer, preferably dark,
or ¾ cup bottled dark beer

2 teaspoons vegetable oil

Dark Beer BBQ Sauce (recipe follows)

YOU'LL ALSO NEED:

2 cups wood chips or chunks (preferably
hickory or cherry), soaked for 1 hour in water
and/or beer to cover, then drained

1 clean empty 12-ounce beer can (optional) or a
vertical chicken roaster (optional)

1. Make the marinade: Place the beer, mustard, soy sauce, lemon juice, onion, garlic, hot sauce, salt, and pepper in a deep nonreactive bowl and whisk to mix.

2. Remove the packet of giblets from the body cavity of the chicken and set aside for another use. Remove and discard the fat just inside the body and neck cavities. Rinse the chicken, inside and out, under cold running water and then drain and blot dry, inside and out, with paper towels. Place the chicken in the bowl with the marinade or place the chicken and marinade in a large resealable plastic bag. Let marinate in the refrigerator, covered, for at least 4 hours, preferably overnight, turning the bird several times so it marinates evenly.

3. Make the rub: Put the paprika, mustard, salt, pepper, cumin, celery seed, and nutmeg in a small bowl and stir to mix. Set aside.

4. If the beer is canned: Pop the tab off
the beer can and pour half of the beer (¾ cup) over
the soaking wood chips or chunks or reserve for
another use.

If the beer is bottled: Fill an empty can
halfway or fill a vertical chicken roaster, following
the manufacturer's instructions.

5. Set aside the half-filled can of beer or filled
chicken roaster.

6. Remove the chicken from the marinade
and pat dry with paper towels. Discard the marinade. Sprinkle 1 teaspoon of the rub inside the
body cavity and ½ teaspoon inside the neck cavity
of the bird. Drizzle the oil over the outside and rub
or brush it all over the skin. Sprinkle the outside of
the bird with 1 tablespoon of the rub and rub it all
over the skin. Spoon the remaining rub into the
beer through the hole in the top of the can or into
the beer in the vertical chicken roaster. Don't worry
if the beer foams up: This is normal.

7. If cooking on a can: Using a church key-
style can opener, make 2 additional holes in the top
of the can. Hold the bird upright, with the opening
of the body cavity at the bottom, and lower it onto
the beer can so the can fits into the cavity. Pull the
chicken legs forward to form a sort of a tripod, so
the bird stands upright. The rear leg of the tripod is
the beer can.

If cooking on a roaster: Position the
chicken on top, following the manufacturer's
instructions.

8. Tuck the tips of the wings behind the
chicken's back.

9. Set up the grill for indirect grilling (see
page 9 for both charcoal and gas) and preheat to

medium. If using a charcoal grill, place a large drip pan in the center. If using a gas grill, place all the wood chips or chunks in the smoker box or in a smoker pouch (see page 12) and preheat on high until you see smoke, then reduce the heat to medium.

10. When ready to cook, if using a charcoal grill, toss all of the wood chips or chunks on the coals. Stand the chicken up in the center of the hot grate, over the drip pan and away from the heat. Cover the grill and cook the chicken until the skin is a dark golden brown and very crisp and the meat is cooked through (about 180°F on an instant-read meat thermometer inserted in the thickest part of a thigh, but not touching the bone), 1¼ to 1½ hours (see page 27 for other tests for doneness). If using a charcoal grill, you'll need to add 12 fresh coals per side after 1 hour. If the chicken skin starts to brown too much, loosely tent the bird with aluminum foil.

11. If cooking on a can: Using tongs, hold the bird by the can and carefully transfer it in an upright position to a platter.

If cooking on a roaster: Use oven mitts or pot holders to remove the bird from the grill while it's still on the vertical roaster.

12. Present the bird to your guests. Let the chicken rest for 5 minutes, then carefully lift it off

its support. Take care not to spill the hot beer or otherwise burn yourself. Halve, quarter, or carve the chicken and serve with the Dark Beer Barbecue Sauce.

SERVES 2 to 4

Dark Beer BBQ Sauce

Use a dark beer with a lot of character for this recipe. Good candidates include Newcastle Brown Ale, Samuel Smith Oatmeal Stout, or Dragon Stout from Jamaica.

1 tablespoon butter

1 slice bacon, minced

1 medium-size onion, finely chopped

1 cup dark beer

1 cup ketchup

¼ cup Worcestershire sauce

¼ cup firmly packed dark brown sugar, or more to taste

3 tablespoons Dijon mustard

1 tablespoon fresh lemon juice

1 to 3 teaspoons of your favorite hot sauce,
   such as Tabasco sauce

1 teaspoon liquid smoke

Coarse salt (kosher or sea) and freshly
   ground black pepper

1. Melt the butter in a saucepan over medium heat. Add the bacon and onion and cook until both are a deep golden brown, 5 to 8 minutes. If the onion starts to burn, reduce the heat.

2. Add the beer and boil until reduced by half. Add the ketchup, Worcestershire sauce, brown sugar, mustard, lemon juice, hot sauce, liquid smoke, and ½ cup water. Let the sauce simmer until mellow, thick, and richly flavored, about 10 minutes, stirring often with a wooden spoon. Taste for seasoning, adding salt and pepper to taste; the sauce should be highly seasoned. Let the sauce cool to room temperature before serving. The sauce can be refrigerated, covered, for up to 1 week. Let return to room temperature before serving.

MAKES about 2½ cups

INDIRECT GRILLING

CHICKEN CARBONNADE

North Americans don't have a monopoly on cooking with beer. Just ask a Belgian or a Frenchman from the northeast of France. The local specialty in these parts is carbonnade, pot roast braised in a robust mixture of garlic, beer, and caramelized onions. That set me thinking about a carbonnade sauce you could serve with chicken instead of pot roast, and a new beer-can chicken was born.

ADVANCE PREPARATION:
1 hour for marinating the chicken

> **TIP:** Belgians make some of the greatest beers on the planet and I strongly suggest you use one for this recipe. But being serious beer drinkers, Belgians avoid cans, so you'll need to transfer the beer to an empty beer can or use a vertical chicken roaster. By the way, excellent Belgian-style beers are made in the United States by the Brewery Ommegang in Cooperstown, New York.

1 chicken (3½ to 4 pounds)
12 ounces Belgian beer, plus 1 can (12 ounces)
   beer, or ¾ cup bottled Belgian beer
2 tablespoons olive oil
1 medium-size onion, thinly sliced
2 cloves garlic, finely chopped
1 teaspoon dried thyme
1 bay leaf
Freshly ground black pepper
Coarse salt (kosher or sea)
2 teaspoons vegetable oil
Carbonnade Sauce (recipe follows)

YOU'LL ALSO NEED:

2 cups wood chips or chunks (preferably hickory or cherry), soaked for 1 hour in water and/or beer to cover, then drained

1 clean empty 12-ounce beer can (optional) or a vertical chicken roaster (optional)

1. Remove the packet of giblets from the body cavity of the chicken and set aside for another use about 1½ hours before you plan to grill. Remove and discard the fat just inside the body and neck cavities. Rinse the chicken, inside and out, under cold running water and then drain and blot dry, inside and out, with paper towels. Place the chicken in a deep bowl or in a large resealable plastic bag. Add 12 ounces of beer and the olive oil, onion, garlic, thyme, bay leaf, and ½ teaspoon of pepper. Let marinate in the refrigerator, covered, for 1 hour, turning the bird several times so it marinates evenly.

2. If the beer is canned: Pop the tab off the beer can and pour half of the beer (¾ cup) over the soaking wood chips or chunks or reserve for another use.

If the beer is bottled: Fill an empty can halfway or fill a vertical chicken roaster following the manufacturer's instructions.

3. Set aside the half-filled can of beer or filled chicken roaster.

4. Remove the chicken from the marinade and pat dry with paper towels. Discard the marinade. Generously season the body and neck cavities of the chicken with salt and pepper. Drizzle the oil over the outside of the bird and rub or brush it all over the skin. Season the outside of the bird with more salt and pepper.

5. If cooking on a can: Using a church key-style can opener, make 2 additional holes in the top of the can. Hold the bird upright, with the opening of the body cavity at the bottom, and lower it onto the beer can so the can fits into the cavity. Pull the chicken legs forward to form a sort of tripod, so the bird stands upright. The rear leg of the tripod is the beer can.

If cooking on a roaster: Position the chicken on top, following the manufacturer's instructions.

6. Tuck the tips of the wings behind the chicken's back.

7. Set up the grill for indirect grilling (see page 9 for both charcoal and gas) and preheat to medium. If using a charcoal grill, place a large drip pan in the center. If using a gas grill, place all the wood chips or chunks in the smoker box or in a smoker pouch (see page 12) and preheat on high until you see smoke, then reduce the heat to medium.

8. When ready to cook, if using a charcoal grill, toss all of the wood chips or chunks on the coals. Stand the chicken up in the center of the hot grate, over the drip pan and away from the heat. Cover the grill and cook the chicken until the skin is a dark golden brown and very crisp and the meat is cooked through (about 180°F on an instant-read meat thermometer inserted in the thickest part of a thigh, but not touching the bone), 1¼ to 1½ hours (see page 27 for other tests for doneness). If using

a charcoal grill, you'll need to add 12 fresh coals per side after 1 hour. If the chicken skin starts to brown too much, loosely tent the bird with aluminum foil.

9. If cooking on a can: Using tongs, hold the bird by the can and carefully transfer it in an upright position to a platter.

If cooking on a roaster: Use oven mitts or pot holders to remove the bird from the grill while it's still on the vertical roaster.

10. Present the bird to your guests. Let the chicken rest for 5 minutes, then carefully lift it off its support. Take care not to spill the hot beer or otherwise burn yourself. Halve, quarter, or carve the chicken and serve with the Carbonnade Sauce on the side.

SERVES 2 to 4

Carbonnade Sauce

Caramelized onion and beer give this sauce a distinctively Belgian flavor. I've suggested a range of quantities of beer—the more flavorful, the less you need. Too much beer will make your sauce bitter. If you use only a quarter cup of beer, add an extra quarter cup of chicken stock. For the best results, use homemade chicken stock.

2 tablespoons butter
1 large onion, thinly sliced
3 cloves garlic, minced
1 large ripe tomato, peeled, seeded, and diced
1 bay leaf
1 tablespoon flour
2 tablespoons tomato paste
¼ to ½ cup beer
1½ to 1¾ cups homemade chicken stock (page 52) or low-sodium canned chicken broth

1 teaspoon Dijon mustard

½ teaspoon honey

1 scallion, both white and green parts, trimmed
    and finely chopped

3 tablespoons finely chopped fresh parsley or cilantro

Coarse salt (kosher or sea) and freshly ground
    pepper

1. Melt the butter in a large saucepan, over medium heat. Add the onion and garlic and cook until the onions are golden brown, 8 to 12 minutes, reducing the heat to medium-low after a few minutes should the onions start to burn.

2. Add the tomato and bay leaf and cook over medium heat for 2 minutes. Stir in the flour and cook over medium heat for 2 minutes. Stir in the tomato paste and cook for 2 minutes. Add the beer, increase the heat to high, and bring to a boil, stirring with a wooden spoon as the sauce thickens. Stir in the chicken stock, mustard, honey, scallion, and 2 tablespoons of the parsley and bring to a boil.

3. Reduce the heat to medium and simmer the sauce until thick and richly flavored, 5 minutes longer, stirring as needed. Remove and discard the bay leaf. Add the remaining 1 tablespoon of parsley and salt and pepper to taste; the sauce should be highly seasoned. Keep the sauce warm in a pot on the edge of the grill or on the stove until ready to serve.

MAKES about 2 cups

TOMATO TIPS:

TO SEED A TOMATO: Cut it in half crosswise. Working over a bowl or the sink, squeeze each tomato half in the palm of your hand, cut side down, to wring out the seeds. If necessary, use the handle of a spoon to scrape out the seeds. If peeling and seeding the tomato seems like too much trouble, just skip it. The sauce will still be great.

TO PEEL A TOMATO: Cut out the stem end, cut an X in the opposite end, and plunge the tomato in a pot of boiling water. When the skin starts to loosen (about 45 seconds), remove the tomato, rinse under cold water, and drain again. You will be able to pull off the skin with your fingers.

BRINED BIG BOY

A roaster is a big bird, but if you've ever had complaints that your barbecued chicken is tough or dry, this is the one for you. Despite the bird's size (6 to 7 pounds), the meat will be squirting moist and fork-tender. The secret is to brine the roaster, that is, marinate it overnight in a salt water solution prior to barbecuing it on a beer can. By the miracle of osmosis, the brine adds moistness and flavor to the meat, resulting in a bird that is almost lascivious in its succulence.

ADVANCE PREPARATION: 12 hours for brining the roaster

FOR THE BRINE:

1 large can (16 ounces) beer

¾ cup coarse salt (kosher or sea), plus
    salt for seasoning the chicken skin

1 quart hot water

2 quarts cold water

2 bay leaves

1 small onion, quartered

4 cloves

2 strips lemon zest (½ by 2½ inches, removed
    with a vegetable peeler)

3 cloves garlic, peeled and gently crushed with
    the side of a cleaver

3 slices peeled fresh ginger (¼ inch thick),
    gently crushed with the side of a cleaver

8 peppercorns

1 roasting chicken (6 to 7 pounds)

2 tablespoons melted butter

Coarse salt (kosher or sea),
    freshly ground black pepper,
    and sweet paprika

Your choice of barbecue sauce,
    for serving

YOU'LL ALSO NEED:

2 cups wood chips or chunks
    (preferably hickory or oak),
    soaked for 1 hour in water
    to cover, then drained

Vertical chicken roaster (optional)

1. Pop the tab off the beer
can. Pour half of the beer
(1 cup) into a large deep pot
(one just deep and wide enough
to hold the chicken). If cooking
the chicken on the can, using a
church key-style can opener,
make 2 additional holes in the
top. Cover the half-filled beer
can with aluminum foil and
refrigerate until ready to cook.

TIP: *A roasting chicken is bigger than a fryer, so you'll need a larger beer can—a 16-ounce "tall boy." If you prefer, you could brine a 3 1/2 - to 4-pound frying chicken and roast it on a regular beer can. In this case, cut the brining time to 6 hours. The main trick to brining is to not overdo it. Excessive brining will make the meat taste salty and commercial.*

2. Make the brine: Add ¾ cup salt and
1 quart hot water to the pot with the beer and
whisk until the salt dissolves. Whisk in the cold
water. Pin the bay leaves to 2 of the onion quarters
with cloves and add to the pot. Pin the strips of
lemon zest to the other 2 onion quarters with cloves
and add to the pot. Add the garlic, ginger, and peppercorns. Let the brine cool to room temperature.

3. Remove the packet of giblets from the
body cavity of the chicken and set aside for another
use. Remove and discard the fat just inside the
body and neck cavities. Rinse the chicken, inside
and out, under cold running water and then drain

and blot dry, inside and out, with paper towels. Add the chicken to the cooled brine. Place a saucepan or a plate on top to keep the bird submerged. Let the chicken brine in the refrigerator, covered, for 12 hours.

4. Remove the chicken from the brine and discard the brine. Blot the chicken dry with paper towels. Brush the outside of the chicken all over with the melted butter. Sprinkle the outside of the bird with salt, pepper, and paprika (go easy on the salt—the chicken will already be quite salty from the brine).

5. If cooking on a can: Hold the bird upright, with the opening of the body cavity at the bottom, and lower it onto the beer can so the can fits into the body cavity. Pull the chicken legs forward to form a sort of tripod, so the bird stands upright. The rear leg of the tripod is the beer can.

If cooking on a roaster: Fill it with the remaining 1 cup of beer and position the chicken on top, following the manufacturer's instructions.

6. Tuck the tips of the wings behind the chicken's back.

7. Set up the grill for indirect grilling (see page 9 for both charcoal and gas) and preheat to medium. If using a charcoal grill, place a large drip pan in the center. If using a gas grill, place all the wood chips or chunks in the smoker box or in a smoker pouch (see page 12) and preheat on high until you see smoke, then reduce the heat to medium.

8. When ready to cook, if using a charcoal grill, toss all of the wood chips or chunks on the coals. Stand the chicken upright in the center of the hot grate, over the drip pan and away from the heat. Cover the grill and cook the chicken until the skin is golden brown and very crisp and the meat is cooked through (about 180°F on an instant-read meat thermometer inserted in the thickest part of a thigh, but not touching the bone), about 2 hours (see page 27 for other tests for doneness). If using a charcoal grill, you'll need to add 12 fresh coals per side after 1 hour. If the chicken skin starts to brown too much, loosely tent the bird with aluminum foil.

9. If cooking on a can: Using tongs, hold the bird by the can and carefully transfer it in an upright position to a platter.

If cooking on a roaster: Use oven mitts or pot holders to remove the bird from the grill while it's still on the vertical roaster.

10. Present the bird to your guests. Let the chicken rest for 5 minutes, then carefully lift it off the support. Take care not to spill the hot beer or otherwise burn yourself. Halve, quarter, or carve the chicken and serve with your favorite barbecue sauce (there are quite a few in this book to choose from).

SERVES 6 to 8

INDIRECT GRILLING

SMOKED CHICKEN STOCK

Chicken broth is one of the cornerstones of great cooking. Just ask a French, Italian, or Chinese chef. A number of the recipes in this book call for chicken stock, and while you *could* use canned stock, self-respecting pit masters will want to make their own. Why? Because canned stock tends to be unnaturally salty. And when you make your own, you can start with a home-smoked chicken. This produces a stock of such flavor, depth, and substance that it would make a French chef green with envy. You can smoke the chicken on a beer can or directly on the grate, and you don't have to fire up your grill specially just to make stock. Simply smoke the chicken at the same time you make another recipe in this book and use the bird to make stock later.

> 1 chicken (about 3½ pounds) or 2 pounds
> chicken parts (such as backs, necks, or wings)
> 5 sprigs fresh parsley
> 5 black peppercorns
> 2 bay leaves
> 2 sprigs fresh thyme, or 1 teaspoon dried thyme
> 1 clove
> 1 medium onion, quartered
> 1 large carrot, cut into 1-inch pieces
> 2 ribs celery, cut into 1-inch pieces
> 4 cloves garlic, cut in half
> 10 to 12 cups cold water, or
> more as needed

YOU'LL ALSO NEED:

> **2 cups wood chips or chunks (optional; preferably hickory or oak), soaked in water to cover for 1 hour, then drained**
>
> **6-inch square piece of cheesecloth and butcher's string (optional)**

1. **REMOVE THE PACKET** of giblets from the body cavity of the chicken and set aside for another use. Remove and discard any fat just inside the body and neck cavities. Rinse the chicken, inside and out, under cold running water and then drain and blot dry, inside and out, with paper towels.

2. **SET UP THE GRILL** for indirect grilling (see page 9 for both charcoal and gas) and preheat to medium. If using a charcoal grill, place a large drip pan in the center. If using a gas grill, place all of the wood chips or chunks in the smoker box or in a smoker pouch (see page 12) and pre-heat on high until you see smoke, then reduce the heat to medium.

3. **WHEN READY TO COOK,** if using a charcoal grill, toss all of the wood chips or chunks on the coals. Place the chicken in the center of the hot grate, over the drip pan and away from the heat. Cover the grill and cook the chicken until the skin is a dark golden brown and very crisp and the meat is cooked through (about 180°F on an instant-read meat thermometer inserted in the thickest part of a thigh, but not touching the bone), 1¼ to 1½ hours (see page 27 for other tests for doneness). If using a charcoal grill, you'll need to add 12 fresh coals per side after 1 hour. (If the chicken skin starts to brown too much, loosely tent the bird with aluminum foil.) If cooking chicken pieces, it will take about 45 minutes. Transfer the chicken to a plate and let cool. The recipe can be prepared to this stage up to 3 days ahead.

TIP: *For the best broth, start with a whole chicken, but you can also make great stock with the more economical chicken backs, wings, or necks. For that matter, you can save the carcasses from other beer-can chickens (store them in a resealable plastic bag in the freezer) and make stock with them; you'll need two. Or if you're really in a hurry, make the stock with a fresh (unsmoked) chicken—it will still be plenty tasty.*

4. MAKE THE STOCK: Tie the parsley, peppercorns, bay leaves, thyme, and clove in a piece of cheesecloth or wrap in aluminum foil and poke holes in the bundle with a fork. Place the herb bundle, smoked chicken, onion, carrot, celery, and garlic in a large pot and add enough water to cover by 2 inches.

5. BRING TO A BOIL over high heat. Skim off any fat or foam that rises to the surface. Immediately lower the heat to medium and let simmer gently until the stock is richly flavored, about 1 hour, adding cold water as needed to keep the chicken covered. Skim the stock often with a ladle to remove any fat or impurities that rise to the surface (the best time to skim is after an addition of cold water; the water will bring the fat to the surface). If making stock with a raw chicken or chicken parts, simmer until cooked through, about 1 hour.

6. LINE A STRAINER with paper towels and place it over a large bowl. Transfer the chicken to a plate (see Note). Ladle the stock through the strainer, changing the paper towels as needed. Let the strained stock cool to room temperature, then refrigerate until cold. Skim off any congealed fat that rises to the surface. I like to freeze chicken stock in 1- or 2-cup containers so I always have a premeasured amount on hand; it will keep for up to 3 months.

MAKES ABOUT **2 quarts**

NOTE: Since the chicken has been grilled and boiled, it will have given up just about all its flavor to the stock. If it still feels wasteful to discard it, allow the chicken to cool, pull the meat off the bones, and use it in salad.

INDIRECT GRILLING

COUSIN ROB'S CAJUN CHICKEN

Introducing my cousin Rob Raichlen, sports publicist, accomplished griller, and supernice guy. Rob learned to make beer-can chicken from a college roommate from Louisiana (hence the Cajun seasoning here). As for using Old Bay seasoning, well, our family comes from Baltimore—the place where the spice mix was born. Put them together and you get a beer-can chicken that explodes with the flavors of Louisiana *and* the Chesapeake Bay.

ADVANCE PREPARATION: 45 minutes for marinating the chicken

FOR THE RUB:

1½ tablespoons Cajun Seasoning (recipe follows)

1½ tablespoons Old Bay Seasoning

FOR THE CHICKEN:

1 can (12 ounces) beer

1 teaspoon liquid smoke

1 chicken (3½ to 4 pounds)

2 teaspoons vegetable oil

YOU'LL ALSO NEED:

2 cups wood chips or chunks (preferably hickory or cherry), soaked for 1 hour in water and/or beer to cover, then drained

Vertical chicken roaster (optional)

TIP: *If you don't have time to make your own, commercial Cajun seasoning is widely available and it works great in this recipe.*

1. Make the rub: Put the Cajun and Old Bay seasonings in a small bowl and stir to mix.

2. Pop the tab off the beer can and pour half of the beer (¾ cup) over the soaking wood chips or chunks or reserve for another use. If cooking the chicken on the can, using a church key-style can opener, make 2 additional holes in its top. Pour the liquid smoke into the beer can. Don't worry if the beer foams up: This is normal. Insert a chopstick or skewer into the beer can and gently stir to mix the liquid smoke and beer.

3. Remove the packet of giblets from the body cavity of the chicken and set aside for another use. Remove and discard the fat just inside the body and neck cavities. Rinse the chicken, inside and out, under cold running water and then drain and blot dry, inside and out, with paper towels. Place the chicken in a large bowl on its side or in a resealable plastic bag and pour half the smoke-flavored beer over it. Let marinate in the refrigerator, covered, for 45 minutes, turning the chicken twice. Make sure each breast side and the back have each marinated for 15 minutes. Set aside the can with the remaining smoke-flavored beer.

4. Remove the chicken from the marinade and pat dry with paper towels. Discard the marinade. Sprinkle 2 teaspoons of the rub inside the body cavity and 1 teaspoon inside the neck cavity of the chicken. Drizzle the oil over the outside of the bird and rub or brush it all over the skin. Sprinkle the outside of the bird with 1 tablespoon of the rub and rub it all over the skin. Spoon the remaining rub into the beer through a hole in the top of the can.

5. If cooking on a can: Hold the bird upright, with the opening of the body cavity at the bottom, and lower it onto the beer can so the can fits into the cavity. Pull the chicken legs forward to form a sort of tripod, so the bird stands upright. The rear leg of the tripod is the beer can.

If cooking on a roaster: Fill it with the beer mixture and position the chicken on top, following the manufacturer's instructions.

6. Tuck the tips of the wings behind the chicken's back.

7. Set up the grill for indirect grilling (see page 9 for both charcoal and gas) and preheat to medium. If using a charcoal grill, place a large drip pan in the center. If using a gas grill, place all the wood chips or chunks in the smoker box or in a smoker pouch (see page 12) and preheat on high until you see smoke, then reduce the heat to medium.

8. When ready to cook, if using a charcoal grill, toss all of the wood chips or chunks on the coals. Stand the chicken upright in the center of the hot grate, over the drip pan and away from the heat. Cover the grill and cook the chicken until the skin is a dark golden brown and very crisp and the meat is cooked through (about 180°F on an instant-read meat thermometer inserted in the thickest part of a thigh, but not touching the bone), 1¼ to 1½ hours (see page 27 for other tests for doneness). If using a charcoal grill, you'll need to add 12 fresh coals per side after 1 hour. If the chicken skin starts to brown too much, loosely tent the bird with aluminum foil.

9. If cooking on a can: Using tongs, hold the bird by the can and carefully transfer it in an upright position to a platter.

If cooking on a roaster: Use oven mitts

or pot holders to remove the bird from the grill while it's still on the vertical roaster.

10. Present the bird to your guests. Let the chicken rest for 5 minutes, then carefully lift it off the support. Take care not to spill the hot beer or otherwise burn yourself. Halve, quarter, or carve the chicken and serve.

SERVES 2 to 4

Cajun Seasoning

This pungent mixture of spices first appeared in *The Barbecue! Bible*. It's one I keep coming back to again and again. Apply it to almost any seafood or meat at least 30 minutes before grilling for delicious results.

¼ cup coarse salt
   (kosher or sea)
2 tablespoons garlic
   powder
2 tablespoons onion
   powder
2 tablespoons dried thyme
2 tablespoons dried oregano
2 tablespoons sweet paprika
1 tablespoon freshly ground black pepper
1 tablespoon freshly ground white pepper
1 to 3 teaspoons cayenne pepper, to taste

Combine all the ingredients in a jar, twist the lid on airtight, and shake to mix. Store away from heat and light for up to 6 months.

MAKES about 1 cup

BEER-CAN TANDOORI

Blessings can come disguised as bad luck sometimes. When Meena Patel lost her job of eight years as a buyer of fine jewelry for a department store, she turned to a dream she had nurtured since childhood: to open a restaurant. And, thank goodness for me, she happened to open Anokha near where I live in Miami, Florida. Born in Indore, in the central Indian state of Madhya Pradesh, Meena is one of those instinctive cooks whose taste buds lead her to utterly transform everyday dishes by the simple addition of an unexpected ingredient. Consider her tandoori chicken—a pit-roasted bird marinated in an explosive mixture of yogurt, lemon juice, ginger, garlic, and spices. Those are the ingredients found in every tandoori recipe, of course, but Meena adds a fillip of fiery mustard oil. You've simply never tasted tandoori until you've sampled Meena's. Indians would roast the chicken in a tandoor—a superhot, vertical barbecue pit—but the preparation works great for beer canning, which, after all, is another form of vertical roasting.

TIP: *Kingfisher is India's most famous beer. It comes only in bottles, but you could certainly transfer it to an empty can or a vertical chicken roaster.*

ADVANCE PREPARATION: 4 to 12 hours for marinating the chicken

FOR THE CHICKEN AND "WASH":
¼ cup fresh lemon juice
1 teaspoon coarse salt (kosher or sea)
1 chicken (3½ to 4 pounds)

FOR THE MARINADE:
2 cloves garlic, minced
1 tablespoon minced peeled fresh ginger
1 teaspoon coarse salt (kosher or sea)
⅔ cup whole milk yogurt
⅓ cup mustard oil or vegetable oil
  (see Note)
2 teaspoons prepared Chinese mustard
  (if using vegetable oil; optional)
1 tablespoon fresh lemon juice
1 teaspoon ground cumin
½ teaspoon ground mace
½ teaspoon ground nutmeg
½ teaspoon ground cardamom
½ teaspoon ground turmeric
½ teaspoon cayenne pepper
½ teaspoon freshly ground black pepper
½ teaspoon red food coloring (optional;
  Indians like their chicken very red)

FOR COOKING AND SERVING:
1 can (12 ounces) beer, or ¾ cup bottled
  Indian beer
½ red onion, thinly sliced
½ cup rough-chopped cilantro
1 lemon, cut into wedges and seeds removed

YOU'LL ALSO NEED:
1 clean empty 12-ounce beer can (optional) or a
  vertical chicken roaster (optional)

1. Make the "wash": Combine the lemon juice and salt in a deep nonreactive bowl or in a large resealable plastic bag and stir to mix.

2. Remove the packet of giblets from the body cavity of the chicken and set aside for another use. Remove and discard the fat just inside the body and neck cavities. Rinse the chicken, inside and out, under cold running water and then drain and blot dry, inside and out, with paper towels. Remove the chicken skin if desired, pulling it off the meat and cutting it off at the joints as needed. Using a sharp knife, make two deep slashes in each leg (one in each drumstick and one in each thigh) and two in each breast. This helps the absorption of the marinade.

TIP: *Indians always skin chickens for barbecuing—first, because the skin impedes the absorption of the marinade, then because it often burns in the blistering heat of the tandoor. This may seem a little fussy so, if you prefer, leave the skin on in this recipe.*

3. Place the chicken on its side in the bowl with the lemon juice. Let marinate in the "wash" in the refrigerator, covered, for 15 minutes, turning twice. Make sure each breast side and the back have each marinated for 5 minutes.

4. Prepare the marinade: Place the garlic, ginger, and salt in the bottom of a large mixing bowl and mash to a paste with the back of a spoon. Add the yogurt, oil, Chinese mustard, if using, lemon juice, cumin, mace, nutmeg, cardamom, turmeric, cayenne pepper, black pepper, and food coloring, if using, and whisk to mix. Spoon the mixture over the "washed" chicken. Cover the bowl or reseal the bag and let the chicken continue marinating in the refrigerator for at least 4 hours, preferably overnight, turning the bird several times so it marinates evenly.

5. If the beer is canned: Pop the tab off the can and pour out half of the beer (3/4 cup) and reserve it for another use. Using a church key-style can opener, make 2 additional holes in the top of the can.

If the beer is bottled: Fill an empty can halfway or fill a vertical chicken roaster, following the manufacturer's instuctions.

6. Set aside the half-filled can of beer or filled chicken roaster.

7. Remove the chicken from the marinade and discard the marinade.

8. If cooking on a can: Hold the bird upright, with the opening of the body cavity at the bottom, and lower it onto the beer can so the can fits into the cavity. Pull the chicken legs forward to form a sort of tripod, so the bird stands upright. The rear leg of the tripod is the beer can.

If cooking on a roaster: Position the chicken on top, following the manufacturer's instructions.

9. Tuck the tips of the wings behind the chicken's back.

10. Set up the grill for indirect grilling (see page 9 for both charcoal and gas) and preheat to medium-high. If using a charcoal grill, place a large drip pan in the center.

11. When ready to cook, stand the chicken up in the center of the hot grate, over the drip pan and away from the heat. Cover the grill and cook the chicken until nicely browned on the outside and the meat is cooked through (about 180°F on an instant-read meat thermometer inserted in the thickest part of a thigh, but not touching the bone), 1 to 1¼ hours for skinless chicken, 1¼ to 1½ hours for a bird with skin (see page 27 for other tests for doneness). If using a charcoal grill, you'll need to add 12 fresh coals per side after 1 hour. If the chicken skin starts to brown too much, loosely tent the bird with aluminum foil.

12. If cooking on a can: Using tongs, hold the bird by the can and carefully transfer it in an upright position to a platter.

If cooking on a roaster: Use oven mitts or pot holders to remove the bird from the grill while it's still on the vertical roaster.

13. Present the bird to your guests. Let the chicken rest for 5 minutes, then carefully lift it off the support. Take care not to spill the hot beer or otherwise burn yourself. Halve, quarter, or carve the chicken. Place the sliced onion and chopped cilantro each in a small serving bowl. Serve the chicken with lemon wedges for squeezing and the onion and cilantro for sprinkling over the meat.

SERVES 2 to 4

NOTE: In order to be strictly authentic, you'd make this chicken with mustard oil, available at Indian grocery stores (or see Mail-Order Sources, page 311). If you can't find mustard oil, prepare the recipe with vegetable oil, if possible adding 2 teaspoons prepared Chinese mustard (available in plastic packages from a Chinese carryout).

INDIRECT GRILLING

BEIJING CHICKEN

Why should Americans have all the fun? There are some terrific beers in the Far East (I'm partial to the Chinese beer Tsingtao) and Asians love roast chicken. Put them together and you get a bird the likes of which has never been seen on the barbecue circuit in the United States.

> **TIP:** *Two ingredients are essential for this recipe: star anise and Chinese five-spice powder. Star anise is a star-shaped spice with a smoky, licoricey flavor. Chinese five-spice powder is a blend of four to seven spices that can include cinnamon, cloves, fennel seeds, white pepper, Szechuan peppercorns, and star anise. Both can be found at Asian markets or gourmet shops.*

FOR THE FLAVORED BEER:

1 can (12 ounces) beer, preferably Asian, or ½ cup bottled Asian beer

2 tablespoons soy sauce

2 tablespoons Chinese rice wine or dry sherry

2 tablespoons honey

1 tablespoon Asian (dark) sesame oil

1 whole star anise

1 cinnamon stick (3 inches)

2 scallions, trimmed, white parts cut into 1-inch pieces, green parts finely chopped

1 slice peeled fresh ginger (1¼ inches thick), flattened with the side of a cleaver

1 clove garlic, flattened with the side of a cleaver

FOR THE CHICKEN AND RUB:

1 tablespoon coarse salt (kosher or sea)

1 tablespoon sugar

2 teaspoons Chinese five-spice powder

1 teaspoon freshly ground black pepper

1 chicken (3½ to 4 pounds)

YOU'LL ALSO NEED:

2 cups wood chips or chunks (preferably oak, maple, or cherry), soaked for 1 hour in water and/or beer to cover, then drained

1 clean empty 12-ounce beer can (optional) or a vertical chicken roaster (optional)

1. Pour ½ cup beer into a nonreactive mixing bowl. Pour the remaining beer, if any, over the soaking wood chips or chunks or reserve for another use. Add the soy sauce, rice wine, honey, and 1 teaspoon of sesame oil to the beer in the mixing bowl. Gently stir the ingredients to mix.

2. If cooking on a can: Use a church key-style can opener to make 2 additional holes in the top of the can. Using a funnel, pour the flavored beer back into the can.

3. Add the star anise (you may need to break it into pieces), cinnamon stick, scallion pieces, ginger slice, and garlic to the beer can, if using, or to the ingredients in the bowl. Set aside the flavored beer.

4. Make the rub: Put the salt, sugar, five-spice powder, and pepper in a small bowl and stir to mix.

5. Remove the packet of giblets from the body cavity of the chicken and set aside for another use. Remove and discard the fat just inside the body and neck cavities. Rinse the chicken, inside and out, under cold running water and then drain and blot dry, inside and out, with paper towels. Sprinkle 1 teaspoon of the rub inside the body cavity and $\frac{1}{2}$ teaspoon inside the neck cavity of the chicken. Drizzle the remaining 2 teaspoons of sesame oil on the outside of the bird and rub or brush it all over the skin. Sprinkle the outside of the bird with 1 tablespoon of the rub and rub it all over the skin. Spoon the remaining rub into the beer through a hole in the top of the can.

6. If cooking on a can: Hold the bird upright, with the opening of the body cavity at the bottom, and lower it onto the beer can so the can fits into the cavity. Pull the chicken legs forward to form a sort of tripod, so the bird stands upright. The rear leg of the tripod is the beer can.

If cooking on a roaster: Fill it with the flavored beer mixture and position the chicken on top, following the manufacturer's instructions.

7. Tuck the tips of the wings behind the chicken's back.

8. Set up the grill for indirect grilling (see page 9 for both charcoal and gas) and preheat to medium. If using a charcoal grill, place a large drip pan in the center. If using a gas grill, place all the wood chips or chunks in the smoker box or in a smoker pouch (see page 12) and preheat on high until you see smoke, then reduce the heat to medium.

9. When ready to cook, if using a charcoal grill, toss all of the wood chips or chunks on the coals. Stand the chicken upright in the center of the hot grate, over the drip pan and away from the heat. Cover the grill and cook the chicken until the skin is a dark golden brown and very crisp and the meat is cooked through (about 180°F on an instant-read meat thermometer inserted in the thickest part of a thigh, but not touching the bone), $1\frac{1}{4}$ to $1\frac{1}{2}$ hours (see page 27 for other tests for doneness). If using a charcoal grill, you'll need to add 12 fresh coals per side after 1 hour. If the chicken skin starts to brown too much, loosely tent the bird with aluminum foil.

10. If cooking on a can: Using tongs, hold the bird by the can and carefully transfer it in an upright position to a platter.

    If cooking on a roaster: Use oven mitts or pot holders to remove the bird from the grill while it's still on the vertical roaster.

11. Present the bird to your guests. Let the chicken rest for 5 minutes, then carefully lift it off the support. Take care not to spill the hot beer or otherwise burn yourself. Halve, quarter, or carve the chicken and serve.

SERVES 2 to 4

INDIRECT GRILLING

CHICKEN AQUAVIT

Scandinavia and barbecue? It's not the first place that comes to mind when you think of grilling. But a classic Scandinavian dish—gravlax—was the inspiration for this singular version of beer-can chicken. Gravlax (cured salmon) owes its vibrancy to a cure made of salt, sugar, and dill. This sounded an awful lot like a barbecue rub to me and it turns out to be a great flavoring for chicken. To complete the motif, I add a splash of aquavit—a Scandinavian liquor. What results is a chicken bursting with Nordic flavors. Skoal!

TIP: *Aquavit is rather like vodka that's been flavored with caraway and other spices. Look for it at a well-stocked liquor store or substitute your favorite flavored vodka.*

1 can (12 ounces) beer

2 tablespoons aquavit or vodka

2 sprigs fresh dill (optional)

2 tablespoons dried dill

1 tablespoon coarse salt (kosher or sea)

1 tablespoon light brown sugar

1 teaspoon dry mustard

1 teaspoon garlic powder

1 teaspoon freshly ground black pepper

1 chicken (3½ to 4 pounds)

2 teaspoons olive oil

Creamy Mustard-Dill Sauce (recipe follows)

YOU'LL ALSO NEED:

**2 cups wood chips or chunks
(optional; preferably hickory or
cherry), soaked for 1 hour in
water and/or beer to cover,
then drained**

Vertical chicken roaster (optional)

> **TIP:** *Since gravlax
> is cured, not smoked,
> I've made wood smoke
> optional for this chicken.*

1. Pop the tab off the beer can. Pour half of
the beer over the soaking wood chips or chunks, if
using, or reserve for another use. If cooking the
chicken on the can, using a church key-style opener,
make 2 additional holes in its top. Using a funnel,
add the aquavit to the beer can and insert the dill
sprigs, if using, through one of the holes in the can's
top. Set the can of beer aside.

2. Make the rub: Put the dried dill, salt,
brown sugar, dry mustard, garlic powder, and pepper in a small bowl and stir to mix.

3. Remove the packet of giblets from the
body cavity of the chicken and set aside for
another use. Remove and discard the fat just inside the body and neck cavities. Rinse the chicken,
inside and out, under cold running water and then
drain and blot dry, inside and out, with paper
towels. Sprinkle half of the rub inside the body
and neck cavities of the chicken. Drizzle the olive
oil over the outside of the bird and rub or brush it
all over the skin. Sprinkle the outside of the bird
with the remaining rub and rub it all over the skin.

4. If cooking on a can: Hold the bird upright, with the opening of the body cavity at the
bottom, and lower it onto the beer can so the can
fits into the cavity. Pull the chicken legs forward to
form a sort of tripod, so the bird stands upright.
The rear leg of the tripod is the beer can.

If cooking on a roaster: Fill it with the
beer mixture, add the dill sprigs, if using, and

position the chicken on top, following the manufacturer's instructions.

5. Tuck the tips of the wings behind the chicken's back.

6. Set up the grill for indirect grilling (see page 9 for both charcoal and gas) and preheat to medium. If using a charcoal grill, place a large drip pan in the center. If using a gas grill, place all the wood chips or chunks, if using, in the smoker box or in a smoker pouch (see page 12) and preheat on high until you see smoke, then reduce the heat to medium (smoking is optional, but the chicken will definitely taste richer if you use wood).

7. When ready to cook, if using a charcoal grill, toss all of the wood chips or chunks, if using, on the coals. Stand the chicken upright in the center of the hot grate, over the drip pan and away from the heat. Cover the grill and cook the chicken until the skin is a dark golden brown and very crisp and the meat is cooked through (about 180°F on an instant-read meat thermometer inserted in the thickest part of a thigh, but not touching the bone), 1¼ to 1½ hours (see page 27 for other tests for doneness). If using a charcoal grill, you'll need to add 12 fresh coals per side after 1 hour. If the chicken skin starts to brown too much, loosely tent the bird with aluminum foil.

8. If cooking on a can: Using tongs, hold the bird by the can and carefully transfer it in an upright position to a platter.

 If cooking on a roaster: Use oven mitts or pot holders to remove the bird from the grill while it's still on the vertical roaster.

9. Present the bird to your guests. Let the chicken rest for 5 minutes, then carefully lift it off the support. Take care not to spill the hot beer or otherwise burn yourself. Halve, quarter, or carve the chicken and serve with Creamy Mustard-Dill Sauce. Ice-cold aquavit served in equally ice-cold shot glasses would make a terrific accompaniment.

SERVES 2 to 4

Creamy Mustard-Dill Sauce

Quick and piquant, this mustard sauce makes a great accompaniment to roast chicken, and, as you might suspect, it's also good with smoked or grilled seafood.

1 tablespoon dry mustard
1 tablespoon fresh lemon juice, or more to taste
¾ cup mayonnaise
⅓ cup sour cream
¼ cup grainy mustard, such as Meaux
2 tablespoons chopped fresh dill
1 teaspoon light brown sugar or granulated sugar
Coarse salt (kosher or sea) and freshly ground
   black pepper

1. Place the dry mustard and lemon juice in a nonreactive mixing bowl and stir with a fork to form a smooth paste. Let sit for 3 minutes.

2. Add the mayonnaise, sour cream, grainy mustard, dill, and sugar to the mustard mixture and whisk. Taste for seasoning, adding salt, pepper, and more lemon juice if necessary. The sauce can be refrigerated, covered, for up to a day. Let it return to room temperature before serving.

MAKES about 1½ cups

LACQUERED SAIGON CHICKEN

Mention *poulet laqué* ("lacquered" chicken) to a Vietnamese and his eyes will light and mouth water. When properly prepared, the bird will have crackling crisp, mahogany-colored skin that shines like Asian lacquer. The effect is achieved by marinating the bird overnight in a fragrant mixture of soy sauce, sesame oil, and wine, then roasting it vertically in a hot oven. In short, it's just the sort of preparation that's ideal for grilling on a beer can. The only even remotely challenging thing about this recipe is remembering to marinate the chicken ahead of time.

ADVANCE PREPARATION: 12 to 24 hours for marinating the chicken

FOR THE MARINADE:

¼ cup soy sauce

3 tablespoons rice wine or dry white wine

1 tablespoon Asian (dark) sesame oil

2 cloves garlic, minced

½ teaspoon ground coriander

¼ teaspoon Chinese five-spice powder

¼ teaspoon ground cinnamon

1 chicken (3½ to 4 pounds)

1 clove garlic, lightly smashed with the side
   of a cleaver

1 slice peeled fresh ginger (¼ inch thick),
   gently crushed with the side of a cleaver

1 can (12 ounces) beer

Spicy Peanut Sauce (recipe follows)

YOU'LL ALSO NEED:

2 cups wood chips or chunks
   (optional; preferably apple or
   cherry), soaked for 1 hour in
   water and/or beer to cover,
   then drained

Vertical chicken roaster
   (optional)

> **TIP:** *Smoking isn't really common in Vietnam, so I've made wood chips optional.*

1. Make the marinade: Place the soy sauce, wine, sesame oil, garlic, coriander, five-spice powder, and cinnamon in a large nonreactive bowl and whisk to mix.

2. Remove the packet of giblets from the body cavity of the chicken and set aside for another use. Remove and discard the fat just inside the body and neck cavities. Rinse the chicken, inside and out, under cold running water and then drain and blot dry, inside and out, with paper towels. Place the garlic and ginger in the main cavity of the chicken. Place the chicken in the bowl with the marinade or place the chicken and marinade in a large resealable plastic bag. Let marinate in the refrigerator, covered, for 12 to 24 hours, turning the bird several times so it marinates evenly.

3. Pop the tab off the beer can. Pour half of the beer over the soaking wood chips or chunks, if using, or reserve for another use. If cooking the chicken on the can, using a church key-style opener, make 2 additional holes in its top. Set the can of beer aside.

4. Remove the chicken from the marinade and discard the marinade.

5. If cooking on a can: Hold the bird upright, with the opening of the body cavity at the bottom, and lower it onto the beer can so the can fits into the cavity. Pull the chicken legs forward to form a sort of tripod, so the bird stands upright. The rear leg of the tripod is the beer can.

If cooking on a roaster: Fill it with the beer and position the chicken on top, following the manufacturer's instructions.

6. Tuck the tips of the wings behind the chicken's back.

7. Set up the grill for indirect grilling (see page 9 for both charcoal and gas) and preheat to medium. If using a charcoal grill, place a large drip pan in the center. If using a gas grill, place all the wood chips or chunks, if using, in the smoker box or in a smoker pouch (see page 12) and preheat on high until you see smoke, then reduce the heat to medium.

8. When ready to cook, if using a charcoal grill, toss all of the wood chips or chunks, if using, on the coals. Stand the chicken upright in the center of the hot grate, over the drip pan and away from the heat. Cover the grill and cook the chicken until the skin is a dark golden brown and very crisp and the meat is cooked through (about 180°F on an instant-read meat thermometer inserted in the thickest part of a thigh, but not touching the bone), 1¼ to 1½ hours (see page 27 for other tests for doneness). If using a charcoal grill, you'll need to add 12 fresh coals per side after 1 hour. If the chicken skin starts to brown too much, loosely tent the bird with aluminum foil.

9. If cooking on a can: Using tongs, hold the bird by the can and carefully transfer it in an upright position to a platter.

If cooking on a roaster: Use oven mitts or pot holders to remove the bird from the grill while it's still on the vertical roaster.

10. Present the bird to your guests. Let the chicken rest for 5 minutes, then carefully lift it off the support. Take care not to spill the hot beer or otherwise burn yourself. Halve, quarter, or carve the chicken and serve with Spicy Peanut Sauce.

SERVES 2 to 4

Spicy Peanut Sauce

Throughout Southeast Asia, peanut sauces are enjoyed. Indeed, you'll find two in this book. But this one is the simplest, containing few ingredients—all of which come from jars or bottles. Hoisin sauce is a salty-sweet, purplish sauce made from soybeans, sugar, and spices. The Thai sweet chile sauce, *nuoe cham ga,* is syrupy and only mildly spicy. For extra spice, you could add a spoonful of fiery *tuong ot tuoi,* a Vietnamese chile paste, or Indonesian *sambal oelek* (also a chile paste). These ingredients are readily available at Asian markets, natural foods stores, and in the ethnic foods section of most supermarkets. The peanut sauce will keep for several months in a covered container in the refrigerator, but, trust me, it's so good you won't have it around for more than a week.

⅓ cup smooth or chunky peanut butter

⅓ cup hoisin sauce

2 tablespoons Thai sweet chile sauce (nuoe cham ga)

1 tablespoon Vietnamese or Indonesian hot chile paste (tuong ot tuoi or sambal oelek; optional)

Combine the peanut butter, hoisin sauce, sweet chile sauce, hot chile paste, if using, and 1 tablespoon water in a small bowl and whisk to mix. Add up to 3 tablespoons more water if needed to thin the sauce to a pourable consistency.

MAKES about 1 cup

INDIRECT GRILLING

TRUFFLED CHICKEN

Unless Bubba hails from Alba, this isn't like any beer-can chicken he has ever made. Alba, in the Piedmont in northern Italy, is the world capital of the *tartufo bianco,* the white truffle, a perfumed (some might say malodorous), tannish-gray fungus that grows underground. Its powerful aroma and distinctive flavor have made the fresh white truffle one of the most prized and costly foods in the world. (Last year, white truffles sold for $3,200 a pound.) That's the bad news. The good news is that a little of the incredibly aromatic tuber goes a long way. A quarter of an ounce will be plenty to make one of the most heavenly beer-can chickens on earth. In the best of all possible worlds, you'd buy a small but fragrant white truffle. The way to maximize the truffle's flavor is to slice it paper-thin, and I mean paper-thin. This recipe may seem a little extravagant (even a lot extravagant), but beer canning is the perfect way to cook a truffled chicken.

TIP: *Fresh white truffles are available from October through December at gourmet shops or by mail order from Marché aux Delices (see page 313). You'll probably have some truffle left over. Store what's left in a jar full of arborio rice, which you'll eventually use to make risotto (a perfect accompaniment to truffled beer-can chicken). If you'd rather not invest in a truffle, you could substitute a few drops of truffle oil, which is widely available at gourmet shops.*

The penetrating truffle aroma perfumes the bird from the inside out. I'm sure Signore Bubba would agree.

1 can (12 ounces) beer
¼ ounce fresh truffle, or 2 teaspoons
truffle oil
1 chicken (3½ to 4 pounds)
Coarse salt (kosher or sea) and freshly ground
white pepper
2 teaspoons olive oil or
truffle oil
Garlic-Truffle Cream Gravy
(recipe follows)

YOU'LL ALSO NEED:
A truffle shaver (optional)
Vertical chicken roaster
(optional)

1. Pop the tab off the beer can, pour out half of the beer from the can, and reserve for another use. If cooking the chicken on the can, using a church key-style opener, make 2 additional holes in its top. Using a truffle shaver or a very sharp paring knife, cut 3 paper-thin slices of truffle. Place 1 in the beer can and set the can aside. (If using truffle oil, add 1 teaspoon to the beer can.)

2. Remove the packet of giblets from the body cavity of the chicken and set aside for another use. Remove and discard the fat just inside the body and neck cavities. Rinse the chicken, inside and out, under cold running water and then drain and blot dry, inside and out, with paper towels. Generously, and I mean generously, season the inside of the chicken with salt and pepper. Place 1 truffle slice in the neck cavity and 1 in the body cavity. (If using truffle oil, rub ½ teaspoon in the body cavity and

½ teaspoon inside the neck cavity.) Drizzle 2 teaspoons of olive oil over the outside of the bird and rub or brush it all over the skin. Generously season the outside of the bird with more salt and pepper.

3. If cooking on a can: Hold the bird upright, with the opening of the body cavity at the bottom, and lower it onto the beer can so the can fits into the cavity. Pull the chicken legs forward to form a sort of tripod, so the bird stands upright. The rear leg of the tripod is the beer can.

If cooking on a roaster: Fill it with the beer and add the remaining truffle slice. (If using truffle oil, add the remaining teaspoon to the vertical roaster.) Position the chicken on top, following the manufacturer's instructions.

4. Tuck the tips of the wings behind the chicken's back.

5. Set up the grill for indirect grilling (see page 9 for both charcoal and gas) and preheat to medium. If using a charcoal grill, place a large drip pan in the center.

6. When ready to cook, stand the chicken upright in the center of the hot grate, over the drip pan and away from the heat. Cover the grill and cook the chicken until the skin is a dark golden brown and very crisp and the meat is cooked through (about 180°F on an instant-read meat thermometer inserted in the thickest part of a thigh, but not touching the bone), 1¼ to 1½ hours (see page 27 for other tests for doneness). If using a charcoal grill, you'll need to add 12 fresh coals per side after 1 hour. If the chicken skin starts to brown too much, loosely tent the bird with aluminum foil.

7. If cooking on a can: Using tongs, hold the bird by the can and carefully transfer it in an upright position to a platter.

If cooking on a roaster: Use oven mitts or pot holders to remove the bird from the grill while it's still on the vertical roaster.

8. Present the bird to your guests. Let the chicken rest for 5 minutes, then carefully lift it off the support. Take care not to spill the hot beer or otherwise burn yourself. Halve, quarter, or carve the chicken and serve with Garlic-Truffle Cream Gravy.

SERVES 2 to 4

NOTE: The chicken is roasted, not smoked, in this recipe since you'll want to keep all the focus on the flavor of the truffle.

Garlic-Truffle Cream Gravy

Designed to enrich and moisten the chicken, this simple sauce enhances the flavor of the truffle. To get the full effect, I recommend using homemade chicken stock or broth. If you must use canned chicken broth, choose a low-sodium brand.

3 cups unsalted homemade chicken stock
   (page 52) or low-sodium canned chicken
   broth
1 clove garlic, peeled but not crushed
1 cup heavy (whipping) cream, or more as needed
2 or 3 paper-thin slices fresh white truffle, or
   ½ teaspoon truffle oil
Coarse salt (kosher or sea) and freshly ground
   white pepper

1. Place the chicken stock and garlic in a wide heavy saucepan over medium-high heat. Bring to a boil and boil until the stock is reduced to 1 cup, 10 to 15 minutes. Add 1 cup of the cream and the truffle slices, if using, and continue boiling, whisking occasionally, until reduced to 1 cup, about 10 minutes. (Keep your eye on the gravy; if beads of oil appear, the sauce is about to separate.) Remove the pan from the heat and whisk until slightly cooled.

2. Remove and discard the garlic clove. If using truffle oil, whisk it in now. Season the gravy, adding salt and pepper to taste. Keep the gravy in a shallow pan of warm water until ready to serve. Or to reheat, whisk the gravy over medium heat. Whisking should prevent the gravy from separating, but if it does, whisk in a couple more tablespoons of cream.

MAKES 1 cup

CHICKEN RETSINA

Long before vintners stored wine in bottles, or even barrels, they used amphorae sealed with pine resin. Resin may also have been added as a preservative. In any case, the flavor the resin imparted survives today in a curious Greek wine called retsina. To make retsina, a simple red, white, or rosé is flavored with resin, exactly as it would have been done in the age of Homer. The resin gives the wine a fresh woodsy pungency that makes it highly refreshing on a hot summer day. Retsina goes great with chicken, which gave me the idea to grill a bird on a beer can filled with it. To complete the Greek theme, I marinate the chicken in retsina and oregano and serve it with a Greek "salsa." Homer never knew what he was missing!

ADVANCE PREPARATION: 1 to 3 hours for marinating the chicken

1 chicken (3½ to 4 pounds)

1 small onion, thinly sliced

2 cloves garlic, crushed

2½ teaspoons dried oregano, preferably Greek

2 tablespoons extra-virgin olive oil, plus

    2 teaspoons for rubbing the chicken

1 bottle retsina

1 tablespoon coarse salt (kosher or sea)

1½ teaspoons dried mint

1 teaspoon freshly ground black pepper

Greek "Salsa" (recipe follows)

YOU'LL ALSO NEED:

2 cups wood chips or chunks
    (preferably oak), soaked for
    1 hour in water to cover, then
    drained

1 clean empty 12-ounce beer can
    or a vertical chicken roaster

TIP: *Retsina can be found in a well-stocked wine shop or liquor store in a Greek neighborhood. The wine is available as a red or rosé, but the white works best for this recipe because it doesn't discolor the chicken.*

1. Remove the package

of giblets from the body cavity of the chicken and set aside for another use. Remove and discard the fat just inside the body and neck cavities. Rinse the chicken, inside and out, under cold running water and then drain and blot dry, inside and out, with paper towels.

2. Place the onion, garlic, 1 teaspoon of

oregano, and 2 tablespoons of olive oil in a deep nonreactive bowl or large resealable plastic bag. Add the chicken. Pour out ¾ cup of the retsina and set aside. Pour enough of the remaining retsina in the bowl or bag to cover the chicken. Let the chicken marinate in the refrigerator, covered, for at least 1 hour, preferably 3 hours, turning the bird several times so it marinates evenly.

3. Make the rub: Put the salt, mint, pepper,

and remaining 1½ teaspoons of oregano in a small bowl and stir to mix. Remove the chicken from the

marinade and pat dry with paper towels. Discard
the marinade. Sprinkle 1 teaspoon of the rub inside
the body cavity and ½ teaspoon inside the neck
cavity of the chicken. Drizzle the remaining 2 teaspoons of olive oil over the outside of the bird and
rub or brush it all over the skin. Sprinkle the outside of the bird with the remaining rub, and rub it
all over the skin.

4. If cooking on a can: Using a church
key-style can opener, make 2 additional holes in
the top of the empty beer can. Using a funnel, pour
the reserved ¾ cup of retsina into the beer can.
Hold the bird upright, with the opening of the
body cavity at the bottom, and lower it onto the
beer can so the can fits into the cavity. Pull the
chicken legs forward to form a sort of tripod, so
the bird stands upright. The rear leg of the tripod
is the beer can.

If cooking on a roaster: Fill it with the
reserved ¾ cup of retsina and position the chicken
on top, following the manufacturer's instructions.

5. Tuck the tips of the wings behind the
chicken's back.

6. Set up the grill for indirect grilling (see
page 9 for both charcoal and gas) and preheat to
medium. If using a charcoal grill, place a large drip
pan in the center. If using a gas grill, place all the
wood chips or chunks in the smoker box or in a
smoker pouch (see page 12) and preheat on high
until you see smoke, then reduce the heat to
medium.

7. When ready to cook, if using a charcoal
grill, toss all of the wood chips or chunks on the
coals. Stand the chicken up in the center of the hot
grate, over the drip pan and away from the heat.
Cover the grill and cook the chicken until the skin
is a dark golden brown and very crisp and the

meat is cooked through (about 180°F on an instant-read meat thermometer inserted in the thickest part of a thigh, but not touching the bone), 1¼ to 1½ hours (see page 27 for other tests for doneness). If using a charcoal grill, you'll need to add 12 fresh coals per side after 1 hour. If the chicken skin starts to brown too much, loosely tent the bird with aluminum foil.

8. If cooking on a can: Using tongs, hold the bird by the can and carefully transfer it in an upright position to a platter.

If cooking on a roaster: Use oven mitts or pot holders to remove the bird from the grill while it's still on the vertical roaster.

9. Present the bird to your guests. Let the chicken rest for 5 minutes, then carefully lift it off the support. Take care not to spill the hot retsina or otherwise burn yourself. Halve, quarter, or carve the chicken and serve with Greek "Salsa" and well-chilled retsina.

SERVES 2 to 4

Greek "Salsa"

Nothing more than the ingredients for a Greek salad cut small, this "salsa" is delicious with grilled chicken. For that matter, it's pretty terrific eaten all by itself. The recipe makes a little more "salsa" than you need for one chicken. Serve any leftovers on grilled bread slices as an hors d'oeuvre or as a salad.

1 clove garlic, minced

½ teaspoon coarse salt (kosher or sea), or more
    to taste

½ teaspoon freshly ground black pepper

1 tablespoon red wine vinegar, or more to taste

2 tablespoons extra-virgin olive oil, preferably
    Greek

1 cucumber

1 large or 2 medium luscious, ripe red tomatoes

½ medium red onion, finely diced

½ green bell pepper, finely diced

¼ cup kalamata olives

2 ounces feta cheese, drained and crumbled

1. Place the garlic, salt, and black pepper in the
bottom of a nonreactive mixing bowl and mash to a
paste with the back of a wooden spoon. Add the
vinegar and stir until the salt crystals are dissolved.
Stir in the olive oil.

2. Using a vegetable peeler, partially peel the
cucumber (remove the peel in lengthwise strips,
leaving a little green showing for color). Cut the
cucumber in half lengthwise, scrape out the seeds
with a melon baller or spoon, and cut the flesh into
¼-inch dice. Cut the tomato(es) in half crosswise
and gently squeeze each half over the sink, cut side
down, to wring out the seeds. Cut the tomato
halves into ¼-inch dice.

3. Add the diced cucumber and tomato(es),
onion, bell pepper, olives, and feta to the bowl with
the dressing and gently toss to mix. Taste for seasoning, adding salt or vinegar as necessary.

MAKES 3 cups

INDIRECT GRILLING

SAKE CHICKEN

Nowadays, you can hardly pick up a magazine without reading about sake, Japan's smooth, dry rice wine, which can be sipped either hot or cold. Although commonly described as wine, sake is technically a sort of beer. I needed no more invitation than that to try it for beer-can chicken. In fact, in Japan you can buy sake in cans. In the United States, it comes in bottles, so to grill this you'll have to use a clean, empty beer can or a vertical chicken roaster.

TIP: *You can spend every bit as much money for sake as you can for a fine vintage wine or for a single malt scotch. The screw-top variety works fine for this recipe (unlike grape wines, many sakes come in screw-top bottles).*

FOR THE RUB:

2 teaspoons sesame seeds

2 teaspoons wasabi powder

2 teaspoons coarse salt
    (kosher or sea)

1 teaspoon freshly ground black pepper

1 chicken (3½ to 4 pounds)

2 tablespoons Asian (dark) sesame oil

¾ cup sake

2 strips lemon zest

Lime "Teriyaki" Glaze (recipe follows)

YOU'LL ALSO NEED:

1 clean empty 12-ounce beer can or a vertical chicken roaster

TIP: *Wasabi is a fiery Japanese root similar to Western horseradish. It's commonly sold powdered in tiny cans in Asian markets or gourmet shops.*

1. Make the rub: Put the sesame seeds, wasabi, salt, and pepper in a spice mill or coffee grinder and grind to a fine powder.

2. Remove the packet of giblets from the body cavity of the chicken and set aside for another use. Remove and discard the fat just inside the body and neck cavities. Rinse the chicken, inside and out, under cold running water and then drain and blot dry, inside and out, with paper towels. Sprinkle half of the rub inside the body and neck cavities of the chicken. Drizzle 1 tablespoon of sesame oil over the outside of the bird and rub or brush it all over the skin. Sprinkle the outside of the bird with the remaining rub and rub it all over the skin.

3. If cooking on a can: Using a church key-style can opener, make 2 additional holes in the top of the empty beer can. Using a funnel, pour the sake into the beer can. Add the lemon zest to the beer can through one of the holes in the top. Hold the bird upright, with the opening of the body cavity at the bottom, and lower it onto the beer can so the can fits into the cavity. Pull the chicken legs forward to form a sort of tripod, so the bird stands upright. The rear leg of the tripod is the beer can.

If cooking on a roaster: Fill it with the sake, add the lemon zest, and position the chicken on top, following the manufacturer's instructions.

4. Tuck the tips of the wings behind the chicken's back.

5. Set up the grill for indirect grilling (see page 9 for both charcoal and gas) and preheat to medium. If using a charcoal grill, place a large drip pan in the center.

6. When ready to cook, stand the chicken upright in the center of the hot grate, over the drip pan and away from the heat. Cover the grill and cook the chicken until the skin is a dark golden brown and very crisp and the meat is cooked through (about 180°F on an instant-read meat thermometer inserted in the thickest part of a thigh, but not touching the bone), 1¼ to 1½ hours (see page 27 for other tests for doneness). If using a charcoal grill, you'll need to add 12 fresh coals per side after 1 hour. Baste the chicken with the remaining 1 tablespoon of sesame oil once or twice during the last 30 minutes of cooking, taking care not to knock the bird over. If the chicken skin starts to brown too much, loosely tent the bird with aluminum foil.

7. If cooking on a can: Using tongs, hold the bird by the can and carefully transfer it in an upright position to a platter.

If cooking on a roaster: Use oven mitts or pot holders to remove the bird from the grill while it's still on the vertical roaster.

8. Present the bird to your guests. Let the chicken rest for 5 minutes, then carefully lift it off the support. Take care not to spill the hot beer or otherwise burn yourself. Halve, quarter, or carve the chicken and serve with Lime "Teriyaki" Glaze and well-chilled sake.

SERVES 2 to 4

Lime "Teriyaki" Glaze

A creation of my chef son, Jake, this edgy takeoff on teriyaki sauce is simplicity itself, containing only four ingredients. It's an irresistible condiment, the fresh lime juice adding a whole new dimension to familiar ingredients. Take care not to let the sauce boil too rapidly or you'll scorch the soy sauce. The glaze will seem a bit thin when it comes off the stove, but it thickens on cooling. Stored, covered, in the refrigerator, it will keep for several months. Bring to room temperature before serving or reheat over low heat just to warm it up.

½ cup soy sauce, such as Kikkoman
1 cup sugar
2 cloves garlic, peeled and flattened with the side of a cleaver
¼ cup fresh lime juice

1. Combine the soy sauce, sugar, and garlic in a heavy saucepan and stir to mix. Cook over medium-high heat, stirring often with a wooden spoon, until the sugar is dissolved and the mixture is thick, like molasses, 4 to 6 minutes.

2. Stir in the lime juice and briskly simmer until the glaze thickens slightly, 5 minutes. (It will thicken more as it cools.) Discard the garlic cloves and serve the glaze warm or at room temperature.

MAKES about 1 cup

BEERLESS BIRDS

Looking for new challenges a few years ago, I popped open a can of root beer and inserted it in a chicken. What came off the grill was a fork-tender bird exquisitely perfumed with sassafras, wintergreen, and cloves (you'll find a version for game hens on page 153). Since then, I've experimented with ginger ale, cola, and even black cherry soda, not to mention poultry roasted over peach nectar, cranberry juice, lemonade, and even iced tea. The bottom line is that virtually any flavorful liquid can be used to barbecue chicken with finger-licking felicitous results. Who says you need beer to make great beer-can chicken?

COLA-CAN CHICKEN

Highbrow chefs operate under a major handicap: Coca-Cola—or any other cola, for that matter—is seldom an ingredient in restaurant kitchens. As any pit boss worth his salt knows, the complex interplay of sweet, tart, spicy, and aromatic flavors in Coke, Pepsi, and other colas makes them a valuable addition to marinades, bastes, and barbecue sauces. This truth is appreciated elsewhere in the Americas—in Venezuela, for example, where pot roast braised in Coke is something of a national treasure. I've taken the idea one step further by barbecuing a chicken on a cola can. This is a great way to make "beer"-can chicken for people who don't drink alcohol.

FOR THE RUB:

1 tablespoon mild chili powder

2 teaspoons salt

2 teaspoons light brown sugar

1 teaspoon freshly ground black pepper

1 teaspoon ground cumin

½ teaspoon garlic powder

¼ teaspoon cayenne pepper, or more to taste

1 can (12 ounces) cola

1 chicken (3½ to 4 pounds)

2 teaspoons vegetable oil

Cola Barbecue Sauce (recipe follows)

YOU'LL ALSO NEED:

**2 cups wood chips or chunks
(preferably hickory),
soaked for 1 hour in water to
cover, then drained**
**Vertical chicken roaster
(optional)**

1. Make the rub: Put the
chili powder, salt, brown sugar,
black pepper, cumin, garlic powder, and cayenne in a small bowl
and stir to mix.

2. Pop the tab off the soda
can. Pour half of the cola
(¾ cup) into a measuring cup
and set aside for the sauce. If
cooking the chicken on the can,
using a church key-style can opener, make
2 additional holes in its top.

TIP: *Coke and Pepsi
are the two most obvi-
ous candidates for this
recipe, but don't hesi-
tate to try a different
cola. (Do I hear Inka
Kola from Peru?) You
could also vary the rub
or use your favorite
commercial mix.*

3. Remove the packet of giblets from the
body cavity of the chicken and set aside for another
use. Remove and discard the fat just inside the
body and neck cavities. Rinse the chicken, inside
and out, under cold running water and then drain
and blot dry, inside and out, with paper towels.
Sprinkle 1 teaspoon of the rub inside the body
cavity and ½ teaspoon inside the neck cavity of the
chicken. Drizzle the oil over the outside of the bird
and rub or brush it all over the skin. Sprinkle the
outside of the bird with 1 tablespoon rub and rub it
all over the skin. Spoon the remaining rub through a
hole in the top of the can. Don't worry if the cola
foams up: This is normal.

4. If cooking on a can: Hold the bird
upright, with the opening of the body cavity at the
bottom, and lower it onto the can so the can fits
into the cavity. Pull the chicken legs forward to

form a sort of tripod, so the bird stands upright. The rear leg of the tripod is the can.

If cooking on a roaster: Fill it with the flavored cola and add the remaining rub. Position the chicken on top, following the manufacturer's instructions.

5. Tuck the tips of the wings behind the chicken's back.

6. Set up the grill for indirect grilling (see page 9 for both charcoal and gas) and preheat to medium. If using a charcoal grill, place a large drip pan in the center. If using a gas grill, place all the wood chips or chunks in the smoker box or in a smoker pouch (see page 12) and preheat on high until you see smoke, then reduce the heat to medium.

7. When ready to cook, if using a charcoal grill, toss all of the wood chips or chunks on the coals. Stand the chicken up in the center of the hot grate, over the drip pan and away from the heat. Cover the grill and cook the chicken until the skin is a dark golden brown and very crisp and the meat is cooked through (about 180°F on an instant-read meat thermometer inserted in the thickest part of a thigh, but not touching the bone), 1¼ to 1½ hours (see page 27 for other tests for doneness). If using a charcoal grill, you'll need to add 12 fresh coals per side after 1 hour. If the chicken skin starts to brown too much, loosely tent the bird with aluminum foil.

8. If cooking on a can: Using tongs, hold the bird by the can and carefully transfer it in an upright position to a platter.

If cooking on a roaster: Use oven mitts or pot holders to remove the bird from the grill while it's still on the vertical roaster.

9. Present the bird to your guests. Let the chicken rest for 5 minutes, then carefully lift it off the support. Take care not to spill the hot cola or otherwise burn yourself. Halve, quarter, or carve the chicken and serve with the barbecue sauce.

SERVES 2 to 4

Cola Barbecue Sauce

What better way to spice up a barbecue sauce than with one of the most popular soft drinks in the United States? Obviously, cola barbecue sauce goes great with chicken, but you can also serve it with pork, brisket, ribs, and even salmon.

1 tablespoon butter

¼ cup minced onion

1 tablespoon minced peeled fresh
   ginger

1 clove garlic, minced

¾ cup cola (reserved from Cola-Can
   Chicken)

¾ cup ketchup

½ teaspoon grated lemon zest

2 tablespoons fresh lemon juice

2 tablespoons Worcestershire sauce

2 tablespoons A.1. steak sauce

½ teaspoon liquid smoke

½ teaspoon freshly ground black pepper,
   or more to taste

Coarse salt (kosher or sea) to taste

1. Melt the butter in a heavy saucepan over medium heat. Add the onion, ginger, and garlic and cook until soft but not brown, about 3 minutes. Stir in the cola, raise the heat to high, and bring the sauce to a boil.

2. Add the ketchup, lemon zest and juice, Worcestershire sauce, steak sauce, liquid smoke, and pepper and bring back to a boil. Reduce the heat to medium and gently simmer the sauce until thick and richly flavored, about 5 minutes. Taste for seasoning, adding salt and more pepper to taste. Serve warm or at room temperature. The sauce can be refrigerated, covered, for up to 1 week. Let return to room temperature or warm over medium heat before serving.

MAKES about 1½ cups

INDIRECT GRILLING

GINGER ALE CHICKEN

Chicken has an affinity for ginger—a penchant appreciated by culinary cultures as diverse as Jamaican, Chinese, and Moroccan. That set me thinking about a beer-can chicken that could be cooked with ginger ale or ginger beer. The "rub" is an aromatic paste made from ginger, garlic, and spices. The ginger ale and ginger barbecue sauce up the flavor even more. Now that's a bird with a kick!

FOR THE GINGER-GARLIC PASTE:

2 tablespoons peeled finely chopped fresh ginger

3 cloves garlic, finely chopped

2 scallions, both white and green parts trimmed and finely chopped

1 teaspoon coarse salt (kosher or sea)

½ teaspoon freshly ground black pepper

2 tablespoons Asian (dark) sesame oil or vegetable oil

1 can or bottle (12 ounces) ginger ale or ginger beer

1 chicken (3½ to 4 pounds)

2 slices peeled fresh ginger (each ¼ inch thick)

Ginger Barbecue Sauce (recipe follows)

YOU'LL ALSO NEED:

2 cups wood chips or chunks (preferably hickory), soaked for 1 hour in water and/or beer to cover, then drained

1 clean empty 12-ounce beer or soda can with 2 additional holes made in its top (optional) or a vertical chicken roaster (optional)

1. Make the ginger-garlic paste:

Combine the ginger, garlic, scallions, salt, pepper, and oil in a mini-chopper or blender and purée to a paste. Set aside 1 tablespoon of this paste for the sauce.

2. If the ginger ale is canned: Pop the

tab off the can and pour half of the ginger ale (¾ cup) into a measuring cup and set aside for the sauce. If cooking the chicken on the can, using a church key-style can opener, make 2 additional holes in its top.

If the ginger ale is bottled: Fill an empty can halfway or fill a vertical chicken roaster, following the manufacturer's instructions.

3. Set aside the half-filled

can or filled chicken roaster.

> **TIP:** Ginger ale will produce a great beer-can chicken. Its Caribbean cousin, ginger beer, is stronger, spicier, and less sweet, and also makes wonderful chicken. But most ginger beer comes in bottles only, so if you use it, you'll need to funnel it into an empty can.

4. Remove the packet

of giblets from the body cavity of the chicken and set aside for another use. Remove and discard the fat just inside the body and neck cavities. Rinse the chicken, inside and out, under cold running water and then drain and blot dry, inside and out, with paper towels. Place half of the ginger-garlic paste in the body and neck cavities of the chicken and rub the remainder over the outside of the bird. Put a slice of ginger in the body cavity and in the neck cavity of the chicken.

5. If cooking on a can: Hold the bird

upright, with the opening of the body cavity at the bottom, and lower it onto the can so the can fits into the cavity. Pull the chicken legs forward to form a sort of tripod, so the bird stands upright. The rear leg of the tripod is the can.

If cooking on a roaster: Position the chicken on top, following the manufacturer's instructions.

6. Tuck the tips of the wings behind the chicken's back.

7. Set up the grill for indirect grilling (see page 9 for both charcoal and gas) and preheat to medium. If using a charcoal grill, place a large drip pan in the center. If using a gas grill, place all the wood chips or chunks in the smoker box or in a smoker pouch (see page 12) and preheat on high until you see smoke, then reduce the heat to medium.

8. When ready to cook, if using a charcoal grill, toss all of the wood chips or chunks on the coals. Stand the chicken up in the center of the hot grate, over the drip pan and away from the heat. Cover the grill and cook the chicken until the skin is a dark golden brown and very crisp and the meat is cooked through (about 180°F on an instant-read meat thermometer inserted in the thickest part of a thigh, but not touching the bone), 1¼ to 1½ hours (see page 27 for other tests for doneness). If using a charcoal grill, you'll need to add 12 fresh coals per side after 1 hour. If the chicken skin starts to brown too much, loosely tent the bird with aluminum foil.

9. If cooking on a can: Using tongs, hold the bird by the can and carefully transfer it in an upright position to a platter.

If cooking on a roaster: Use oven mitts or pot holders to remove the bird from the grill while it's still on the vertical roaster.

10. Present the bird to your guests. Let the chicken rest for 5 minutes, then carefully lift it off the support. Take care not to spill the hot ginger ale or otherwise burn yourself. Halve, quarter, or carve the chicken and serve with the Ginger Barbecue Sauce.

SERVES 2 to 4

Ginger Barbecue Sauce

Hoisin sauce, a thick, sweet, purplish-brown, Chinese condiment made from fermented soy bean paste, garlic, and spices, is central to the flavor of this barbecue sauce, adding a musky sweetness. It is available in the ethnic foods section of most supermarkets (not to mention at Asian markets and gourmet shops). Good brands include Amoy, Koon Chun, and Pearl River Bridge.

¾ cup ginger ale or ginger beer (reserved from Ginger Ale Chicken)

¼ cup rice wine or dry sherry

¼ cup hoisin sauce

3 tablespoons ketchup

2½ tablespoons fresh lime juice, or more to taste

2 tablespoons brown sugar

1 tablespoon ginger-garlic paste reserved from Ginger Ale Chicken

Coarse salt (kosher or sea) and freshly ground pepper to taste

1. Place the ginger ale and rice wine in a heavy saucepan, bring to a boil over high heat, and let boil for 2 minutes.

2. Whisk in the hoisin sauce, ketchup, lime juice, brown sugar, and ginger paste. Reduce the heat to medium and let the sauce simmer gently until thick and flavorful, 6 to 10 minutes, whisking from time to time. Taste for seasoning, adding salt and pepper to taste. The sauce can be refrigerated, covered, for up to 1 week. Let return to room temperature before serving.

MAKES about 1 cup

CEL-RAY CHICKEN

Celery soda? One of the most curious beverages on the planet, Dr. Brown's Cel-Ray is soda pop flavored with celery seed. A staple at Jewish delicatessens, the drink has been sipped by untold generations of Americans to wash down corned beef and pastrami sandwiches.

> **TIP:** Dr. Brown's Cel-Ray is available at delicatessens and at many supermarkets. If you can't find it, substitute Sprite or 7UP.

It's virtually unknown outside of these circles, but if you haven't already, there are at least three reasons you should try it. Cel-Ray is delectably different, it's incredibly refreshing, and the celery mitigates the cloying sweetness associated with most soda pops. Give me a canned beverage and I'll create a new version of beer-can chicken. This one is accompanied by a New Orleans-style celery and olive relish.

FOR THE RUB:

1 tablespoon paprika

1 tablespoon brown sugar

2 teaspoons celery salt

1 teaspoon freshly ground black pepper

1 teaspoon dried oregano

1 teaspoon garlic powder

½ teaspoon hot red pepper flakes

¼ teaspoon celery seed

1 can (12 ounces) Dr. Brown's Cel-Ray soda

2 tablespoons salted butter

1 chicken (3½ to 4 pounds)

2 teaspoons vegetable oil

Celery-Olive Relish (recipe follows)

YOU'LL ALSO NEED:

2 cups wood chips or chunks (preferably hickory
or oak), soaked for 1 hour in water to cover,
then drained

Vertical chicken roaster (optional)

1. Make the rub: Put the paprika, brown
sugar, celery salt, black pepper, oregano, garlic
powder, hot red pepper flakes, and celery seed
in a small bowl and stir to mix.

2. Pop the tab off the Cel-Ray can. Pour out
half of the Cel-Ray (¾ cup), setting aside 2 tablespoons for making the basting mixture and reserving the rest for another use. If cooking the chicken
on the can, using a church key-style can opener,
make 2 additional holes in its top.

3. Make the basting mixture: Melt the
butter in a small saucepan over low heat. Add the
2 tablespoons of Cel-Ray and stir to mix. Keep warm.

4. Remove the packet of giblets from the
body cavity of the chicken and set aside for another
use. Remove and discard the fat just inside the

body and neck cavities. Rinse the chicken, inside and out, under cold running water and then drain and blot dry, inside and out, with paper towels. Sprinkle 1 teaspoon of the rub inside the body cavity and ½ teaspoon inside the neck cavity of the chicken. Drizzle the oil over the outside of the bird and rub or brush it all over the skin. Sprinkle the outside of the bird with 1 table-spoon of rub and rub it all over the skin. Spoon the remaining rub into the Cel-Ray through a hole in the top of the can. Don't worry if the Cel-Ray foams up: This is normal.

5. If cooking on a can: Hold the bird upright, with the opening of the body cavity at the bottom, and lower it onto the can so the can fits into the cavity. Pull the chicken legs forward to form a sort of tripod, so the bird stands upright. The rear leg of the tripod is the can.

If cooking on a roaster: Fill it with the flavored Cel-Ray and position the chicken on top, following the manufacturer's instructions.

6. Tuck the tips of the wings behind the chicken's back.

7. Set up the grill for indirect grilling (see page 9 for both charcoal and gas) and preheat to medium. If using a charcoal grill, place a large drip pan in the center. If using a gas grill, place all the wood chips or chunks in the smoker box or in a smoker pouch (see page 12) and preheat on high until you see smoke, then reduce the heat to medium.

8. When ready to cook, if using a charcoal grill, toss all of the wood chips or chunks on the

coals. Stand the chicken up in the center of the hot
grate, over the drip pan and away from the heat.
Cover the grill and cook the chicken until the skin is
a dark golden brown and very crisp and the meat
is cooked through (about 180°F on an instant-read
meat thermometer inserted in the thickest part of a
thigh, but not touching the bone), 1¼ to 1½ hours
(see page 27 for other tests for doneness). If using a
charcoal grill, you'll need to add 12 fresh coals per
side after 1 hour. Baste the chicken with the Cel-Ray
and butter mixture after it has grilled for 30 minutes
and again 30 minutes later, taking care not to knock
the bird over. If the chicken skin starts to brown too
much, loosely tent the bird with aluminum foil.

9. If cooking on a can: Using tongs, hold
the bird by the can and carefully transfer it in an
upright position to a platter.

If cooking on a roaster: Use oven mitts
or pot holders to remove the bird from the grill
while it's still on the vertical roaster.

10. Present the bird to your guests. Let the
chicken rest for 5 minutes, then carefully lift it off
the support. Take care not to spill the hot beer or
otherwise burn yourself. Halve, quarter, or carve
the chicken and serve with the Celery-Olive Relish.

SERVES 2 to 4

Celery-Olive Relish

You can certainly serve this relish
15 minutes after you've made it. But, for a
more authentic New Orleans flavor, prepare
it a day or so ahead of time to let the
flavors marry in the refrigerator.

½ teaspoon salt, or more to taste

1 clove garlic

2 tablespoons red wine vinegar, or more
    to taste

1 cup thinly sliced celery

½ cup sliced pimiento-stuffed green olives

½ cup sliced pitted black olives

⅓ cup finely diced onion

1 teaspoon dried oregano

½ teaspoon freshly ground black pepper

½ teaspoon hot red pepper flakes

3 tablespoons extra-virgin olive oil

1. Place the salt in the bottom of a nonreactive mixing bowl. Add the garlic and mash to a paste with the back of a spoon. Add the vinegar and stir until the salt dissolves.

2. Stir in the celery, green and black olives, onion, oregano, black pepper, hot red pepper flakes, and olive oil. Let the mixture stand for at least 15 minutes, or ideally for several hours or even overnight, before serving.

MAKES about 2 cups

INDIRECT GRILLING

BLACK CHERRY SODA CHICKEN

Poultry and cherries seem made for each other—a relationship appreciated by anyone who has enjoyed Persian duck with sour cherries or French *canard aux cerises* (duck with cherries). These gave me the idea for a beer-can chicken made with black cherry soda.

> **TIP:** A reddish, lemony spice, sumac is made from a Middle Eastern berry. Look for it at Middle Eastern grocery stores. Lemon pepper is a distant substitute, but it will work.

The green tea rub I use was inspired by Ann Wilder, owner of Baltimore-based Vann's Spices. Green tea and sumac may seem like odd ingredients to pair with cherries, but the earthy flavor of the tea and tartness of the sumac balance the sweetness of the soda beautifully. I've included my version of the tea rub, but you can also order it ready-made from Vann's.

FOR THE RUB:

1 tablespoon dried green tea

1 tablespoon ground sumac, or 2 teaspoons
    lemon pepper

1 tablespoon dried onion or shallot flakes

1½ teaspoons coarse salt (kosher or sea)

1 teaspoon freshly ground black pepper
    (if using sumac; omit if using lemon pepper)

1 can (12 ounces) black cherry soda

1 chicken (3½ to 4 pounds)

2 teaspoons vegetable oil

Black Cherry Barbecue Sauce (recipe follows)

YOU'LL ALSO NEED:

2 cups wood chips or chunks (preferably hickory
    or cherry), soaked for 1 hour in water to
    cover, then drained

Vertical chicken roaster (optional)

1. Make the rub: Put the green tea, sumac,
onion flakes, salt, and black pepper, if using, in a
spice mill or coffee grinder and grind them to a fine
powder.

2. Pop the tab off the black cherry soda can.
Pour half of the soda (¾ cup) into a measuring cup
and set aside for the sauce. If cooking the chicken
on the can, using a church key-style can opener,
make 2 additional holes in its top. Set the soda
can aside.

3. Remove the packet of giblets from the
body cavity of the chicken and set aside for another
use. Remove and discard the fat just inside the
body and neck cavities. Rinse the chicken, inside
and out, under cold running water and then drain
and blot dry, inside and out, with paper towels.
Sprinkle 1 teaspoon of the rub inside the body
cavity and ½ teaspoon inside the neck cavity of the
chicken. Drizzle the oil over the outside of the bird

and rub or brush it all over the skin. Sprinkle the outside of the bird with 1 tablespoon of the rub and rub it all over the skin. Spoon the remaining rub into the soda through a hole in the top of the can. Don't worry if the soda foams up: This is normal.

4. If cooking on a can: Hold the bird upright, with the opening of the body cavity at the bottom, and lower it onto the beer can so the can fits into the cavity. Pull the chicken legs forward to form a sort of tripod, so the bird stands upright. The rear leg of the tripod is the can.

If cooking on a roaster: Fill it with the flavored soda and position the chicken on top, following the manufacturer's instructions.

5. Tuck the tips of the wings behind the chicken's back.

6. Set up the grill for indirect grilling (see page 9 for both charcoal and gas) and preheat to medium. If using a charcoal grill, place a large drip pan in the center. If using a gas grill, place all the wood chips or chunks in the smoker box or in a smoker pouch (see page 12) and pre-heat on high until you see smoke, then reduce the heat to medium.

7. When ready to cook, if using a charcoal grill, toss all of the wood chips or chunks on the coals. Stand the chicken up in the center of the hot grate, over the drip pan and away from the heat. Cover the grill and cook the chicken until the skin is a dark golden brown and very crisp and the meat is cooked through (180°F on an instant-read meat thermometer inserted in the thickest part of a thigh, but not touching the bone), 1¼ to 1½ hours (see page 27 for other tests for doneness). If using a charcoal grill, you'll need to add 12 fresh coals per side after

1 hour. If the chicken skin starts to brown too much, loosely tent the bird with aluminum foil.

8. If cooking on a can: Using tongs, hold the bird by the can and carefully transfer it in an upright position to a platter.

If cooking on a roaster: Use oven mitts or pot holders to remove the bird from the grill while it's still on the vertical roaster.

9. Present the bird to your guests. Let the chicken rest for 5 minutes, then carefully lift it off the support. Take care not to spill the hot soda or otherwise burn yourself. Halve, quarter, or carve the chicken and serve with the Black Cherry Barbecue Sauce.

SERVES 2 to 4

Black Cherry Barbecue Sauce

A triple blast of fruit flavor here comes from black cherry soda, cherry preserves, and canned Bing cherries. The purist would start with fresh cherries. (You'd need to pit about a pound.) For the sake of simplicity, use the canned.

¾ cup black cherry soda (reserved from
   Black Cherry Soda Chicken)
1 can Bing cherries (17 ounces), drained
3 tablespoons cherry preserves
2 tablespoons fresh lemon juice, or more to
   taste
2 tablespoons butter
1 tablespoon sugar, or more to taste
½ teaspoon ground cinnamon
¼ cup dry red wine
1 tablespoon cornstarch
Coarse salt (kosher or sea) and freshly
   ground black pepper

1. Put the cherry soda, cherries, cherry preserves, lemon juice, butter, sugar, cinnamon, and
3 tablespoons of the wine in a heavy saucepan
and bring to a boil over high heat. Reduce the heat
to medium and let the sauce simmer gently for
5 minutes.

2. Put the remaining 1 tablespoon wine and the
cornstarch in a small bowl and stir to form a slurry
(thick paste). Whisk this paste into the cherry
sauce. Bring the sauce to a boil over high heat to
thicken, about 1 minute.

3. Taste for seasoning, adding more sugar or
lemon juice to adjust the sweetness and salt and
pepper to taste; the sauce should be highly seasoned. Serve warm or at room temperature. The
sauce can be refrigerated, covered, for up to 1 week.
Let return to room temperature or warm over
medium heat before serving.

MAKES about 2 cups

PEACH NECTAR CHICKEN

If you have savored barbecue

in Georgia, you know that the brassy flavor of peach makes a great combo with the smoky tang of barbecued chicken. This peach nectar chicken, with its peach barbecue sauce, will delight everyone who loves a ripe peach—and who doesn't?

TIP: *Peach nectar is available in cans in the juice section of most supermarkets. You want an aluminum can with a baked-on label, not one of the old-fashioned soldered cans with a paper label. Be sure to shake the can well before opening it. You could also make this savory bird with apricot or nectarine nectar.*

FOR THE RUB:

2 teaspoons brown sugar

2 teaspoons sweet paprika

1 teaspoon coarse salt (kosher or sea)

1 teaspoon freshly ground black pepper

1 teaspoon garlic powder

1 teaspoon ground cinnamon

¼ teaspoon ground cardamom

1 can (12 ounces) peach nectar

1 cinnamon stick (3 inches)

1 chicken (3½ to 4 pounds)

2 teaspoons vegetable oil

Peach Barbecue Sauce

 (recipe follows)

YOU'LL ALSO NEED:

2 cups wood chips or chunks (preferably peach
or apple), soaked for 1 hour in
water to cover, then drained
Vertical chicken roaster (optional)

> **TIP:** *Peach wood chips can be purchased from Nature's Own and Peoples Woods (see Mail-Order Sources, page 311).*

1. Make the rub: Put the
brown sugar, paprika, salt, pepper, garlic powder, cinnamon,
and cardamom in a small bowl and stir to mix.

2. Pop the tab off the can of peach nectar.
Pour half of the peach nectar (³⁄₄ cup) into a measuring cup and set aside for the sauce. If cooking the
chicken on the can, using a church key-style can
opener, make 2 additional holes in its top, then
place the cinnamon stick in the nectar can and set
aside. If using a vertical chicken roaster, fill with the
³⁄₄ cup peach nectar remaining in the can, add the
cinnamon stick, and set aside.

3. Remove the packet of giblets from the
body cavity of the chicken and set aside for another
use. Remove and discard the fat just inside the
body and neck cavities. Rinse the chicken, inside
and out, under cold running water and then drain
and blot dry, inside and out, with paper towels.
Sprinkle 1 teaspoon of the rub inside the body
cavity and ¹⁄₂ teaspoon inside the neck cavity of the
chicken. Drizzle the oil over the outside of the bird
and rub or brush it all over the skin. Sprinkle the
outside of the bird with 1 tablespoon of the rub and
rub it all over the skin.

4. If cooking on a can: Spoon the remaining rub into the can of peach nectar through a hole
in its top. Hold the bird upright, with the opening of
the body cavity at the bottom, and lower it onto the
can so the can fits into the cavity. Pull the chicken
legs forward to form a sort of tripod, so the bird
stands upright. The rear leg of the tripod is the can.

If cooking on a roaster: Spoon the remaining rub into the peach nectar in the vertical roaster. Position the chicken on top, following the manufacturer's instructions.

5. Tuck the tips of the wings behind the chicken's back.

6. Set up the grill for indirect grilling (see page 9 for both charcoal and gas) and preheat to medium. If using a charcoal grill, place a large drip pan in the center. If using a gas grill, place all the wood chips or chunks in the smoker box or in a smoker pouch (see page 12) and preheat on high until you see smoke, then reduce the heat to medium.

7. When ready to cook, if using a charcoal grill, toss all of the wood chips or chunks on the coals. Stand the chicken up in the center of the hot grate, over the drip pan and away from the heat. Cover the grill and cook the chicken until the skin is a dark golden brown and very crisp and the meat is cooked through (about 180°F on an instant-read meat thermometer inserted in the thickest part of a thigh, but not touching the bone), 1¼ to 1½ hours (see page 27 for other tests for doneness). If using a charcoal grill, you'll need to add 12 fresh coals per side after 1 hour. If the chicken skin starts to brown too much, loosely tent the bird with aluminum foil.

8. If cooking on a can: Using tongs, hold the bird by the can and carefully transfer it in an upright position to a platter.

If cooking on a roaster: Use oven mitts or pot holders to remove the bird from the grill while it's still on the vertical roaster.

9. Present the bird to your guests. Let the chicken rest for 5 minutes, then carefully lift it off

the support. Take care not to spill the hot nectar or otherwise burn yourself. Halve, quarter, or carve the chicken and serve with the Peach Barbecue Sauce.

SERVES 2 to 4

Peach Barbecue Sauce

Barbecue sauce made with peaches is a great accompaniment for regular beer-can chicken, as well as Peach Nectar Chicken, and it's equally outrageous with pork or ribs.

¾ cup peach nectar (reserved from Peach
    Nectar Chicken)
½ cup ketchup
2 tablespoons peach or apricot preserves
1 tablespoon honey, or more to taste
1 tablespoon Worcestershire sauce
1 tablespoon peach schnapps or dark rum
½ teaspoon soy sauce
¼ teaspoon liquid smoke
Coarse salt (kosher or sea) and freshly ground
    black pepper to taste

1. Combine the peach nectar, ketchup, peach preserves, honey, Worcestershire sauce, schnapps, soy sauce, and liquid smoke with ¼ cup water in a heavy saucepan and slowly bring to a boil, over medium-high heat.

2. Reduce the heat to medium and let the sauce simmer gently until thick and richly flavored, 8 to 10 minutes, stirring often. Taste for seasoning, adding salt, pepper, and additional honey to taste.

3. Serve the sauce warm or at room temperature. In the unlikely event you have any left over, store it in the refrigerator, covered, where it will keep for up to a week.

MAKES about 2 cups

PILGRIM CHICKEN

I'm not sure what the first European settlers in New England would have made of beer-can chicken, but they did drink lots of beer, and they did discover cranberries at their first settlement, Plimoth, in southeastern Massachusetts. The refreshing astringency of cranberry juice inspired this variation on beer-can chicken. The bird gets a triple blast of cranberry flavor: first from the juice in the can, then from a cranberry butter glaze, and finally from a fresh cranberry salsa served on the side.

FOR THE RUB:

1 tablespoon brown sugar
1 tablespoon coarse salt
  (kosher or sea)
1 teaspoon freshly ground black pepper
1½ teaspoons ground coriander
½ teaspoon ground cinnamon

1 can (12 ounces) cranberry juice
3 tablespoons salted butter, melted
1 chicken (3½ to 4 pounds)
Cranberry Salsa (recipe follows)

YOU'LL ALSO NEED:

2 cups wood chips or chunks
  (preferably oak, apple, or cherry), soaked for
  1 hour in water to cover, then drained
Vertical chicken roaster (optional)

TIP: *Cranberry juice is most commonly available in bottles. If you can't find it canned at the supermarket, look for it in vending machines that sell fruit juices. Or pour it into an empty beer can.*

1. Make the rub: Put the brown sugar, salt, pepper, coriander, and cinnamon in a small bowl and stir to mix.

2. Pop the tab off the cranberry juice can. Pour half of the cranberry juice (¾ cup) into a small heavy saucepan. If cooking the chicken on the can, using a church key-style can opener, make 2 additional holes in its top. Set the juice can aside.

3. Boil the cranberry juice in the saucepan over high heat until only ¼ cup remains, about 5 minutes. Add 2 tablespoons of the butter and 1 teaspoon of the rub and simmer until syrupy, about 2 minutes. Set the glaze aside.

4. Remove the packet of giblets from the body cavity of the chicken and set aside for another use. Remove and discard the fat just inside the body and neck cavities. Rinse the chicken, inside and out, under cold running water and then drain and blot dry, inside and out, with paper towels. Sprinkle 1 teaspoon of the rub inside the body cavity and ½ teaspoon inside the neck cavity of the chicken. Brush the outside of the bird with the remaining 1 tablespoon of melted butter. Sprinkle the outside of the bird with 1 tablespoon of the rub and rub it all over the skin. Spoon the remaining rub into the cranberry juice through the holes in the top of the can.

5. If cooking on a can: Hold the bird upright, with the opening of the body cavity at the bottom, and lower it onto the can so the can fits into the cavity. Pull the chicken legs forward to form a sort of tripod, so the bird stands upright. The rear leg of the tripod is the can.

If cooking on a roaster: Fill the can with the cranberry juice mixture and position the chicken on top, following the manufacturer's instructions.

6. Tuck the tips of the wings behind the chicken's back.

7. Set up the grill for indirect grilling (see page 9 for both charcoal and gas) and preheat to medium. If using a charcoal grill, place a large drip pan in the center. If using a gas grill, place all the wood chips or chunks in the smoker box or in a smoker pouch (see page 12) and preheat on high until you see smoke, then reduce the heat to medium.

8. When ready to cook, if using a charcoal grill, toss all of the wood chips or chunks on the coals. Stand the chicken upright in the center of the hot grate, over the drip pan and away from the heat. Cover the grill and cook the chicken until the skin is a dark golden brown and very crisp and the meat is cooked through (about 180°F on an instant-read meat thermometer inserted in the thickest part of a thigh, but not touching the bone), 1¼ to 1½ hours (see page 27 for other tests for doneness). If using a charcoal grill, you'll need to add 12 fresh coals per side after 1 hour. Baste the chicken with the cranberry glaze 15 minutes before taking it off the grill, taking care not to knock it over. If the chicken skin starts to brown too much, loosely tent the bird with aluminum foil. Baste the bird one last time before it comes off the grill.

9. If cooking on a can: Using tongs, hold the bird by the can and carefully transfer it in an upright position to a platter.

 If cooking on a roaster: Use oven mitts or pot holders to remove the bird from the grill while it's still on the vertical roaster.

10. Present the bird to your guests. Let the chicken rest for 5 minutes, then carefully lift it off the support. Take care not to spill the hot cranberry juice or otherwise burn yourself. Halve, quarter, or carve the chicken and serve with Cranberry Salsa on the side.

SERVES 2 to 4

Cranberry Salsa

You'll find that this recipe makes more salsa than you need for one chicken. Well, maybe. Actually, my wife and I have been known to eat a whole batch at a single sitting. In the event that you have any left over, it'll keep for several days in the refrigerator.

1 bag (12 ounces) fresh cranberries
1 clove garlic, minced
1 to 3 jalapeño peppers, seeded and minced
   (for a hotter salsa, leave the seeds in)
¼ cup chopped fresh cilantro
3 scallions, both white and green parts,
   trimmed and finely chopped
⅓ cup sugar, or more to taste
¼ cup fresh lime juice, or more to taste
Coarse salt (kosher or sea) and freshly ground
   black pepper

1. Bring 2 cups of water to a boil in a large saucepan over high heat. Add the cranberries and cook 1 to 2 minutes. Drain the cranberries in a colander and rinse under cold water until cool. Drain well.

2. Place the cooled cranberries in a nonreactive mixing bowl and gently stir in the garlic, jalapeño(s), cilantro, scallions, sugar, and lime juice. Taste for seasoning, adding salt and pepper and more sugar or lime juice as necessary; the salsa should be sweet, tart, and spicy.

MAKES about 2 cups

LEMONADE CHICKEN

A cold glass of lemonade on a hot summer day—is there anything quite as refreshing? This is the inspiration for another twist on beer-can chicken: a bird roasted upright over an open can of lemonade. The rub is made with powdered lemonade mix (the "secret" ingredient in a lot of Kansas City rubs), while the barbecue sauce combines lemonade, brown sugar, and mustard.

FOR THE LEMONADE RUB:

1 tablespoon lemonade powder

1 tablespoon brown sugar

1 tablespoon paprika

2 teaspoons hickory-smoked salt

1 teaspoon lemon pepper

1 teaspoon garlic powder

1 teaspoon onion powder

¼ teaspoon celery seed

1 can (12 ounces) lemonade

1 chicken (3½ to 4 pounds)

2 teaspoons vegetable oil

Lemonade-Mustard Sauce (recipe follows)

YOU'LL ALSO NEED:

2 cups wood chips or chunks (preferably hickory or oak), soaked for 1 hour in water to cover, then drained

Vertical chicken roaster (optional)

BUYING TIPS:

CANNED LEMONADE can be found in convenience store cold cases and at many supermarkets. Choose yellow lemonade if possible. Be sure to use a can of lemonade, not frozen lemonade concentrate.

HICKORY-SMOKED SALT AND LEMON PEPPER are often sold in the supermarket spice rack. If unavailable, use regular salt and pepper.

1. Make the lemonade rub: Put the lemonade powder, brown sugar, paprika, hickory salt, lemon pepper, garlic and onion powders, and celery seed in a small bowl and stir to mix.

2. Pop the tab off the lemonade can. Pour half of the lemonade (¾ cup) into a measuring cup and set aside for the sauce. If cooking the chicken on the can, using a church key-style can opener, make 2 additional holes in its top. Set the can aside.

3. Remove the packet of giblets from the body cavity of the chicken and set aside for another use. Remove and discard the fat just inside the body and neck cavities. Rinse the chicken, inside and out, under cold running water and then drain and blot dry, inside and out, with paper towels. Sprinkle 1 teaspoon of the rub inside the body cavity and ½ teaspoon inside the neck cavity of the chicken. Drizzle the oil over the outside of the bird and rub or brush it all over the skin. Sprinkle the outside of the bird with 1 tablespoon rub and rub it all over the skin. Set aside 2 teaspoons of rub for the sauce. Spoon the remaining rub into the lemonade through a hole in the top of the can.

4. If cooking on a can: Hold the bird upright, with the opening of the body cavity at the bottom, and lower it onto the can so the can fits into the cavity. Pull the chicken legs forward to form a sort of tripod, so the bird stands upright. The rear leg of the tripod is the can.

If cooking on a roaster: Fill it with the lemonade mixture and position the chicken on top, following the manufacturer's instructions.

5. Tuck the tips of the wings behind the chicken's back.

6. Set up the grill for indirect grilling (see page 9 for both charcoal and gas) and preheat to medium. If using a charcoal grill, place a large drip pan in the center. If using a gas grill, place all the wood chips or chunks in the smoker box or in a smoker pouch (see page 12) and preheat on high until you see smoke, then reduce the heat to medium.

7. When ready to cook, if using a charcoal grill, toss all of the wood chips or chunks on the coals. Stand the chicken up in the center of the hot grate, over the drip pan and away from the heat. Cover the grill and cook the chicken until the skin is a dark golden brown and very crisp and the meat is cooked through (about 180°F on an instant-read meat thermometer inserted in the thickest part of a thigh, but not touching the bone), 1¼ to 1½ hours (see page 27 for other tests for doneness). If using a charcoal grill, you'll need to add 12 fresh coals per side after 1 hour. If the chicken skin starts to brown too much, loosely tent the bird with aluminum foil.

8. If cooking on a can: Using tongs, hold the bird by the can and carefully transfer it in an upright position to a platter.

If cooking on a roaster: Use oven mitts or pot holders to remove the bird from the grill while it's still on the vertical roaster.

9. Present the bird to your guests. Let the chicken rest for 5 minutes, then carefully lift it off the support. Take care not to spill the hot lemonade or otherwise burn yourself. Halve, quarter, or carve the chicken and serve with Lemonade-Mustard Sauce.

SERVES 2 to 4

1
2
3

LEMONADE-MUSTARD SAUCE

What started as a mustard sauce in the finest South Carolina tradition gets an uncommon piquancy with the addition of lemon juice, lemon zest, and lemonade. It goes great with any sort of poultry, with pork, and even with rich, grilled fish, such as swordfish or salmon.

1 tablespoon butter

2 to 3 shallots, or 1 small onion, finely chopped (about ½ cup)

¾ cup lemonade (reserved from Lemonade Chicken)

½ cup firmly packed light brown sugar

6 tablespoons Dijon mustard

3 tablespoons fresh lemon juice, or more to taste

½ teaspoon grated fresh lemon zest

Coarse salt (kosher or sea) and freshly ground black pepper

1. Melt the butter in a heavy saucepan over medium heat. Add the shallots and cook until just beginning to brown, about 4 minutes.

2. Add the lemonade, raise the heat to high, and let boil until reduced to 2 tablespoons, about 5 minutes.

3. Stir in the brown sugar, mustard, lemon juice, and lemon zest. Lower the heat to medium and let the sauce simmer until thick and richly flavored, about 5 minutes, whisking from time to time. Taste for seasoning, adding salt, pepper, and more lemon juice to taste.

MAKES about 1¼ cups

INDIRECT GRILLING

THAI COCONUT CHICKEN

I'm certainly not alone in declaring coconut milk one of my favorite ingredients for barbecue. Throughout Southeast Asia, this "cream" of the tropics is used for marinades, bastes, and barbecue sauces. I love its tropical fragrance and the way its high fat content keeps foods moist during grilling. Here coconut milk comes into play in three stages: as a steaming agent in the beer can, as a baste for the chicken, and to enrich the peanut barbecue sauce. And since Thais don't go in much for smoked foods, I've made the wood chips optional.

ADVANCE PREPARATION: 1 hour for marinating the chicken

TIP: *Most of the coconut milk you'll find comes in cans that are about 14 ounces, which are a little too big to fit in a chicken. But you can certainly transfer the coconut milk to an empty beer can. You'll find coconut milk at Asian and Latino markets, gourmet shops, and at an increasing number of supermarkets (look for it in the ethnic foods section). You must use unsweetened coconut milk, not the sugary coconut cream used for making piña coladas. Two good Thai brands are Chaokoh and A Taste of Thai.*

FOR THE RUB:

1 tablespoon ground coriander

1 tablespoon coarse salt (kosher or sea)

1 tablespoon freshly ground black pepper

2 cloves garlic, minced

2 tablespoons minced fresh cilantro

1 tablespoon minced fresh lemongrass, or 1 teaspoon finely grated lemon zest

1 tablespoon minced peeled fresh ginger

3 to 4 tablespoons vegetable oil

1 can coconut milk (about 13½ ounces)

1 stalk lemongrass, trimmed (see Note), or 2 strips lemon zest (each 2 by ½ inches)

1 chicken (3½ to 4 pounds)

Coconut-Peanut Sauce (recipe follows)

YOU'LL ALSO NEED:

2 cups wood chips or chunks (optional; preferably oak or apple), soaked for 1 hour in water to cover, then drained

1 clean empty 12-ounce beer or soda can with 2 additional holes made in its top or a vertical chicken roaster

> **TIP:** *Lemongrass is an Asian herb with long, slender fibrous stalks. The flavor is perfumed, lemony, and herbacious but not the least bit tart. In a pinch, you can substitute ½-by-2-inch strips of lemon zest.*

1. Make the rub paste:

Put the coriander, salt, pepper, garlic, cilantro, minced lemongrass, and ginger in a blender and purée, adding enough oil to make a paste.

2. Shake the can of

coconut milk well. Place ¼ cup coconut milk and 1 tablespoon of the rub paste in a small bowl and set aside. You'll use this mixture for basting the chicken. Using a funnel, pour ¾ cup coconut milk into a clean empty beer can or vertical chicken roaster. Add the lemongrass stalk and set aside.

3. Remove the packet of giblets from the body cavity of the chicken and set aside for another use. Remove and discard the fat just inside the body and neck cavities. Rinse the chicken, inside and out, under cold running water and then drain and blot dry, inside and out, with paper towels. Smear the remaining rub paste over the chicken inside and out. Place the chicken in a resealable plastic bag or covered bowl and let marinate in the refrigerator for 1 hour.

4. If cooking on a can: Hold the bird upright, with the opening of the body cavity at the bottom, and lower it onto the coconut milk-filled beer can so the can fits into the cavity. Pull the chicken legs forward to form a sort of tripod, so the chicken stands upright. The rear leg of the tripod is the can.

   If cooking on a roaster: Position the chicken on top, following the manufacturer's instructions.

5. Tuck the tips of the wings behind the chicken's back.

6. Set up the grill for indirect grilling (see page 9 for both charcoal and gas) and preheat to medium. If using a charcoal grill, place a large drip pan in the center. If using a gas grill, place all the wood chips or chunks, if using, in the smoker box or in a smoker pouch (see page 12) and preheat on high until you see smoke, then reduce the heat to medium.

7. When ready to cook, if using a charcoal grill, toss all of the wood chips or chunks, if using, on the coals. Stand the chicken up in the center of the hot grate, over the drip pan and away from the heat. Cover the grill and cook the chicken until the skin is a dark golden brown and very crisp and the meat is cooked through (about 180°F on an instant-read meat thermometer inserted in the thickest part of a thigh, but not touching the bone), 1¼ to 1½ hours (see page 27 for other tests for doneness). Start basting the chicken with the coconut milk mixture after 45 minutes and baste it every 15 minutes, taking care not to knock the bird over. Do not baste the chicken immediately before you remove it from the grill. If using a charcoal grill, you'll need to add 12 fresh coals per side after 1 hour. If the chicken skin starts to brown too much, loosely tent the bird with aluminum foil.

8. If cooking on a can: Using tongs, hold the bird by the can and carefully transfer it in an upright position to a platter.

If cooking on a roaster: Use oven mitts or pot holders to remove the bird from the grill while it's still on the vertical roaster.

9. Present the bird to your guests. Let the chicken rest for 5 minutes, then carefully lift it off the support. Take care not to spill the hot coconut milk or otherwise burn yourself. Halve, quarter, or carve the chicken and serve with Coconut-Peanut Sauce.

SERVES 2 to 4

NOTE: To trim lemongrass, cut off the root end and green leafy tops, leaving a core section that's 3 to 5 inches long. Strip off the outer leaves. The core should be pale green or cream colored.

Coconut-Peanut Sauce

Order grilled chicken in Indonesia, Singapore, Malaysia, and Thailand and this is what you'll get as a barbecue sauce. Peanut butter makes it nutty and rich, while fried shallots, garlic, ginger, and chiles provide pungency. Don't be put off by the large number of ingredients: The sauce can be prepared in less than 15 minutes.

2 tablespoons vegetable oil
2 to 3 shallots, finely chopped (about ½ cup)
2 cloves garlic, minced
1 tablespoon minced peeled fresh ginger
1 to 2 Thai chile(s) or serrano or jalapeño pepper(s), seeded and minced (for a hotter sauce, leave the seeds in)
1 teaspoon ground coriander
¾ cup coconut milk (reserved from Thai Coconut Chicken)
¾ cup chunky peanut butter
2 tablespoons soy sauce or Asian fish sauce, or more to taste
1 tablespoon fresh lime juice, or more to taste
2 teaspoons sugar
½ teaspoon freshly ground black pepper
2 tablespoons chopped fresh cilantro

> **TIP:** *Fish sauce is a malodorous condiment made from fermented anchovies. I've made it optional in the peanut barbecue sauce, calling for commonplace soy sauce instead.*

1. Heat the oil in a wok or deep saucepan over high heat. Add the shallots, garlic, ginger, chile(s), and coriander and stir-fry until golden brown, about 3 minutes, stirring with a wooden spoon.

2. Stir in the coconut milk and bring to a boil. Stir in the peanut butter, soy sauce, lime juice, sugar, and black pepper, reduce the heat to medium, and let simmer until thick and richly flavored, about 5 minutes. Stir in the cilantro and cook for 1 minute. Taste for seasoning, adding soy sauce and/or lime juice as necessary. Serve at room temperature. The sauce can be refrigerated, covered, for up to 3 days. Let return to room temperature and stir to recombine before serving.

MAKES about 2 cups

ICED TEA CHICKEN

Think out of the box—this cutting-edge business philosophy is also good for barbecue. Sweet tea (heavily sweetened iced tea) is so popular at barbecue joints in Texas and the South, I thought, why not use iced tea mix in a barbecue rub and grill the chicken on a can of iced tea? It sounds outrageous. It *is* outrageous. But being outrageous should be one of the goals of a grill master. And, besides, you'll be surprised how well the tea flavor marries with smoke and spice in this chicken.

TIP: *Be sure to use an iced tea made with real sugar, not with an artificial sweetener. The latter will give the chicken a chemical taste.*

FOR THE RUB:

1 tablespoon powdered iced tea mix

1 tablespoon paprika

2 teaspoons ground coriander

1 teaspoon sugar

1 teaspoon coarse salt (kosher or sea)

½ teaspoon freshly ground black pepper

½ teaspoon garlic powder

¼ teaspoon celery seed

1 can (12 ounces) iced tea

1 chicken (3½ to 4 pounds)

2 teaspoons vegetable oil

Iced Tea Barbecue Sauce (recipe follows)

YOU'LL ALSO NEED:

2 cups wood chips or chunks (preferably hickory
**   or cherry), soaked for 1 hour in water to**
**   cover, then drained**
Vertical chicken roaster (optional)

1. Make the rub: Put the iced tea mix,
paprika, coriander, sugar, salt, pepper, garlic powder, and celery seed in a small bowl and stir to mix.

2. Pop the tab off the iced tea can. Pour half
the tea (¾ cup) into a measuring cup and set aside
for the sauce. If cooking the chicken on the can,
using a church key-style can opener, make 2 additional holes in its top. Set the can aside.

3. Remove the packet of giblets from the
body cavity of the chicken and set aside for
another use. Remove and discard the fat just
inside the body and neck cavities. Rinse the
chicken, inside and out, under cold running water
and then drain and blot dry, inside and out, with
paper towels. Sprinkle 1 teaspoon of the rub inside
the body cavity and ½ teaspoon inside the neck
cavity of the chicken. Drizzle the oil over the outside of the bird and rub or brush it all over the
skin. Sprinkle the outside of the bird with 1 tablespoon of the rub and rub it all over the skin.
Spoon the remaining rub into the iced tea
through a hole in the top of the can.

4. If cooking on a can: Hold the bird
upright, with the opening of the body cavity at the
bottom, and lower it onto the can so the can fits
into the cavity. Pull the chicken legs forward to
form a sort of tripod, so the bird stands upright.
The rear leg of the tripod is the can.

   If cooking on a roaster: Fill it with the
iced tea mixture and position the chicken on top,
following the manufacturer's instructions.

5. Tuck the tips of the wings behind the chicken's back.

6. Set up the grill for indirect grilling (see page 9 for both charcoal and gas) and preheat to medium. If using a charcoal grill, place a large drip pan in the center. If using a gas grill, place all the wood chips or chunks in the smoker box or in a smoker pouch (see page 12) and preheat on high until you see smoke, then reduce the heat to medium.

7. When ready to cook, if using a charcoal grill, toss all of the wood chips or chunks on the coals. Stand the chicken up in the center of the hot grate, over the drip pan and away from the heat. Cover the grill and cook the chicken until the skin is a dark golden brown and very crisp and the meat is cooked through (about 180°F on an instant-read meat thermometer inserted in the thickest part of a thigh, but not touching the bone), 1¼ to 1½ hours (see page 27 for other tests for doneness). If using a charcoal grill, you'll need to add 12 fresh coals per side after 1 hour. If the chicken skin starts to brown too much, loosely tent the bird with aluminum foil.

8. If cooking on a can: Using tongs, hold the bird by the can and carefully transfer it in an upright position to a platter.

If cooking on a roaster: Use oven mitts or pot holders to remove the bird from the grill while it's still on the vertical roaster.

9. Present the bird to your guests. Let the chicken rest for 5 minutes, then carefully lift it off the support. Take care not to spill the hot iced tea or otherwise burn yourself. Halve, quarter, or carve the chicken and serve with Iced Tea Barbecue Sauce.

SERVES 2 to 4

Iced Tea Barbecue Sauce

The annals of barbecue have seen some pretty strange sauces. This one may seem over-the-top, and yet, canned iced tea has a lot in common with the flavor profile of a good barbecue sauce. It's sweet. It's tart. It's earthy and aromatic. What more could you ask for? Think of the bragging you'll get to do the next time someone admires this sauce and asks you what's in it.

¾ **cup canned iced tea**
  (reserved from Iced Tea Chicken)
¾ **cup ketchup**
2 **tablespoons Worcestershire sauce**
2 **tablespoons A.1. steak sauce**
2 **tablespoons brown sugar, or more to**
  taste
1 **tablespoon fresh lemon**
  juice, or more to taste
½ **teaspoon liquid smoke**
½ **teaspoon onion powder**
½ **teaspoon garlic powder**
½ **teaspoon freshly ground**
  black pepper

1. Combine the iced tea, ketchup, Worcestershire sauce, steak sauce, brown sugar, lemon juice, liquid smoke, onion and garlic powders, and pepper in a heavy saucepan with ¼ cup of water and gradually bring to a boil over medium-high heat.

2. Reduce the heat to medium to obtain a gentle simmer. Let the sauce simmer gently until slightly reduced, thick, and richly flavored, 6 to 8 minutes. Taste for seasoning, adding brown sugar or lemon juice as necessary; the sauce should be highly seasoned. If sauce is too thick or intense, thin with a little more water.

3. Transfer the sauce to a bowl or clean jar and let cool to room temperature before serving. Any leftover sauce (in the unlikely event that you have it) will keep in the refrigerator, covered, for several weeks. Let return to room temperature before serving.

MAKES about 2 cups

OTHER BIRDS MEET THE CAN

Beer-can chicken is a way of life for me. That is to say, I use the beer-canning process not just with chicken but with all manner of poultry, from diminutive quail to oversize turkeys. The secret is the choice of beverage and the size of the can. A 6-ounce juice can is just small enough to accommodate a small bird like that quail, while a 32-ounce can of Australian Foster's lager can handle a whole Thanksgiving turkey. Along the way in this chapter, you'll find duck barbecued on a "tall boy" (an oversize 16-ounce beer can), some game hens that are fair game for beer canning; and a partridge cooked on my kind of pear tree—a can of pear nectar. Who said beer-can chicken is only good for chicken? It's a whole new ball game out there, and here are some of the latest star players.

INDIRECT GRILLING

PINEAPPLE JUICE QUAIL

He wouldn't. He couldn't. Human decency simply wouldn't allow a person to force such a small, delicate bird as a quail onto a beer can. True, but what about using a smaller can, say a 6-ounce can of pineapple juice? Pineapple juice is an indispensable barbecue ingredient in Hawaii, and it makes a knockout barbecue sauce for quail. These little soldiers lined up on their juice cans look cool, and when you serve them, everyone will admire your ingenuity.

> **TIP:** *Quail are almost always sold frozen, so buy them the day before you plan to use them and let them thaw in the refrigerator. Many are sold partially boned, with wire frames to hold them flat. You'll need to remove the wire before cooking. If your quail is not boned, you may need to make a cut on either side of the backbone, using poultry shears, to make it easier to fit the bird on the can.*

8 cans (6 ounces each) pineapple juice

2 tablespoons Asian (dark) sesame oil or vegetable oil, plus vegetable oil for oiling the cans

8 quail (about 2 pounds total)

Coarse salt (kosher or sea) and freshly ground black pepper

Pineapple Sauce (recipe follows)

YOU'LL ALSO NEED:

2 cups wood chips or chunks (optional; preferably apple or cherry), soaked for 1 hour in water to cover, then drained

Poultry shears (optional)

1. Pop the tab off each juice can. Pour half of the juice (6 tablespoons per can, 3 cups total) into a large heavy saucepan and set aside for the sauce. Using a church key-style can opener, make 1 additional hole in the top of each can. Generously rub the outside of the cans with vegetable oil (this facilitates removing the quail) and set aside.

2. Remove the wire frames from the quail, if necessary. Rinse the quail under cold running water and then drain and blot dry with paper towels. Generously season the inside of each quail with salt and pepper. Drizzle some of the sesame oil over the outside of each quail and rub or brush it all over the skin. Season the outsides of the quail with salt and pepper, rubbing them all over the skin.

3. Holding a quail upright, with the opening of the body cavity at the bottom, lower it onto the juice can so the can fits into the cavity. You'll need to do some tugging and pulling. If the fit is really tight, using poultry shears, make cuts on either side of the backbone, starting at the tail and going about halfway up the back. Repeat with the remaining quail. Tuck the wing tips behind the back of each quail.

4. Set up the grill for indirect grilling (see page 9 for both charcoal and gas) and preheat to medium-high. If using a charcoal grill, place a large drip pan in the center. If using a gas grill, place all the wood chips or chunks, if using, in the smoker box or in a smoker pouch (see page 12) and preheat on high until you see smoke, then reduce the heat to medium-high.

5. When ready to cook, if using a charcoal grill, toss all of the wood chips or chunks, if using, on the coals. Arrange the quail in the center of the hot grate, over the drip pan and away from the heat. The quail legs won't be long enough to reach the grate, so you'll need to balance the cans so the quail stand upright. Cover the grill and cook the quail until the skins are a dark golden brown and very crisp and the meat is cooked through (the breast will feel firm to the touch when done), 20 to 30 minutes (see page 27 for other tests for doneness). If the quail start to brown too much, lay a sheet of aluminum foil over them.

6. Using tongs to take hold of the can, carefully transfer the quail one by one in an upright position on its juice can to a platter and present them to your guests. Let the quail rest for 5 minutes, then carefully lift them off the cans (you may need to twist them gently). Wear a kitchen mitt to protect your fingers. Take care not to spill the hot pineapple juice or otherwise burn yourself. Serve the quail whole, 2 per person, with Pineapple Sauce.

SERVES 4

Pineapple Sauce

Sweet, acidic, fruity, and distinctively perfumed, pineapple juice has the perfect flavor profile for a barbecue sauce. This sauce has an Asian accent and you can make it as fiery or mild as you desire, depending on how much chili sauce you add.

> **TIP:** Pineapple juice comes in two sorts of cans—the old-fashioned soldered tin can with a paper label and the new-style aluminum can with a label baked into the metal. Use the latter.

3 cups pineapple juice (reserved from Pineapple
   Juice Quail)

3 tablespoons brown sugar

2 tablespoons soy sauce

1 to 3 teaspoons Sriracha
   (Thai hot sauce) or your
   favorite hot sauce

2 tablespoons chopped fresh
   cilantro

1 tablespoon minced peeled
   fresh ginger

2 tablespoons butter

Coarse salt (kosher or sea) and
   freshly ground black pepper to taste

1. Put the pineapple juice, brown sugar, soy
sauce, hot sauce, cilantro, and ginger in a large
heavy saucepan. Bring the mixture to a boil over
high heat, then reduce the heat to medium and
simmer, stirring occasionally, until thick, richly
flavored, and reduced to about 2 cups, 15 to 20
minutes.

2. Remove the pan from the heat and whisk in
the butter. Season with salt and pepper to taste.

MAKES about 2 cups

INDIRECT GRILLING

QUAIL ON A THRONE

What is it about prunes? They get so little respect in the United States. A very different attitude prevails in Europe, where Italians eat prune gelato; Yugoslavians sip prune brandy; and the French consume prunes in everything from duck to yogurt to Armagnac. The truth is that the prune is a superb fruit, and here I've given it the royal treatment. I think you'll find prune juice, with its rich earthy flavors, makes a compelling barbecue sauce.

FOR THE RUB:
1 tablespoon coarse salt (kosher or sea)
1 tablespoon brown sugar
1½ teaspoons freshly ground black pepper
1½ teaspoons ground coriander
1 teaspoon ground cinnamon

8 cans (6 ounces each) prune juice
8 quail (about 2 pounds total)
2 tablespoons walnut oil or olive oil
Vegetable oil for oiling the cans
Cinnamon-Prune Sauce (recipe
follows)

TIP: *You want to use prune juice that comes in an aluminum can with a baked-on label for the quail, not in a soldered tin can with a paper label.*

YOU'LL ALSO NEED:
2 cups wood chips or chunks (optional;
preferably hickory or oak), soaked for 1 hour
in water or beer to cover, then drained
Poultry shears (optional)

1. Make the rub: Put the salt, brown sugar, pepper, coriander, and cinnamon in a small bowl and stir to mix.

2. Pop the tab off each juice can. Pour half of the juice (6 tablespoons per can, 3 cups total) into a large heavy saucepan and set aside for the sauce. Using a church key-style opener, make 1 additional hole in the top of each can. Generously oil the outside of the cans (this facilitates removing the quail) and set aside.

3. Remove the wire frames from the quail, if necessary. Rinse the quail under cold running water and then drain and blot dry with paper towels. Season the inside of each quail with some of the rub. Drizzle some of the walnut oil over the outside of each quail and rub or brush it all over the skin. Sprinkle the outside of the quail with the remaining rub and rub it all over the skin.

> **TIP:** The delicate nutty flavor of walnut oil, which is pressed from walnuts, goes great with prunes. Look for it in gourmet shops and natural foods stores or substitute olive oil.

4. Holding a quail upright, with the opening of the body cavity at the bottom, lower it onto the juice can so the can fits into the cavity. You'll need to do some tugging and pulling. If the fit is really tight, using poultry shears, make cuts on either side of the backbone, starting at the tail and going about halfway up the back. Repeat with the remaining quail. Tuck the wing tips behind the back of each quail.

5. Set up the grill for indirect grilling (see page 9 for both charcoal and gas) and preheat to medium-high. If using a charcoal grill, place a large drip pan in the center. If using a gas grill, place all the wood chips or chunks, if using, in the smoker box or in a smoker pouch (see page 12) and preheat on high until you see smoke, then reduce the heat to medium-high.

6. When ready to cook, if using a charcoal grill, toss all of the wood chips or chunks, if using, on the coals. Arrange the quail in the center of the hot grate, over the drip pan and away from the heat. Their legs won't be long enough to reach the grate, so you'll need to balance the cans so the quail stand upright. Cover the grill and cook the quail until the skins are a dark golden brown and very crisp and the meat is cooked through (the breast will feel firm to the touch when done) 20 to 30 minutes (see page 27 for other tests for doneness). If the quail start to brown too much, lay a sheet of aluminum foil over them.

7. Using tongs to take hold of the can, carefully transfer the quail one by one in an upright position on its juice can to a platter and present them to your guests. Let the quail rest for 5 minutes, then carefully lift them off the cans (you may need to twist them gently). Take care not to spill the hot prune juice or otherwise burn yourself. Serve the quail whole, 2 per person, with Cinnamon-Prune Sauce.

SERVES 4

Cinnamon-Prune Sauce

Prune juice may seem like a strange ingredient for a barbecue sauce—until you pause to consider that prune juice possesses sweetness, acidity, and all sorts of interesting plummy and fruity flavors. In short, it has just the sort of flavor profile you'd look for in any barbecue sauce.

3 cups prune juice (reserved from
    Quail on a Throne)
2 cinnamon sticks (3 inches each)
2 tablespoons hoisin sauce
2 tablespoons honey
2 tablespoons brown sugar
2 tablespoons fresh lemon juice
2 tablespoons ketchup
1/2 teaspoon liquid smoke
2 tablespoons butter
Coarse salt (kosher or
    sea) and freshly
    ground black pepper

1. Put the prune juice, cinnamon sticks, hoisin sauce, honey, brown sugar, lemon juice, ketchup, and liquid smoke in a large heavy saucepan. Bring the mixture to a boil over medium-high heat and cook until thick, richly flavored, and reduced to about 2 cups, about 10 minutes, whisking from time to time.

2. Remove the pan from the heat and discard the cinnamon sticks. Whisk in the butter. Season with salt and pepper to taste. If the sauce is too thick or concentrated, add a little water. The sauce can be refrigerated, covered, for up to 2 weeks. Let return to room temperature before serving.

MAKES about 2 cups

INDIRECT GRILLING

PARTRIDGE ON A PEAR CAN

The dark, rich meat of a partridge is, like most game, quite lean, so the challenge in cooking it is to keep the meat moist. What better way to accomplish this than by roasting it upright over an open can of fruit juice? Game has a natural affinity for autumn fruit, which gave me the idea to pair the partridge with a pear barbecue sauce. I think you'll find the combination quite irresistible.

> **TIP:** Partridges are available from D'Artagnan (see Mail-Order Sources, page 311); however, they are seasonal and not available in the summer. If you can't get them, the recipe is plenty tasty made with chicken or game hen, although then you don't get to say "partridge on a pear can," which is half the fun of this recipe.

4 partridges (about 14 ounces each)
Coarse salt (kosher or sea) and freshly
    ground pepper
4 bay leaves
6 tablespoons (¾ stick) salted butter,
    melted
4 cans (5½ ounces each) pear nectar
Vegetable oil for oiling the cans
Pear Sauce (recipe follows)

YOU'LL ALSO NEED:
2 cups wood chips or chunks (preferably
    apple or cherry), soaked for 1 hour in
    water to cover, then drained
Poultry shears (optional)

1. Rinse the partridges, inside and out, under cold running water, then drain and blot dry, inside and out, with paper towels. Season the body and neck cavities of the birds with salt and pepper. Place a bay leaf in the body cavity of each bird. Brush the outside of each bird with some of the melted butter and season generously with salt and pepper.

2. Pop the tabs off the pear nectar cans. Pour half of the pear nectar from each can (about 1½ cups in all) into a large heavy saucepan and set aside for the sauce. Using a church key-style can opener, make 1 additional hole in the top of each can. Oil the outsides of the nectar cans.

> **TIP:** Look for pear nectar in aluminum cans with baked-on labels; you don't want to use soldered cans with paper labels.

3. Holding a partridge upright, with the opening of the body cavity at the bottom, lower it onto the nectar can so the can fits into the cavity. It may take a little twisting to get the can to fit. If the fit is really tight, using poultry shears, make cuts on either side of the backbone, starting at the tail and going about halfway up the back. Repeat with remaining partridge.

4. Set up the grill for indirect grilling (see page 9 for both charcoal and gas) and preheat to medium-high. If using a charcoal grill, place a large drip pan in the center. If using a gas grill, place all the wood chips or chunks in the smoker box or in a smoker pouch (see page 12) and preheat on high until you see smoke, then reduce the heat to medium-high.

5. When ready to cook, if using a charcoal grill, toss all of the wood chips or chunks on the coals. Stand the partridges in the center of the hot grate, over the drip pan and away from the heat.

Cover the grill and cook the partridges until the skins are a dark golden brown and very crisp and the meat is cooked through (about 160°F on an instant-read meat thermometer inserted in the thickest part of a thigh, but not touching the bone), 30 minutes (see page 27 for other tests for doneness). Baste the partridges with melted butter after 10 minutes of cooking, taking care not to knock the birds over, and again when the partridges are cooked. If the birds start to brown too much, loosely tent them with aluminum foil.

6. Using tongs, hold a partridge by the can and carefully transfer it in an upright position to a platter. Repeat with the remaining partridge. Let the partridges rest for 5 minutes, then carefully lift them off the cans. Take care not to spill the hot nectar or otherwise burn yourself. Serve the partridges with the Pear Sauce.

SERVES 4

Pear Sauce

The wonderful earthy fruitiness of this sauce comes from pear nectar, while the butter will bathe the partridge meat, ensuring that it's moist. You can substitute white rum for *eau-de-vie de poire Williams*, but if you can find the pear spirit (try a premium wine and spirits shop), it adds an extra dose of pear flavor.

1½ cups pear nectar (reserved from Partridge
   on a Pear Can)

1 stick salted butter, cut into ½-inch pieces

½ cup beer

⅓ cup ketchup

3 tablespoons Worcestershire sauce

3 tablespoons brown sugar

2 tablespoons eau-de-vie de poire Williams or
   white rum

Coarse salt (kosher or sea) and freshly ground
   black pepper

A few drops fresh lemon juice (optional)

1. Put the pear nectar in a large heavy saucepan.
Bring it to a boil over high heat and let boil until
reduced to ⅔ cup, 6 to 10 minutes.

2. Reduce the heat to medium and whisk in the
butter, beer, ketchup, Worcestershire sauce, brown
sugar, and eau-de-vie. Let the sauce simmer over
medium heat until richly flavored and slightly
thickened, about 5 minutes. Taste for seasoning,
adding salt and pepper and a few drops of lemon
juice, if desired, to taste. The sauce can be served
warm or at room temperature. It will keep refrigerated, covered, for several weeks. Let return to
room temperature or reheat over medium heat
before serving.

MAKES about 2 cups

INDIRECT GRILLING

BEER-CAN GAME HENS

Pity the game hen— it's one of the most under-appreciated barbecue foods in the United States. Leaner than a full-grown chicken, its diminutive size gives it a high ratio of crackling crisp skin to meat. One bird makes a nice single serving, and it looks mighty impressive on a plate. One more advantage: Game hens cook faster than chickens, always handy if you're short on time.

TIP: The biggest challenge to preparing this recipe will be to find small 8-ounce cans of beer. Some supermarkets carry these and so do many liquor stores. In a worst-case scenario, which isn't such a bad case at all, you can cook the hens on full-size 12-ounce beer cans. You may need to do a little twisting to get the cans into the cavities and the legs will dangle without touching the grill, so you'll need to take extra care to balance the cans on the grate. With either size can, the look of beer-can game hens is cool. No matter what, you'll wind up a winner.

FOR THE RUB:

**1 tablespoon coarse salt
(kosher or sea)**

1 tablespoon brown sugar

1 tablespoon sweet paprika

2 teaspoons freshly ground black pepper

2 teaspoons dry mustard

1 teaspoon ground cumin

1 teaspoon garlic powder

½ teaspoon cayenne pepper

4 cans (8 or 12 ounces each) beer

**4 game hens (about 1 pound each), thawed in
the refrigerator if frozen**

2 tablespoons olive oil

**Cola Barbecue Sauce (page 95), Black Cherry
Barbecue Sauce (page 110), or your favorite
commercial barbecue sauce, for serving**

YOU'LL ALSO NEED:

**2 cups wood chips or chunks (preferably oak or
hickory), soaked for 1 hour in water and/or
beer to cover, then drained**

1. Make the rub: Put the salt, brown sugar, paprika, black pepper, mustard, cumin, garlic powder, and cayenne in a small bowl and stir to mix. Set aside.

2. Pop the tabs off the beer cans. Pour half of the beer from each can over the soaking wood chips or chunks or reserve for another use. Using a church key-style can opener, make 2 additional holes in the top of each of the cans. Set the cans of beer aside.

3. Remove the packets of giblets (if any) from the body cavities of the hens and set aside for another use. Remove and discard the fat just inside the body and neck cavities. Rinse the hens, inside and out, under cold running water and then drain and blot dry, inside and out, with paper towels. Sprinkle ¾ teaspoon of the rub inside the body cavity and ¼ teaspoon inside the neck cavity of each hen. Drizzle 1½ teaspoons of olive oil over the outside of each hen and rub or brush it all over the skin. Sprinkle the outside of each bird with 1½ teaspoons of rub and rub it all over the skin. Spoon the remaining rub through the holes in the tops of the beer cans, dividing it evenly among them. Don't worry if the beer foams up: This is normal.

4. Holding a game hen upright, with the opening of the body cavity at the bottom, lower it onto a beer can so the can fits into the cavity. It will be a tight fit—tighter than with a chicken—but with a little twisting and jiggling, you should be able to work the can into the cavity. Repeat with the remaining hens, then tuck the wing tips behind the hens' backs.

TIP: *I've suggested serving Cola or Black Cherry Barbecue Sauce with the game hens, but really just about any sauce from this book would be a good accompaniment.*

5. Set up the grill for indirect grilling (see page 9 for both charcoal and gas) and preheat to medium. If using a charcoal grill, place a large drip pan in the center. If using a gas grill, place all the wood chips or chunks in the smoker box or in a smoker pouch (see page 12) and preheat on high until you see smoke, then reduce the heat to medium.

6. When ready to cook, if using a charcoal grill, toss all of the wood chips or chunks on the coals. Line up the hens in the center of the hot grate, over the drip pan and away from the heat. Take special care to balance the hens securely— the legs may not reach the grate, so you'll have to balance the hens solely on the cans. Cover the grill and cook the hens until the skins are a dark golden brown and very crisp and the meat is cooked through (about 170°F on an instant-read meat thermometer inserted in the thickest part of a thigh, but not touching the bone), 40 minutes to 1 hour (see page 27 for other tests for doneness). If the hens start to brown too much, loosely tent them with aluminum foil.

7. Using tongs, hold a hen by the beer can and carefully transfer it in an upright position to a platter. Repeat with the remaining hens, then present them to your guests. Let the hens rest for 5 minutes, then carefully lift them off the beer cans. Take care not to spill the hot beer or otherwise burn yourself. Serve with barbecue sauce on the side.

SERVES 4

ROOT BEER GAME HENS

All-American root beer, like beer-can chicken, is a phenomenon unique to the United States. It was sold as a tonic by pharmacies as early as the eighteenth century. One early recipe (published by a Dr. Chase in 1869) called for hops, burdock, sarsaparilla, dandelion, spruce, sassafras, sugar, and molasses. Even today, there's something sweet and spicy about root beer that makes it a perfect beverage for barbecue.

ADVANCE PREPARATION: 3 hours for marinating the game hens

4 cans (12 ounces each) root beer

4 game hens (about 1 pound each), thawed in
   the refrigerator if frozen

2 cinnamon sticks (3 inches each),
   or ½ teaspoon ground cinnamon

1 tablespoon coriander seeds

4 slices (each ¼ inch thick) peeled fresh
   ginger, crushed with the side of a cleaver

2 cloves garlic, peeled and flattened with the
   side of a cleaver

1 scallion, both white and green parts, trimmed
   and cut into 1-inch pieces

4 tablespoons All-Purpose Barbecue Rub (page
   37), or your favorite commercial brand

2 tablespoons vegetable oil

Root Beer Barbecue Sauce (optional;
   recipe follows)

YOU'LL ALSO NEED:

**2 cups wood chips or chunks (preferably
   hickory or pecan), soaked for 1 hour
   in water to cover, then drained**

1. Pop the tabs off the root beer cans. Pour
half of the root beer from each can into a large
deep bowl. Using a church key-style can opener,
make 2 additional holes in the top of each of the
cans. Set the cans of root beer aside.

2. Remove the packets of giblets (if any)
from the body cavities of the hens and set aside for
another use. Remove and discard the fat just inside
the body and neck cavities. Rinse the hens, inside
and out, under cold running water and then drain
and blot dry, inside and out, with paper towels.
Place the hens in the bowl with the root beer and
add the cinnamon sticks, coriander seeds, ginger,
garlic, and scallion. Let the hens marinate in the
refrigerator, covered, for 3 hours, turning the hens
several times so they marinate evenly. Transfer the
hens to a colander to drain. Discard the marinade.

3. Sprinkle ¾ teaspoon of rub inside the body
cavity and ¼ teaspoon inside the neck cavity of
each hen. Drizzle 1½ teaspoons oil over the outside
of each hen and rub or brush it all over the skin.
Sprinkle the outside of each hen with 2 teaspoons of rub and rub it all
over the skin.

4. Holding a game
hen upright, with the
opening of the body
cavity at the bottom, lower
it onto a root beer can so the can fits
into the cavity. It will be a tight fit—tighter than
with a chicken—but with a little twisting and jiggling, you should be able to work the can into the

cavity. Repeat with the remaining hens, then tuck the wing tips behind the hens' backs.

5. Set up the grill for indirect grilling (see page 9 for both charcoal and gas) and preheat to medium. If using a charcoal grill, place a large drip pan in the center. If using a gas grill, place all the wood chips or chunks in the smoker box or in a smoker pouch (see page 12) and preheat on high until you see smoke, then reduce the heat to medium.

6. When ready to cook, if using a charcoal grill, toss all of the wood chips or chunks on the coals. Line up the hens in the center of the hot grate, over

> **TIP:** *When grilling game hens here, you have two options for cans: 12-ounce cans of root beer or clean, empty 8-ounce "mini" cans of beer. Depending upon where you live, the latter may be available at liquor stores and some supermarkets, and they're just the right size for a 1-pound game hen. However, you can also fit a game hen on a 12-ounce can. It will have the long-necked beauty of a Modigliani portrait, but the hen's legs won't quite reach the grill. So when using 12-ounce cans, take extra care to balance the cans on the grill.*

the drip pan and away from the heat. Take special care to balance the hens securely—the legs may not reach the grate, so you'll have to balance the hens solely on the cans. Cover the grill and cook the hens until the skins are a dark golden brown and very crisp and the meat is cooked through (about 170°F on an instant-read meat thermometer inserted in the thickest part of a thigh, but not touching the bone), 40 minutes to 1 hour (see page 27 for other tests for doneness). If the hens start to brown too much, loosely tent them with aluminum foil.

7. Using tongs, hold a hen by the root beer can and carefully transfer it in an upright position to a platter. Repeat with the remaining hens, then present them to your guests. Let the hens rest for 5 minutes, then carefully lift them off the cans. Take care not to spill the hot root beer or otherwise burn yourself. Serve with Root Beer Barbecue Sauce, if desired. The appropriate beverage? Root beer, of course!

SERVES 4

VARIATION: This recipe calls for game hens, but you could certainly make root beer chicken the same way. You'd use one 3½- to 4-pound chicken and one 12-ounce can of root beer.

Root Beer Barbecue Sauce

Using root beer isn't quite as strange as it sounds. Barbecue sauces flavored with soft drinks are a long-standing tradition in the American South. After all, root beer is sweet and aromatic—the same qualities you expect in a barbecue sauce. Root beer owes its pungency to the presence of mint or wintergreen. The spice flavor comes from nutmeg, cloves, and anise.

1 cup root beer
1 cup ketchup
½ teaspoon grated lemon zest
¼ cup fresh lemon juice, or more to taste
¼ cup fresh orange juice
3 tablespoons Worcestershire sauce
1½ tablespoons brown sugar, or more to taste
1 tablespoon molasses
1 teaspoon liquid smoke
½ teaspoon powdered ginger
½ teaspoon garlic powder
½ teaspoon onion powder
½ teaspoon freshly ground black pepper

1. Put the root beer, ketchup, lemon zest and juice, orange juice, Worcestershire sauce, brown sugar, molasses, liquid smoke, ginger, garlic and onion powders, and pepper in a heavy nonreactive saucepan and gradually bring to a boil over medium heat. Reduce the heat slightly and gently simmer the sauce until thick and richly flavored, 10 to 15 minutes. Taste for seasoning, adding lemon juice, brown sugar, or other ingredients as necessary.

2. Transfer the sauce to a bowl or clean glass jars and let cool to room temperature, then refrigerate, covered, until ready to serve. The sauce can be served chilled or at room temperature. It will keep refrigerated, covered, for several months.

MAKES about 2 cups

INDIRECT GRILLING

DUCKLING "A L'ORANGE"

When I was in cooking school in Paris in the 1970s, duckling *à l'orange* was the highest test of a chef's mettle. The duck had to be roasted just so—skin crackling crisp, meat tender and juicy—and the orange sauce had to strike a perfect balance between the sweetness of the caramelized sugar, the acidity of the fresh orange juice, and the bitterness of the orange peel and marmalade. The garnish involved all sorts of surgical legerdemain, from decoratively fluting orange rinds to placing candles in the hollowed fruit like a jack-o'-lantern. It's a lot easier, and just as tasty, to cook duck on the grill—especially upright on an open beer can. So, here's an orange duck that a bubba can relate to (after all, it's made with orange soda) but that would do a Frenchman proud. **ADVANCE PREPARA-TION: 12 hours for dry-ing the duck (optional)**

TIP: *There are two techniques you can use to maximize the crisp-ness of the duck skin: First, let the duck dry on a rack in the refriger-ator uncovered over-night. I've made this step optional as you may not want to wait that long. Second, prick the skin all over with a sharp fork (I use a carv-ing fork) to allow the fat to escape while grilling. When pricking the skin, be sure not to pierce the meat.*

1 duck (about 5 pounds), thawed in the
    refrigerator if frozen

1 can (16 ounces) beer (see Note)

1 can (12 ounces) orange soda

Coarse salt (kosher or sea) and freshly ground
    black pepper

2 strips orange zest ($\frac{1}{2}$ by $1\frac{1}{2}$ inches each,
    removed with a vegetable peeler)

1 orange, cut in half

1 tablespoon olive oil

Apricot-Orange Sauce (recipe follows)

YOU'LL ALSO NEED:
Vertical chicken roaster (optional)

1. Remove the packet of giblets from the
body cavity of the duck and set aside for another
use. Remove and discard the fat just inside the
body and neck cavities. Rinse the duck, inside and
out, under cold running water and then drain and
blot dry, inside and out, with paper towels. Prick
the duck skin all over with a sharp fork, like a carving fork, taking care not to pierce the meat. Place
the duck on a wire rack on a tray in the refrigerator
and let dry out, uncovered, overnight (this is
optional, but it will help give you crisper skin).

2. Pop the tab off the beer can, pour out three
quarters of the beer ($1\frac{1}{2}$ cups), and reserve for
another use. If cooking the duck on the can, using a
church key-style opener, make 2 additional holes in
the top of the beer can. Using a funnel, add $\frac{1}{2}$ cup
orange soda to the beer can. Don't worry if the
beer foams up a bit: This is normal. Reserve the
remaining orange soda for the sauce.

3. Season the body and neck cavities of the
duck very generously with salt and pepper. Place a
strip of orange zest in the body cavity and in the
neck cavity. Rub the outside of the duck all over
with the cut orange. Drizzle $1\frac{1}{2}$ teaspoons of olive

oil over the duck and rub it all over the skin. Very generously season the outside of the duck with salt and pepper.

4. If cooking on a can: Hold the duck upright, with the opening of the body cavity at the bottom, and lower it onto the beer can so the can fits into the cavity. You'll need to do some twisting. Pull the duck legs forward to form a sort of tripod so the bird stands upright. The rear leg of the tripod is the can.

If cooking on a roaster: Fill it with 1/2 cup beer and 1/2 cup orange soda and position the duck on top, following the manufacturer's instructions.

5. Tuck the tips of the wings behind the duck's back.

6. Set up the grill for indirect grilling (see page 9 for both charcoal and gas) and preheat to medium. If using a charcoal grill, place a large drip pan in the center.

7. When ready to cook, carefully stand the duck up in the center of the hot grate, over the drip pan and away from the heat. Cover the grill and cook the duck until the skin is a dark golden brown and very crisp and the meat is cooked through (about 180°F on an instant-read meat thermometer inserted in the thickest part of a thigh, but not touching the bone), 1 1/2 to 2 hours (see page 27 for other tests for doneness). After 1 hour, prick the duck skin again with a sharp fork, taking care not to pierce the meat. This helps release the fat. Baste the duck with the remaining 1 1/2 teaspoons of olive oil, taking care not to knock the bird over. If using a charcoal grill, you'll need to add 12 fresh coals per side after 1 hour. If the duck skin starts to brown too much, loosely tent the bird with aluminum foil.

8. If cooking on a can: Using tongs, hold the duck by the can and carefully transfer it in an upright position to a platter.

If cooking on a roaster: Use oven mitts or pot holders to remove the duck from the grill while it's still on the vertical roaster.

9. Present the duck to your guests. Let the duck rest for 5 minutes, then carefully lift it off the support. Take care not to spill the hot beer or otherwise burn yourself. Carve the duck or cut it in half or quarters and serve with Apricot-Orange Sauce.

SERVES 2

NOTE: Because of the duck's elongated shape, you'll need a "tall boy"—a 16-ounce can of beer.

Apricot-Orange Sauce

Five stars here, orange soda, orange zest, orange juice, orange marmalade, and orange liqueur, are joined by apricots to deepen the flavor, while lemon juice adds a piquant touch. Try to use a homemade chicken broth or at very least a low-sodium canned broth.

¾ cup orange soda (reserved from Duckling
"à l'Orange")

½ cup homemade chicken stock (page 52) or
low-sodium canned chicken broth

2 strips orange zest (½ by 1 ½ inches each,
removed with a vegetable peeler)

½ cup fresh orange juice

1 cinnamon stick (3 inches), or ½ teaspoon
ground cinnamon

½ cup pitted dried apricots (about 2½ ounces)

3 tablespoons orange marmalade

3 tablespoons brown sugar, or more
to taste

2 tablespoons cider vinegar, or more
to taste

1 tablespoon fresh lemon juice

½ teaspoon cornstarch

1 tablespoon Cointreau or other
orange liqueur

1 tablespoon butter

Coarse salt (kosher or sea) and freshly ground
black pepper

1. Put the orange soda, chicken stock, orange
zest and juice, and cinnamon stick in a heavy
saucepan over high heat, bring to a boil, and let
boil for 3 minutes. Remove the pan from the heat
and add the apricots. Let soak for 30 minutes.
Remove and discard the cinnamon stick.

2. Transfer the apricots and their soaking
liquid to a blender. Add the marmalade, brown
sugar, vinegar, and lemon juice and purée until
smooth. Pour the mixture through a strainer into
a saucepan, forcing the fruit pulp through the
strainer with a spatula (don't forget to scrape
the strained pulp off the bottom of the strainer).

3. Return the sauce to the saucepan and let simmer for 3 minutes over medium-high heat. Dissolve the cornstarch in the orange liqueur and stir this into the sauce. Let simmer for 2 minutes longer; the sauce will thicken slightly. Remove the pan from the heat and whisk in the butter. Add salt, pepper, and additional brown sugar or vinegar to taste. The sauce can be served warm or at room temperature. It can be refrigerated, covered, for up to 5 days. Let return to room temperature or reheat over medium heat.

MAKES about 1¼ cups

INDIRECT GRILLING

PEKING DUCK

No, it's not a bird with a bent for voyeurism. But this Peking duck cooked on a beer can will certainly attract lustful stares. One of the attractions of Peking duck is its rich tender meat and crackling crisp skin. Indirect grilling a duck in a vertical position on a beer can is about the best way I've found (short of the traditional drying and frying) to crisp the skin and keep the duck meat moist. To get the full effect, serve the duck as the Chinese do, with scallion brushes, mandarin pancakes, and Peking duck sauce. If this seems like too much work, the bird is also highly tasty served off the beer can just as is. Note: I omit wood chips in this recipe. The duck has so much flavor you don't need the smoke.

> **TIP:** *Mandarin pancakes are crepe-thin flour pancakes used to wrap sliced Peking duck in before eating. They are also sometimes referred to as Chinese or Peking pancakes or as mu shu wrappers. Although made in a different way and served at the opposite end of the planet, they are similar to Mexican tortillas. Look for them at Asian markets or make your own, following a recipe from a Chinese cookbook. In a pinch you could use flour tortillas.*

ADVANCE PREPARATION:
12 hours for drying the duck (optional);
3 hours for making the scallion brushes (optional)

1 duck (about 5 pounds), thawed in the refrigerator if frozen

8 scallions, for scallion brushes (optional)

1 tablespoon coarse salt (kosher or sea)

1 tablespoon sugar

2 teaspoons freshly ground black pepper

1 teaspoon Chinese five-spice powder

1 tablespoon Asian (dark) sesame oil

1 can (16 ounces) beer (see Note)

8 (6-inch) mandarin pancakes or small flour tortillas

Peking Duck Sauce (recipe follows)

YOU'LL ALSO NEED:
Vertical chicken roaster (optional)

1. Remove the packet of giblets from the body cavity of the duck and set aside for another use. Remove and discard the fat just inside the body and neck cavities. Rinse the duck, inside and out, under cold running water and then drain and blot dry, inside and out, with paper towels. Prick the duck skin all over with a sharp fork, like a carving fork, taking care not to pierce the meat. Place the duck on a wire rack on a tray in the refrigerator and let dry out, uncovered, overnight (this is optional, but it will help give you crisper skin).

2. Make the scallion brushes, if using: Trim the scallions, cutting off the root ends and the dark green tops (reserve the latter for the Peking Duck Sauce). You should be left with pieces of scallion, white and light green, about 3 inches long. Make a series of ¾-inch lengthwise cuts in both ends of each scallion, gradually rotating it to form the "bristles" of the brush. Soak the scallions in a bowl of ice water for 3 hours to swell the ends of the brushes.

3. Make the rub: Put the salt, sugar, pepper, and five-spice powder in a small bowl and stir to mix. Sprinkle 1 teaspoon of the rub inside the body cavity and ½ teaspoon inside the neck cavity of the duck. Drizzle a little sesame oil over the outside of the duck and rub or brush it all over the skin. Sprinkle the outside of the duck with 1 tablespoon rub and rub it all over the skin.

4. Pop the tab off the beer can, pour out half of the beer (1 cup), and reserve for another use. If cooking the duck on the can, using a church key-style opener, make 2 additional holes in the top of the beer can. Spoon the remaining rub into the beer through the hole in the top of the can. Don't worry if the beer foams up: This is normal.

5. If cooking on a can: Hold the duck upright, with the opening of the body cavity at the bottom, and lower it onto the beer can so the can fits into the cavity. You'll need to do some twisting. Pull the duck legs forward to form a sort of tripod so the bird stands upright. The rear leg of the tripod is the can.

If cooking on a roaster: Fill it with the beer mixture and position the duck on top, following the manufacturer's instructions.

6. Tuck the tips of the wings behind the duck's back.

7. Set up the grill for indirect grilling (see page 9 for both charcoal and gas) and preheat to medium. If using a charcoal grill, place a large drip pan in the center.

8. When ready to cook, carefully stand the duck up in the center of the hot grate, over the drip pan and away from the heat. Cover the grill and cook the duck until the skin is a dark golden brown and very crisp and the meat is cooked through (about 180°F on an instant-read meat thermometer inserted in the thickest part of a thigh, but not touching the bone), 1½ to 2 hours (see page 27 for other tests for doneness). After 1 hour, prick the

duck skin again with a sharp fork, taking care not
to pierce the meat. This helps release the fat. Baste
the duck with the remaining sesame oil, taking care
not to knock the bird over. If using a charcoal grill,
you'll need to add 12 fresh coals per side after
1 hour. If the duck skin starts to brown too much,
loosely tent the bird with aluminum foil.

9. If cooking on a can: Using tongs, hold
the duck by the can and carefully transfer it in an
upright position to a platter.

If cooking on a roaster: Use oven mitts
or pot holders to remove the duck from the grill
while it's still on the vertical roaster.

10. Present the duck to your guests, then let
the duck rest for 5 minutes.

11. Meanwhile, warm the mandarin pancakes on the grill, placing them directly over the
flames. This will take 10 to 15 seconds per side:
The pancakes should be warm and pliable but not
browned. Place the pancakes on a plate or in a
basket and cover with a cloth napkin to keep warm.

12. Carefully lift the duck off the support.
Take care not to spill the hot beer or otherwise
burn yourself. The traditional way to serve Peking
duck is to slice the crisp skin off the bird, then cut
off and sliver the meat. To eat it, you brush a pancake with Peking Duck Sauce, using a scallion
brush. Place the scallion brush, duck meat, and
duck skin on the pancake, roll it up, and pop it into
your mouth. Or you could serve the duck halved or
quartered, serving the pancakes, sauce, and scallion brushes on the side.

SERVES 4 as an appetizer, 2 as a main course

NOTE: Because of the duck's elongated shape,
you'll need a "tall boy"—a 16-ounce can of beer.

Peking Duck Sauce

While this barbecue sauce may speak with a Chinese accent, its message will be understood by all brethren of the grill. Hoisin sauce and honey make it sweet; rice vinegar makes it sour; and ginger, garlic, and scallion give it pungency aplenty. After the duck is gone, you might just find your-self serving it with pork chops or even ribs.

⅔ cup hoisin sauce

3 tablespoons rice wine or dry sherry

2 tablespoons soy sauce

2 tablespoons rice vinegar

2 tablespoons honey

1 tablespoon Asian (dark) sesame oil

1 clove garlic, minced

2 teaspoons minced peeled fresh ginger

1 tablespoon minced scallion greens

Combine all of the ingredients with 2 tablespoons of water in a small nonreactive saucepan and let simmer gently over medium heat until thick and richly flavored, 6 to 8 minutes. Let the sauce cool to room temperature before serving. The sauce will keep in the refrigerator, covered, for up to 5 days.

MAKES about 1½ cups sauce

INDIRECT GRILLING

BEER-CAN TURKEY

Don't blame me. It's the fault of the folks who brew Foster's lager in Australia. The moment I saw this oversize can of beer (a whopping 32 ounces), I knew it had a calling. And that calling was to take the revered centerpiece of the American Thanksgiving and turn it on its rear end. I'm talking about beer-can turkey, of course, and once you get over the shock of seeing a turkey in such an undignified (or, should I say, risqué) position, you'll be amazed how crisp-skinned and juicy, how tender and moist, a beer-can turkey can be. Here's the perfect antidote to a bird that's too often

dry, and it's guaranteed to turn heads at your next holiday dinner. The Cranberry Salsa on page 120 makes a great accompaniment.

> **TIP:** Only one can is big enough to handle a turkey: a 32-ounce can of Foster's lager, available at many supermarkets and liquor stores. This big boy can handle up to a 13-pound turkey. (If you'll need more turkey, you're better off cooking two small birds.)

FOR THE RUB:

4 teaspoons coarse salt (kosher or sea)

4 teaspoons sweet paprika

2 teaspoons freshly ground black pepper

2 teaspoons ground sage

2 teaspoons dried oregano

1 teaspoon dried thyme

1 can (32 ounces) Foster's lager

1 turkey (10 to 12 pounds), thawed in the refrigerator if frozen

4 tablespoons (½ stick) unsalted butter, melted

YOU'LL ALSO NEED:

4 cups wood chips or chunks (preferably oak or apple), soaked for 1 hour in water and/or beer to cover, then drained

1. Make the rub: Put the salt, paprika, pepper, sage, oregano, and thyme in a small bowl and stir to mix.

2. Pop the tab off the beer can. Pour half of the beer over the soaking wood chips or chunks or reserve for another use. Using a church key-style opener, make 2 additional holes in the top of the beer can. Set the can of beer aside.

TIP: Some turkeys come with wire trusses that hold the legs together. If yours does, you'll need to remove it to beer can the turkey. Gently wiggle it free or cut it with wire cutters. Be sure to remove the bag of giblets in both the main and front cavities.

3. Remove and discard the trussing clamp if one is holding the turkey legs together. Remove the packet of giblets from the body cavity of the turkey and set aside for another use. Remove and discard the fat just inside the body and neck cavities. Rinse the turkey, inside and out, under cold running water and then drain and blot dry, inside and out, with paper towels. Sprinkle 2 teaspoons of the rub inside the body cavity and

1 teaspoon of the rub inside the neck cavity of the turkey. Brush the outside of the turkey with 1 tablespoon of melted butter. Sprinkle the outside of the turkey with 1 tablespoon of the rub and rub it all over the skin. Stir 2 tablespoons of the rub into the remaining melted butter and set aside.

4. Spoon the remaining rub into the beer through a hole in the top of the can. Don't worry if the beer foams up: This is normal. Holding the turkey upright, with the opening of the body cavity at the bottom, lower it onto the beer can so the can fits into the cavity.

5. Pull the turkey legs forward to form a sort of tripod, so the bird stands upright. The rear leg of the tripod is the beer can. Tuck the wing tips behind the turkey's back.

6. Set up the grill for indirect grilling (see page 9 for both charcoal and gas) and preheat to medium. If using a charcoal grill, place a large drip pan in the center. If using a gas grill, place all the wood chips or chunks in the smoker box or in a smoker pouch (see page 12) and preheat on high until you see smoke, then reduce the heat to medium.

7. When ready to cook, if using a charcoal grill, toss half of the wood chips or chunks on the coals. Stand the turkey up in the center of the hot grate, over the drip pan and away from the heat. Cover the grill and cook the turkey until the skin is a dark golden brown and very crisp and the meat is cooked through (about 180°F on an instant-read meat thermometer inserted in the thickest part of a thigh, but not touching the bone), 2 to 2½ hours (see page 27 for other tests for doneness). If using a charcoal grill, you'll need to add 12 fresh coals per side every hour and toss the remaining wood chips or chunks on the coals after the first hour of grilling. Baste the outside of the turkey with the butter-rub mixture every 30 minutes. If the turkey starts to brown too much (and it will have a tendency to do so at the neck end), loosely tent the bird with aluminum foil.

8. Using tongs, hold the turkey by the can and carefully transfer it in an upright position to a platter. Or use insulated rubber gloves to pick up the turkey on the beer can and remove it from the grill. Present the turkey to your guests. Let the turkey rest for 10 minutes, then carefully lift it off the beer can (see Note). Take care not to spill the hot beer or otherwise burn yourself. Carve the turkey and serve at once.

SERVES 8 to 10

NOTE: A bird this big requires some special treatment when removing it from the grill and the can. Wearing heavy-duty insulated gloves, grab the turkey on both sides and gently slide it, on the can, to a cool part of the grill. Have a buddy hold the beer can with the tongs while you lift the turkey off the can and transfer it to a platter or carving board.

BIRDS OFF THE CAN

Man doesn't live by beer alone, or for that matter by beer-can chicken alone. Sure, beer-can chicken and its variations will amaze your guests and boost your reputation as a grill master, but there comes a time when you'll want to show off some other outlandish grilling techniques. Which brings us to this chapter of recipes that don't happen to require beer cans. Make Welder's Chicken, which involves roasting a fowl swaddled in aluminum foil on the grill and using welder's gloves to turn it. Or spatchcock a chicken—a technique that enables you to grill a whole bird using the direct method and also gives you the opportunity to bandy about the word *spatchcock*. To complete the pyrotechnics, grill a chicken in the style of the devil, grill another in the style of a toad, and yet another under bricks or stones, a technique that keeps the meat moist and makes the skin crisp and the tongues of your guests cluck, as people gather with admiration around your grill.

DIRECT GRILLING

WELDER'S CHICKEN

Our collective pursuit of speed

and convenience has meant the stewing hen (a large old chicken) has virtually disappeared from kitchens in the United States. This is a shame, because what the bird may lack in tenderness, it more than makes up for in flavor. Of course, a stewing chicken (sometimes referred to as a fowl) may seem like a poor candidate for grilling. Not so, says Sean Murphy, who attended a signing of mine at Powell's Books in Portland, Oregon, and told me about a barbecued chicken that his buddy makes. The buddy in question is a welder, and he seasons his hen assertively prior to wrapping it in heavy-duty aluminum foil and then grilling it. The secret to the preparation is a pair of thick welder's gloves (or heavy-duty long-sleeve grill mitts) so you can turn the chicken often (tongs would tear the foil). When you strip off that foil, you wind up with some of the moistest, most flavorful chicken you've ever tasted.

TIP: *The chief challenge in this recipe will be finding a stewing hen. Your best bet will be a kosher or ethnic market or butcher shop. Some supermarkets carry stewing hens in the freezer case. You can certainly make this dish with a regular frying chicken. Reduce the poultry seasoning to 1 tablespoon (or 1½ teaspoons each of dried sage and oregano) and shorten the grilling time to 40 to 60 minutes.*

1 stewing hen or roasting chicken
   (6 to 7 pounds)
1 lemon
3 cloves garlic, peeled and cut in half
2 tablespoons poultry seasoning
Coarse salt (kosher or sea) and
   freshly ground black pepper
5 slices bacon (the smokier,
   the better)

YOU'LL ALSO NEED:
4 pieces heavy-duty aluminum
   foil (30 by 18 inches each)

1. Remove the packet of giblets from the
body cavity of the stewing hen and set aside for
another use. Remove and discard the fat just inside
the body and neck cavities. Rinse the chicken, inside
and out, under cold running water and then drain
and blot dry, inside and out, with paper towels.

2. Using a vegetable peeler, remove
3 strips of zest (the oil-rich outer rind) from the
lemon, taking care not to remove any of the bitter
white pith underneath. Place 1 strip in the neck
cavity and 2 strips in the body cavity of the hen. Cut
the rind and white pith off the lemon and discard.
Cut the lemon crosswise into thin slices and remove
the seeds with a fork.

3. Rub the outside of the hen with cut garlic.
Place 2 garlic cloves (4 halves) in the body cavity
and 1 clove in the neck cavity. Sprinkle 2 teaspoons
of poultry seasoning inside the body cavity and
1 teaspoon inside the neck cavity of the hen. Sprinkle the remaining poultry seasoning on the outside
of the bird. Generously season the bird inside and
out with salt and pepper.

4. Place a piece of heavy-duty aluminum foil
shiny side down on a work surface. Place 2 bacon

slices in the center and place a few lemon slices on top of them. Place the hen breast side up so the backbone is parallel to the long side of the foil, on the bacon. Drape the remaining 3 slices of bacon over the breast and put the remaining lemon slices on the top and sides of the hen. Bring the ends of the aluminum foil up over the hen, folding over the edges several times and crimping them to make a tight seal. Tightly wrap the bird in 3 additional layers of aluminum foil, shiny side out (so it will reflect the heat; see Note) to make a sturdy packet. Be sure all of the bird is covered with foil.

5. Set up the grill for direct grilling (see page 8 for both charcoal and gas) and preheat to medium. When ready to cook, place the foil-wrapped hen on the hot grill and grill until the hen is cooked through (about 180°F on an instant-read thermometer inserted in the hen flesh, but not touching a bone), 1¼ to 1¾ hours, turning and rotating the bird every 15 minutes. If using a charcoal grill, you'll need to add 12 fresh coals per side after 1 hour.

6. Transfer the hen to a platter and, if you like, show it off in its flame-darkened packet to your guests. Let the hen rest for 5 minutes, then, wearing welder's gloves or heavy-duty grill mitts, unwrap the bird. Take care to avoid the escaping steam. Scrape off and discard the bacon. Serve the hen at once.

SERVES 4 to 6

NOTE: If your heavy-duty aluminum foil is 12 inches wide, you'll need to wrap it around the bird like you would a mummy.

VARIATION: You can use the indirect method to grill the stewing hen. It would be easier, but you wouldn't get the sort of browning that occurs when you grill the bird directly.

"STONED" CHICKEN

On a typical book tour morning, I wake up at 5 A.M. and fire up the grill to barbecue at an hour when most people are just having their breakfast. I do have help in doing this, and I was preparing chicken under a brick when my assistant, Monterey-born Julio Martinez, exclaimed, "We do that in Mexico." He proceeded to tell me about *pollo a la piedra,* "stoned" chicken (actually, chicken cooked under a stone). As with the Italian version of the dish, a brick or flat paving stone is placed on top of a chicken breast as it grills. The stone presses the meat into the grill grate, giving you killer grill marks while keeping the breast moist yet crusty. The seasonings here are pure Mexican: garlic, lime juice, and aromatic achiote paste, which is made from ground annatto seeds.

**ADVANCE PREPARATION:
1 to 2 hours
for marinating the
chicken**

2 whole skinless chicken breasts (each 12 to 16
  ounces), or 4 half breasts (each 6 to 8 ounces)
3 cloves garlic, finely chopped
1 teaspoon coarse salt (kosher or sea)
1 teaspoon freshly ground black pepper
1 tablespoon Achiote Paste (recipe
  follows)
2 tablespoons chopped fresh
  cilantro plus 4 sprigs cilantro,
  for garnish
4 tablespoons fresh lime juice
2 tablespoons vegetable oil
4 lime wedges, for serving

YOU'LL ALSO NEED:
2 bricks or pieces of paving stone,
  wrapped in aluminum foil

TIP: *Achiote paste can be found at any Mexican market or see Mail-Order Sources, page 311. You can also make your own paste using annatto seeds, following the recipe on page 180. If you can't find achiote paste or annatto seeds, use 1 tablespoon sweet paprika in their place.*

1. Trim any excess fat or sinews off the chicken breasts and discard. Rinse the breasts under cold running water, then drain and blot dry with paper towels. Arrange the breasts in a nonreactive baking dish.

2. Put the garlic, salt, and pepper in a mixing bowl and mash to a paste with the back of a wooden spoon. Add the achiote paste and chopped cilantro and mash to a paste. Add the lime juice a little at a time and stir until smooth. Stir in the oil. Pour this mixture over the chicken and let marinate in the refrigerator, covered, for 1 to 2 hours.

3. Set up the grill for direct grilling (see page 8 for both charcoal and gas) and preheat to high. When ready to cook, brush and oil the grill grate. Arrange the chicken breasts on the hot grate so that they face the same direction at a 45-degree angle to the bars of the grate. Place the bricks on top of the breasts. Grill the breasts until cooked through, 4 to 6 minutes per side, rotating them 90 degrees after 2 minutes on each side to create an attractive crosshatch of grill marks. To test for doneness, poke a breast in the thickest part with your finger. It should feel firm to the touch. Transfer the chicken to plates or a platter and serve with the cilantro sprigs and lime wedges.

SERVES 4

Āchiote Paste

Also known as annatto, achiote is a rust-colored seed native to the Yucatán. In areas with large Mexican populations, it's often sold in paste form. On the East Coast, it's frequently sold in seed form. Here's how to make a quick achiote paste. It will make more than you need for "Stoned" Chicken; use it any time you want to spice up chicken, pork, or even seafood.

2 tablespoons annatto seeds
2 cloves garlic, minced
2 teaspoons coarse salt (kosher or sea)
2 tablespoons vegetable oil
2 teaspoons red wine vinegar

1. Grind the annatto seeds to a fine powder in a spice mill or coffee grinder (you must use one of these devices—the seed is too hard for a blender).

2. Put the garlic and salt in a small nonreactive bowl and mash to a paste with the back of a spoon.

3. Add the ground annatto seeds and the oil and vinegar and stir until a smooth paste forms. Achiote paste will keep in the refrigerator, covered, for several months.

MAKES about ¼ cup

GAME HENS UNDER BRICKS

I like *pollo al mattone* (Italian chicken grilled under a brick) for four reasons. It's quick and easy to make. It looks great. It produces the most crackling crisp skin and tender juicy meat you can imagine. And, above all, it allows you to use the word *spatchcock,* which is reason enough for preparing it. Spatchcocking means nothing more than cutting out the backbone and breastbone of a chicken or game hen, which makes the bird flatter and maximizes the surface area exposed to the fire, which enables you to grill whole hens using the direct method.

ADVANCE PREPARATION: 1 to 2 hours for marinating the hens

4 game hens (about 1 pound each)

1 tablespoon cracked black peppercorns

1 to 3 teaspoons hot red pepper flakes, to taste

Coarse salt (kosher or sea)

4 cloves garlic, finely chopped

1 bunch fresh sage or rosemary, stemmed and coarsely chopped (about ½ cup; set aside some leaves)

½ cup fresh lemon juice

½ cup extra-virgin olive oil

Lemon wedges, for serving

YOU'LL ALSO NEED:
Poultry shears; 4 bricks wrapped in aluminum foil; water pistol (optional)

1. Remove the packets of giblets (if any) from the body cavities of the game hens and set aside for another use. Remove and discard the fat just inside the body and neck cavities. Rinse the game hens, inside and out, under cold running water and then drain and blot dry, inside and out, with paper towels.

2. Spatchcock a hen: Place a hen on its breast. Using poultry shears and starting at the neck end, cut out the backbone, making one lengthwise cut on either side. Remove and discard the backbone or save it for stock. Fold the game hen open like a book, skin side down. Use a paring knife to cut along each side of the breastbone. Run your thumbs firmly along both sides of the breastbone and white cartilage, then pull them out. Cut off the wing tips and trim off any loose skin. Pull down on the legs to lay them flat. Repeat with the remaining game hens.

> **TIP:** *Spatchcocking is easy: All you need is a pair of poultry shears and a paring knife. I've explained it fully here. A whole chicken could be prepared using this method, in which case increase the cooking time to about 15 minutes per side.*

3. Place the hens in a large nonreactive baking dish, sprinkle both sides with the cracked black peppercorns and hot red pepper flakes and season with salt. Sprinkle the garlic and sage over both sides of the game hens. Pour the lemon juice over the hens, followed by the olive oil, turning the hens to coat both sides. Let the hens marinate in the refrigerator, covered, for 1 to 2 hours.

4. Set up the grill for direct grilling (see page 8 for both charcoal and gas) and preheat to medium. When ready to cook, brush and oil the grill grate. Arrange the spatchcocked game hens skin side down on the grate. Place a brick on top of each hen so that it covers as much of the bird as possible. Grill the game hens until the skin is golden brown, 8 to 10 minutes.

5. Remove the bricks and carefully turn over the hens using tongs and a spatula. Re-cover with the bricks and continue grilling until the second side is a dark golden brown and the hens are cooked through, 8 to 10 minutes more. You may get some flare-ups as melting fat hits the fire. If this happens, move the hens to another section of the grill. You can tame any really serious flare-ups with a squirt from a water pistol (1 or 2 squirts to control the flames are okay, but don't overdo it or you'll put out the fire). The hens are done when an instant-read meat thermometer inserted into the thickest part of a thigh (but not touching the bone) registers 170°F.

6. Transfer the hens to a platter and garnish with sage and lemon wedges.

SERVES 4

TOAD-STYLE CHICKEN

The curious French name *poulet en crapaudine* (chicken in the style of a toad) refers not to its seasonings (although you could use them for frog's legs) but to the way the chicken is cut so that it opens up flat like a book. To the French, this vaguely looks like a frog, and I agree. However, I'm a bigger fan of the English word for this—*spatchcocking*. The simple marinade here is bursting with Mediterranean flavors. If you don't like anchovies, leave them out.

ADVANCE PREPARATION: 2 to 12 hours for marinating the chicken (optional)

FOR THE HERB PASTE:
1 bunch basil leaves, stemmed (2 cups) and roughly chopped
3 cloves garlic, roughly chopped
3 anchovy fillets, roughly chopped (optional)
1½ teaspoons coarse salt (kosher or sea)
1 teaspoon cracked black peppercorns
¼ cup dry vermouth or dry white wine
2 tablespoons Dijon mustard
2 tablespoons fresh lemon juice
½ teaspoon grated lemon zest
6 tablespoons extra-virgin olive oil

1 chicken (3½ to 4 pounds)
Lemon wedges, for serving
Mediterranean Salsa (optional; recipe follows), for serving

YOU'LL ALSO NEED:

**2 cups wood chips or chunks (optional;
   preferably oak or cherry), unsoaked**

Poultry shears

1. Make the herb paste: Place the basil,

garlic, anchovies, if using, salt, and cracked pepper
in a food processor and process to finely chop. Add
the vermouth, mustard, lemon juice and zest, and
olive oil and process to a coarse paste.

2. Remove the packet of giblets from the

body cavity of the chicken and set aside for
another use. Remove and discard the fat just
inside the body and neck cavities. Rinse the
chicken, inside and out, under cold running water
and then drain and blot dry, inside and out, with
paper towels.

3. Spatchcock the chicken: Place the bird

on its breast. Using poultry shears and starting at
the neck end, cut out the back-
bone, making one lengthwise cut
on either side. Remove and discard the backbone or save it for
stock. Fold the chicken open like
a book, skin side down. Use a
paring knife to cut along each
side of the breastbone. Run your
thumbs firmly along both sides
of the breastbone and white
cartilage, then pull them out. Cut
off the wing tips and trim off any
loose skin. Pull down on the legs
to lay them flat. Arrange the
chicken in a nonreactive baking dish. Using a rubber spatula, spread the paste all over the chicken
on both sides. Let marinate in the refrigerator, covered, for at least 2 hours or even overnight; the
longer the chicken marinates, the richer the flavor
will be.

> **TIP:** There are two
> ways to grill spatch-
> cocked birds: using the
> direct or the indirect
> method. The former
> gives you a more robust
> live-fire flavor, but the
> chicken is prone to
> charring and the grill
> to flare-ups. Indirect
> grilling is absolutely
> foolproof. That's the
> method I've used here.

4. Set up the grill for indirect grilling (see page 9 for both charcoal and gas) and preheat to medium. If using a charcoal grill, place a large drip pan in the center. If using a gas grill, place all the wood chips or chunks, if using, in the smoker box or in a smoker pouch (see page 12) and preheat on high until you see smoke, then reduce the heat to medium.

5. When ready to cook, if using a charcoal grill, toss all of the wood chips or chunks, if using,

> **TIP:** *I've made wood chips optional. They'll give you a light smoke flavor similar to what you'd get if you grilled over oak (you want a light wood flavor, so don't soak the chips). But the chicken is plenty tasty without them.*

on the coals. Brush and oil the grate. Place the chicken, skin side up, in the center of the hot grate, over the drip pan and away from the heat. Cover the grill and cook the chicken until the skin is a dark golden brown and very crisp and the meat is cooked through (about 180°F on an instant-read meat thermometer inserted in the thickest part of a thigh, but not touching the bone), about 40 minutes (see page 27 for other tests for doneness). If the chicken skin starts to brown too much, loosely tent the bird with aluminum foil. During the last 5 minutes of grilling, turn the chicken over using tongs and a spatula and move it directly over the fire to char the skin.

6. Transfer the chicken to a platter and serve with lemon wedges and Mediterranean Salsa, if desired.

SERVES 2 to 4

VARIATION: You can use the direct method to grill the chicken. In this case, set up your grill for direct grilling (see page 8 for both charcoal and gas) and preheat to medium. Be sure to leave yourself a fire-free safety zone (see page 9). When ready to grill, brush and oil the grill grate. Start the chicken skin side down and grill until handsomely browned on the outside and cooked through, 15 to 20 minutes per side. Use tongs and a spatula to facilitate turning.

Mediterranean Salsa

A simple Mediterranean salad of fresh tomatoes, olives, capers, and garlic makes a refreshing accompaniment to grilled chicken (or any sort of grilled meat or seafood). You use it exactly as you would a salsa, hence, its name. A recipe like this one lives and dies by the quality of the ingredients: Use vine-ripened tomatoes (the sort that go splat when you hurl them) and quality olive oil. The virtue of this salsa is its freshness: You can chop the ingredients ahead of time, but don't mix them more than 10 minutes before serving.

2 ripe red tomatoes

8 kalamata or other black olives, pitted and
diced

1 tablespoon capers, drained

1 clove garlic, minced

6 fresh basil leaves or flat-leaf parsley sprigs,
thinly slivered

3 tablespoons extra-virgin olive oil

1 tablespoon red wine vinegar

Coarse salt (kosher or sea) and freshly ground
black pepper

Cut the tomatoes in half crosswise and gently
squeeze each half over the sink, cut side down,
to wring out the seeds. Cut the halves into
¼-inch dice. Place the diced tomatoes in a
nonreactive bowl and stir in the olives, capers,
garlic, basil, olive oil, and vinegar. Add salt and
pepper to taste and serve.

MAKES 1½ to 2 cups

INDIRECT GRILLING

DIABOLICAL CHICKEN

A la diable (in the style of the devil) is the French phrase for a grilled chicken or chop topped with a spicy crust of mustard, herbs, and bread crumbs. (Although the flavorings they use are different, the Italians have a similar metaphor for describing their lobster *fra diavolo*.) I first tasted this wicked chicken in Paris in the 1970s, and I still make it whenever I'm short on time or fancy ingredients but I want to impress the hell out of my guests. You'll need to spatchcock the chicken—take out the backbone and breastbone—so it lies flat on the grill, but this is not hard, and the recipe talks you through it.

TIP: *To get the full effect of this dish, you need to use a good imported French mustard and fresh tarragon (or another fresh herb). Ideally, the bread crumbs will be homemade, too (it's a good thing I don't ask for a lot). To toast bread crumbs, spread them in a thin layer on a rimmed baking sheet and bake in a 350°F oven until lightly browned, 8 to 15 minutes, tossing them with a spatula to ensure even browning. Let cool to room temperature, then store in an airtight container. The bread crumbs will keep for several weeks.*

1 chicken (3½ to 4 pounds)

Coarse salt (kosher or sea) and coarsely
    ground black pepper

½ cup Meaux (grainy) or Dijon (smooth)
    French mustard

1 cup toasted bread crumbs

2 tablespoons chopped fresh tarragon

2 cloves garlic, minced

½ teaspoon hot red pepper flakes, or
    more to taste

2 tablespoons melted butter

Lemon wedges, for serving

Tarragon sprigs, for serving

Mustard Sauce (recipe follows), for serving

1. Remove the packet of giblets from the
body cavity of the chicken and set aside for
another use. Remove and discard the fat just
inside the body and neck cavities. Rinse the
chicken, inside and out, under cold running water
and then drain and blot dry, inside and out,
with paper towels.

2. Spatchcock the chicken: Place the bird
on its breast. Using poultry shears and starting at
the neck end, cut out the backbone, making one
lengthwise cut on either side. Remove and discard
the backbone or save it for stock. Fold the chicken
open like a book, skin side down. Use a paring knife
to cut along each side of the breastbone. Run your
thumbs firmly along both sides of the breastbone
and white cartilage, then pull them out. Cut off the
wing tips and trim off any loose skin. Pull down on
the legs to lay them flat.

3. Place the spatchcocked chicken on a
large plate and season very generously on both
sides with salt and pepper. Thickly paint both sides
of the chicken with mustard. Put the bread crumbs,
tarragon, garlic, and hot red pepper flakes in a
large shallow bowl or baking dish and stir to mix.

Lay the chicken skin side down in the crumbs to coat, then turn it over and coat the bone side. Sprinkle crumbs on any bare spots.

4. Set up the grill for indirect grilling (see page 9 for both charcoal and gas) and preheat to medium. If using a charcoal grill, place a large drip pan in the center.

5. When ready to cook, brush and oil the grill grate. Place the chicken, skin side up, in the center of the hot grate, over the drip pan and away from the heat. Drizzle the butter over the top of the chicken. Cover the grill and cook the chicken until the crust is a golden brown and the meat is cooked through (about 180°F on an instant-read meat thermometer inserted in the thickest part of a thigh, but not touching the bone), about 40 minutes. If the crust starts to brown too much, loosely tent the bird with aluminum foil.

6. Transfer the chicken to a platter. Garnish with lemon wedges and tarragon sprigs and serve at once with the Mustard Sauce.

SERVES 2 to 4

VARIATION: You can prepare breasts of game hens or chicken in a mustard crust. Game hens will take about 30 minutes to cook; chicken breasts will be done in about 20 minutes.

Mustard Sauce

Don't reserve this mustard sauce for grilled chicken. It's pretty fantastic alongside grilled pork, veal, and seafood, as well.

⅓ cup mayonnaise

¼ cup Meaux (grainy) or Dijon (smooth)
mustard

1 tablespoon fresh lemon juice

1 tablespoon A.1. steak sauce

½ teaspoon hot red pepper flakes, or more
to taste

Freshly ground black pepper

Put all the ingredients except the black
pepper in a small nonreactive bowl and whisk to
mix. Taste for seasoning, adding black pepper and
more hot red pepper flakes to taste; the sauce
should be highly seasoned. The sauce will keep in
the refrigerator, covered, for up to 1 week. Let
return to room temperature before serving.

MAKES ¾ cup

OFFBEAT MEAT

"A steak is a steak is a steak," goes the saying. Well, if you've ever thought of steak as the plain-Jane of grilling, this chapter will give you a whole new perspective. In the following pages you'll learn how to grill one directly on the embers, in a sugar crust, and even in flaming hay. You'll master the art of roasting a brisket in the coals, a technique that dates from the American Civil War. You'll even find new twists on those barbecue standbys—hot dogs and hamburgers. The franks are stuffed with pickles and cheese and grilled in strips of bacon; the burgers are molded in the shape of a doughnut to maximize crusting. Hot dogs may be a ballpark classic, but when it comes to cooking meat on the grill, it's a whole new ball game.

DIRTY STEAKS

Innovative grill masters Johanne Killeen and George Germon, the owners of Al Forno restaurant in Providence, Rhode Island, are always pushing the limits of what can go on the grill (after all, they invented grilled pizza) or, in the case of the following recipe, what can be grilled without a grill. Dirty steak is nothing more than a strip steak cooked on the glowing coals. George has all sorts of theories about why the result is so tasty, including the intense but irregular charring that results from bringing the meat in direct contact with the embers. Al Forno's owners remain mum on the contents of their steak sauce, so I've paired their steak with a tangy Mushroom-Mustard Sauce of my own.

4 boneless strip or sirloin steaks (each about 1 inch thick and 8 to 10 ounces)
Plenty of coarse salt (kosher or sea) and coarsely ground black pepper
1 piece (2 tablespoons) butter, chilled (optional)
Mushroom-Mustard Sauce (recipe follows)

YOU'LL ALSO NEED:
A charcoal grill
Natural lump charcoal

1. Light the charcoal in a chimney starter (see page 15). When the coals glow red, dump them into the bottom of the grill and rake them into a pile on one side. Let the coals burn until they begin to ash over, 5 to 10 minutes, then fan the coals with a fan or hair drier to blow off the loose ash.

2. Generously season the steaks on both sides with salt and pepper. Lay the steaks directly on the glowing embers. Grill until done to taste, turning once with tongs, 4 to 6 minutes per side for medium-rare.

> **TIP:** *Grilling directly on the embers is an ancient practice, the prehistoric precursor of modern grilling. Lest you envision eating a mouthful of cinders, however, know that the fire is fanned briskly to blow away all the loose ash before placing the meat on the coals. Because the meat comes in such intimate contact with the embers, use natural lump charcoal (see pages 12 to 13), not factory-made briquettes.*

3. Use tongs to hold the steaks over the grill and brush off any loose ash with a pastry brush. Transfer the steaks to plates or a platter and rub the top of the steaks with butter, if desired. If grilling sirloin steaks, slice them on the diagonal. Serve with the Mushroom-Mustard Sauce on the side.

SERVES 4

Mushroom-Mustard Sauce

Beef and mushrooms—they're perfect together, which explains why mushrooms are a traditional accompaniment for steak. And while you don't normally think of combining mushrooms and mustard, they work well in the presence of beef—especially the gutsy Dirty Steaks.

12 ounces button or other mushrooms, cleaned
  and trimmed (see Note)
3 tablespoons butter
2 shallots, minced (about ⅓ cup)
Coarse salt (kosher or sea) and
  freshly ground black pepper
2 teaspoons flour
¼ cup Cognac
1½ cups veal, beef, or homemade chicken stock
  (page 52)
2 teaspoons Worcestershire sauce
2 teaspoons Dijon mustard
½ cup heavy (whipping) cream

1. Working in several batches, place the mushrooms in a food processor and mince, running the machine in short bursts. Don't overprocess or the mushrooms will become watery.

2. Melt the butter in a large saucepan over medium heat. Add the shallots and cook until soft and translucent, but not brown, about 3 minutes. Raise the heat to high, add the mushrooms and a little salt and pepper, and cook until all the liquid has evaporated, 5 minutes. Stir in the flour and cook to blend, about 1 minute. Add the Cognac and bring to a boil. Add the stock, Worcestershire sauce, mustard, and cream and let the sauce simmer until reduced to about 1½ cups, 5 to 8 minutes.

3. Coarsely purée the sauce in a blender, running the machine in short bursts. Don't overblend or the cream may separate. Return the sauce to a saucepan to keep warm. Taste for seasoning, adding salt and pepper as necessary; the sauce should be highly seasoned.

MAKES about 1½ cups

NOTE: The easiest way to clean mushrooms is by wiping them with a damp cloth or paper towel.

DIRECT GRILLING

HAY-SMOKED STEAKS

I've eaten a lot of steak, but this one startled even me. It is based on a recipe from two of my Kansas City barbecue buddies, Ardie "Remus Powers" Davis and Judith Fertig. Ardie first tasted it, or something like it, in Tuscany; Judith penned a recipe in her fine book, *Prairie Home Cooking.* Hay flavors the steak in two ways, first imparting a mild, gentle sweetness to the uncooked meat, then creating a delicate smoke flavor when the hay is tossed on the coals. Above all, there's the novelty factor—after all, how often do you get to see beef cooked on hay?

ADVANCE PREPARATION: 1 to 2 hours for flavoring the steaks

4 generous handfuls of hay
 (4 to 6 cups)
4 boneless strip steaks (each
 about 2 inches thick and 12 to
 14 ounces)
Coarse salt (kosher or sea)
3 to 4 tablespoons extra-virgin
 olive oil
Freshly ground or cracked peppercorns
Lemon wedges, for serving

YOU'LL ALSO NEED:
3 to 4 chunks oak, unsoaked

> **TIP:** *The greatest challenge this recipe presents is finding the hay. Your best bet is a farmers' market, farm stand, or tack shop.*

1. Spread the hay on a platter and arrange the steaks on top. Season the steaks on both sides with 1 tablespoon of salt. Let the steaks come to room temperature, 1 to 2 hours, turning them twice.

> **TIP:** The hay is going to blaze and smoke. Set up your grill on an open patio or in a backyard, well away from buildings or trees. (Do not attempt this recipe on an apartment balcony or closed porch.) If you have long hair, it's a good idea to tie it back; also keep your sleeves rolled up.

2. Meanwhile, set up the grill for direct grilling (see page 8 for both charcoal and gas) and preheat to medium-high (ideally, you'll be cooking on a charcoal grill). About 5 minutes before you plan to put the steaks on the grill, add the wood chunks to the fire. If using a gas grill, position the wood chunks under the grate on the hottest part of the grill, over one of the burners and preheat until you see smoke.

3. Once you see smoke, brush and oil the grill grate. Lift the steaks off the hay, reserving the latter. Arrange the steaks on the hot grate and grill for 3 minutes per side. Using tongs, carefully remove the steaks and grate from the grill. If using a charcoal grill, toss the reserved hay on the fire. If using a gas grill, place the hay under the grate over one of the burners. The hay will catch fire and put out lots of smoke. This is good. Return the grate and steaks to the grill and cover it. If using a gas grill, position the steaks so they are not directly above the hay.

4. Continue grilling the steaks until cooked to taste, 4 to 7 minutes more per side for medium-rare. Turn the steaks several times as they cook to expose both sides to the smoke from the hay.

5. Transfer the steaks to a platter and drizzle with olive oil, turning the meat to coat both sides. Season with pepper and more salt, if desired. Let rest for 3 minutes. Serve with lemon wedges.

SERVES 4 to 8

DIRECT GRILLING

SUGAR-GRILLED STEAKS

Strip steaks crusted with sugar—this seems like the sort of heresy dreamed up after drinking too much beer. I'd heard about it, and eventually my curiosity got the best of me, so I tried "sugar grilling" a steak. I was amazed at just how tasty this unlikely combination could be. You're probably envisioning candied beef, but in fact the sugar creates an unusual crust. The whisper of sweetness goes surprisingly well with the meat.

> **TIP:** *I've prepared the recipe using either brown or white sugar. The latter seems to caramelize a touch better, but both work great. And don't be stingy with the salt—you need it to offset the sweetness. Sugar burns when grilled, so you'll need to choose a steak that's fairly thin and quick cooking: 3/4- to-1-inch thick is ideal. Don't try this on a thick porterhouse. The burnt sugar will become bitter before the meat is cooked through.*

4 boneless strip steaks (each about 3/4 inch thick and 8 ounces)
Plenty of coarse salt (kosher or sea) and freshly ground black pepper
3 to 4 tablespoons granulated sugar or light brown sugar

1. Place the steaks on a large platter and season generously with salt and pepper on both sides. Spread about 1/2 tablespoon of sugar on the top of each steak and rub it into the meat with the back of a spoon. Turn the steaks over and repeat.

2. Set up the grill for direct grilling (see page 8 for both charcoal and gas) and preheat to high. It's a good idea to light the fire in such a way as to have a cooler section on the grill (see page 9); that way, if the sugar starts to burn over high heat, you can move the steaks to a section that is less hot.

3. When ready to cook, brush and oil the grill grate. Arrange the steaks on the hot grate at a 45-degree angle to the bars of the grate so that they all face the same way. Grill the steaks until cooked to taste, 4 to 6 minutes per side for medium-rare, rotating them 90 degrees after 3 minutes to create a handsome crosshatch of grill marks. Check the underside of the steaks as they cook by lifting one edge; if the crusts start to burn, move the steaks to a cooler part of the grill.

4. Transfer the grilled steaks to a platter and reseason with salt and pepper. Let the steaks rest for 2 minutes before serving.

SERVES 4

GRILLING IN THE EMBERS

RUBY'S BRISKET

TIP: *Try to buy a brisket with a thin layer of fat on top. Our briskets are undoubtedly leaner than Ruby's, so I lay strips of bacon underneath and on top. For the full effect of this recipe, cook the meat beneath the embers in a charcoal grill. Gas grillers can get a respectable result by grilling the foil-swaddled brisket directly over a moderate flame.*

The sharp-tongued, backwoods drifter in Charles Frazier's National Book Award-winning Civil War period novel, *Cold Mountain,* Ruby Stobrod is a pragmatic country girl who seems to know how to do everything—from butchering livestock to roasting meat in the embers. Such are the evocative powers of Frazier's writing that, simply by reading about them, you can almost taste the dishes his characters prepare. Consider the following brisket, which Ruby seasons with a simple rub and cooks in the glowing coals of a campfire. (The only thing I've changed is to wrap the brisket in aluminum foil instead of paper.) This gives you a very different sort of

brisket from what you'd get by the more conventional method of smoking. It's also great for campers.

6 slices of thick-sliced smoked bacon
(the smokier, the better)
4 to 6 teaspoons All-Purpose Barbecue Rub
(page 37)
1 center-cut piece of brisket (2½ to 3 pounds)
Your choice of barbecue sauce (optional),
for serving

YOU'LL ALSO NEED:
A charcoal grill
4 pieces of heavy-duty aluminum foil
(24 by 18 inches each)

1. Place a piece of heavy-duty aluminum foil shiny side down on a work surface. Place 3 slices of bacon about 1 inch apart on top of the foil. Sprinkle the rub over the brisket on all sides and rub it onto the meat with your fingers. Lay the brisket on top of the bacon. Lay the remaining bacon on top of the brisket. Bring the ends of the aluminum foil up over the brisket, folding over the edges several times and crimping them to make a tight seal. Tightly wrap the brisket in 3 more layers of aluminum foil, shiny side out (so it will reflect the heat), to make a sturdy packet.

2. Light charcoal or wood chunks in a chimney starter (see page 15). When the coals glow red, dump them into the bottom of the grill and rake into a pile on one side. Let the coals burn until they begin to ash over, 5 to 10 minutes.

3. When ready to cook, lay the wrapped brisket next to the coals. Using a small shovel, long-handled spatula, or tongs, shovel 6 or so glowing embers on top of the brisket.

4. Roast the brisket under the embers until cooked through and tender, about 2 hours. Every 30 minutes, turn and rotate the brisket so that a different side faces the mound of coals (take care not to puncture the foil packet when turning). Place a few fresh coals on top of the foil packet. You'll need to replenish the coals after 45 minutes to 1 hour. Simply place fresh charcoal or wood chunks on top of the mound of coals. They'll light in about 10 minutes. If you've wrapped your brisket well, there won't be any leakage of bacon fat. If the fat does leak, you may get a flare-up in the bottom of the grill. Keep your eye on the grill for flare-ups and move the brisket to a flame-free section of the grill if you see one.

5. Test for doneness by using a long slender metal skewer: It should pierce the meat easily. Rake any coals off the foil packet and transfer it to an aluminum foil pan or roasting pan. Let cool for 10 minutes.

6. Present the brisket in its flame-darkened foil packet to your guests, then remove it to the kitchen for unwrapping and carving. Take care to avoid the escaping steam. Trim off any burnt parts from the brisket. Thinly slice the meat across the grain and serve. By way of an accompaniment, you could serve any of the barbecue sauces in this book or your favorite sauce.

SERVES 6 to 8

VARIATION: To use a gas grill, set it up for direct grilling (see page 8) and preheat to medium-low. Cook the brisket in its foil packet for about 1 hour per side, turning once.

DIRECT GRILLING

"DOUGHNUT" BURGERS

John Willingham may need no introduction. Many visitors to the Smithsonian Institution in Washington, D.C., have seen one of his custom-designed smokers on display in the National Museum of American History. Hundreds of thousands of 'que heads have bought his book, taken his seminars, and dined at his restaurant in Memphis. And this master of smoke and swine has some singular thoughts about hamburgers—he's convinced we've been making them all wrong all these years. "What do people like best about a hamburger?" asks Willingham. "A flame-charred crust and juicy interior." So Willingham has designed a burger that maximizes the crust. He forms the meat into patties with a hole in the center. These doughnut burgers cook quickly and evenly, giving you a perfect crust and moist center. ☼

> **TIP:** *We live in an age when prudence dictates that ground beef be cooked to at least 160°F. This may be more well done than you like your burgers, but with today's risk of bacterial contamination, it's the only sensible thing to do.*

Best of all, they'll make jaws drop at a cookout, ensuring your reputation as a cutting-edge grill meister.

2 pounds ground beef (chuck or round)
1 small onion, minced fine as dust
2 cloves garlic, minced
3 tablespoons chopped flat-leaf parsley
2 teaspoons coarse salt (kosher or sea)
1 teaspoon freshly ground black pepper
8 hamburger buns
Melted butter (optional)
Sliced onion, sliced tomato, lettuce leaves,
    ketchup, mustard, relish, or any other
    topping you may fancy

1. Place the ground beef in a large mixing bowl. Mix in the onion, garlic, parsley, salt, and pepper using your hands, working as quickly as possible so as not to overwork the meat. Divide the beef into 8 even portions and shape each into a patty. Make a hole in the center and shape each burger like a doughnut. The burgers can be made up to 2 hours ahead: Refrigerate them, covered, on a plate lined with plastic wrap.

2. Set up the grill for direct grilling (see page 8 for both charcoal and gas) and preheat to high.

3. When ready to cook, brush and oil the grill grate. Place the burgers on the grill and grill until crusty and golden brown, 3 to 5 minutes per side. If you like, brush the buns with melted butter and grill as well. Put the burgers on the buns and serve them at once with your favorite toppings.

MAKES 8 burgers, SERVES 4 to 8

DIRECT GRILLING

CARDIOLOGIST'S NIGHTMARE

George Cusack of Eugene, Oregon, a visitor to my Web site, barbecuebible.com, describes these as "a cardiac nightmare." And a tasty nightmare at that. Hot dogs, smoked cheese, pickles, peppered bacon, and barbecue sauce—all rolled up in one heart-stopping package! How can you go wrong?!

> **TIP:** *Cusack pins the dogs shut with toothpicks, but I find that string is less likely to catch fire.*

- 4 beef knockwurst or precooked bratwurst (you need a fat hot dog)
- 4 to 5 ounces smoked cheese, thinly sliced, cut into ½-inch-wide strips
- 12 thin dill pickle slices
- 4 strips bacon, preferably pepper bacon
- ¼ cup of your favorite barbecue sauce (I like a mustard-based sauce)
- 8 hot dog buns, lightly brushed with melted butter
- Mustard, ketchup, relish, or your favorite condiments, for serving

YOU'LL ALSO NEED:
- 8 pieces butcher's string (each about 4 inches long)

1. Make 2 lengthwise cuts in each hot dog to remove a slender V-shape strip from the center. The idea is to cut the hot dog almost in half lengthwise, but leave the halves attached at the bottom.

2. Insert cheese strips and pickle slices in the slit. Starting at one end and working on the diagonal, wrap a strip of bacon around each hot dog (the effect will look rather like a candy cane). Tie each hot dog crosswise in two places with butcher's string, cutting off the ends of the string with scissors.

> **TIP:** *The bacon will be easier to use for wrapping if you stretch it slightly by tugging on both ends beforehand.*

3. Set up the grill for direct grilling (see page 8 for both charcoal and gas) and preheat to medium-high.

4. When ready to cook, place the hot dogs on the hot grill, parallel to the bars of the grate, so the bars support them. Grill until the bacon and hot dogs are nicely browned on the bottom and sides, 8 to 10 minutes (use tongs to tilt the hot dogs to brown the sides). During the last few minutes of grilling, baste the dogs with barbecue sauce. Note: The dripping bacon fat may cause flare-ups: Simply move the dogs to another section of the grill, away from the fire. While the hot dogs are cooking, toast the buns on the grill for about 1 minute.

5. Transfer the hot dogs and buns to a platter. Snip off and discard the strings. Serve hot dogs on the buns with your choice of condiment(s).

SERVES 4

FISH OUT OF WATER

What about seafood? Barbecue shouldn't be limited to just birds and beef. There are lots of inventive ways to grill fish. If you need some convincing, let me introduce you to how fish and shellfish are grilled elsewhere on the world's barbecue trail, from Cambodia's *amok,* fish cooked with curry in banana leaves, to France's mussels flamed with pine needles. You'll also learn how to grill salmon on a cedar plank, a specialty of the Pacific Northwest, and how to smoke-roast a whole fish in a salt crust, as they do on the coast of Italy. You'll even get a fresh look at—and new appreciation for—fish sticks, that American childhood favorite.

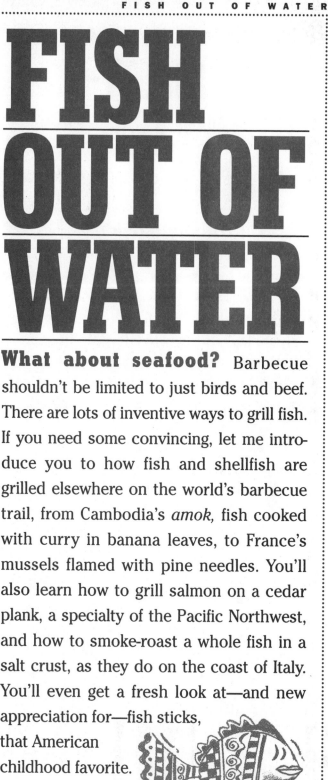

ROSEMARY-TUNA FISH STICKS

I was a finicky eater when I was growing up. (That's putting it mildly!) About the only seafood that would cross my lips was fish sticks. As an adult (and barbecue addict), I still have a soft spot for fish sticks, but now I like to grill them on flavorful skewers, such as rosemary sprigs, strips of sugarcane, and lemongrass stalks. Grilling fish on rosemary sprigs puts a terrific herb flavor *inside* the fish.

ADVANCE PREPARATION: 20 to 30 minutes for marinating the tuna

12 sprigs rosemary, each about
   6 inches long
1½ pounds tuna steaks (about 1 inch thick;
   see Note)
Coarse salt (kosher or sea) and
   cracked black peppercorns
3 cloves garlic, minced
½ to 1 teaspoon hot red
   pepper flakes (optional)
¼ cup fresh lemon juice
¼ cup extra-virgin olive oil, plus oil for grilling
   the grill grate
Lemon wedges, for serving
Mediterranean Salsa, for serving
   (optional; page 187)

1. Strip the leaves off the bottom 4 inches of each rosemary sprig (pull them off between your thumb and forefinger). Finely chop these rosemary leaves and set aside for the marinade. Cut off the very end of the rosemary stem sharply on the diagonal to make a sharp point for easy insertion into the tuna.

> **TIP:** *For the best results, you'll want rosemary sprigs that are about 6 inches long and fairly stiff. You can sometimes find these in the supermarket produce section, but you'll get longer, stiffer sprigs —not to mention a renewable source of rosemary—if you buy a rosemary plant at your local nursery.*

2. Trim any skin or dark or bloody spots off the tuna. Rinse the tuna steaks under cold running water and then blot dry with paper towels. Cut the tuna steaks into strips about 4 inches long and 1 inch wide. Run the bare part of a rosemary stem lengthwise through the center of each strip of tuna (the idea is to create a sort of kebab). Arrange the skewered tuna in a nonreactive baking dish. Sprinkle the fish on all sides with salt and pepper and the garlic, hot red pepper flakes, if using, and chopped rosemary. Pour the lemon juice and olive oil over the fish, turning the kebabs to coat evenly. Let marinate for 20 to 30 minutes, turning once or twice, while you set up the grill.

3. Set up the grill for direct grilling (see page 8 for both charcoal and gas) and preheat to high. Make an aluminum foil shield for the rosemary leaves by folding a 24 by 12-inch sheet of aluminum foil over in half and in half again to make a 12 by 6-inch rectangle.

4. When ready to cook, brush and oil the grill grate. Place the aluminum foil shield on one side of the grill, running parallel to the bars of the grill. Arrange the skewered tuna on the grill so that the tuna portion runs perpendicular to the bars of the grate over the fire and the rosemary portion rests on the aluminum foil shield. Grill the tuna until cooked to taste, 20 to 30 seconds per side (1½ to 2 minutes in all) for medium-rare.

5. Serve the grilled tuna at once, with wedges of lemon for squeezing and the Mediterranean Salsa on the side, if desired.

MAKES 12 fish sticks, SERVES 4

NOTE: You can substitute another firm-fleshed fish, such as swordfish, salmon, or mahimahi, or even shrimp or scallops.

DIRECT GRILLING

MAHIMAHI ON SUGARCANE

I love grilling on sugarcane.

The technique turns up in Vietnam, where cane-grilled shrimp mousse is a traditional appetizer. It's also practiced in the Caribbean and more recently at cutting-edge restaurants in the United States. Sugarcane's firm, fibrous structure makes it great to use as a skewer, and it releases dulcet juices when you bite into it.

ADVANCE PREPARATION:

30 minutes for marinating the fish

FOR THE GLAZE:

4 tablespoons (½ stick) salted butter

¼ cup firmly packed brown sugar

¼ cup dark rum

1 tablespoon soy sauce

½ teaspoon ground cinnamon

¼ teaspoon freshly ground black pepper

Pinch of ground cloves

6 sugarcane swizzle sticks (see Tip; each about 8 inches long)

1½ pounds mahimahi (¾ to 1 inch thick; see Note)

1½ tablespoons vegetable oil

1½ tablespoons jerk seasoning (preferably homemade, recipe follows)

Lime wedges, for serving

TIP: *You can buy whole sections of sugarcane, which you'll need to peel and cut into skewers. It's far less work to find sugarcane swizzle sticks, which are distributed by at least two exotic produce companies (Frieda's and Melissa's—see Mail-Order Sources, page 311). Look for the swizzle sticks at gourmet shops, specialty greengrocers, and very possibly in the produce section of your local supermarket.*

1. Make the glaze: Combine the butter, brown sugar, rum, soy sauce, cinnamon, pepper, and cloves in a small saucepan and bring to a boil over medium-high heat. Boil the mixture until thick and syrupy, 5 minutes, whisking frequently to mix.

2. Cut each swizzle stick in half crosswise sharply on the diagonal, angling your knife so that the cuts form sharp points.

3. Rinse the mahimahi under cold running water and then blot dry with paper towels. Cut the mahimahi into strips about 3½ inches long and 1 inch wide. Using a metal skewer, make a tunnel lengthwise through each strip. Insert a strip of sugarcane through each tunnel. Arrange the skewered fish in a baking dish and drizzle with the oil, turning to coat all sides of the fish. Sprinkle the fish with the jerk seasoning, turning to coat all sides. Let the fish marinate for 30 minutes while you set up the grill.

4. Set up the grill for direct grilling (see page 8 for both charcoal and gas) and preheat to high.

5. When ready to cook, brush and oil the grill grate. Arrange the fish sticks on the grate at a diagonal to the bars. Grill until cooked through, about 30 seconds per side (2 minutes in all), basting with the glaze. Transfer the fish sticks to a platter and drizzle with any remaining glaze (reboil for 2 minutes before serving). Serve with lime wedges.

MAKES 12 fish sticks, SERVES 4

NOTE: Mahimahi is not the only fish that's good grilled on sugarcane. Try preparing this recipe using swordfish or tuna.

Quick Dry Jerk Seasoning

Jamaican jerk seasoning's major flavor notes—the perfume of allspice and cinnamon, the earthy pungency of onion and garlic, the sweetness of sugar, the tang of salt, and the fiery bite of habañero chile pepper—are all singing out in this simple rub. That habañero is available powdered at specialty shops, or you can use cayenne pepper.

1 tablespoon brown sugar

1½ teaspoons coarse salt (kosher or sea)

1½ teaspoons dried coriander

½ teaspoon freshly ground black pepper

½ teaspoon garlic powder

½ teaspoon onion powder

½ teaspoon dried thyme

½ teaspoon ground allspice

¼ to ½ teaspoon habañero powder or cayenne pepper

¼ teaspoon ground cinnamon

Place the brown sugar, salt, coriander, black pepper, garlic and onion powders, thyme, allspice, habañero powder, and cinnamon in a small bowl and stir to mix. Any leftover jerk seasoning can be kept in a jar, covered, for several months in a cool, dry place.

MAKES about 3 tablespoons

SPICY THAI SWORDFISH STICKS

Lemongrass and coconut milk are the twin pillars of Thai cuisine, and they both appear in these explosively flavorful fish sticks—the former serving as skewer, the latter as a base for the marinade.

ADVANCE PREPARATION: 1 hour for marinating the swordfish

FOR THE MARINADE:

2 cloves garlic, roughly chopped

1 tablespoon roughly chopped peeled fresh ginger

1 scallion, trimmed, both white and green part, roughly chopped

2 tablespoons chopped cilantro

2 teaspoons brown sugar

2 teaspoons ground coriander

1/2 teaspoon freshly ground black pepper

1 cup unsweetened coconut milk, or more to taste

3 tablespoons soy sauce, or more to taste

2 tablespoons fresh lime juice, or more to taste

12 thin or 6 thick stalks lemongrass

1 1/2 pounds swordfish steaks (about 1 inch thick)

2 to 3 tablespoons melted butter, for basting (optional)

2 tablespoons finely chopped peanuts, for garnish

2 tablespoons chopped cilantro, for garnish

Spicy Peanut Sauce, page 75, or Coconut-Peanut Sauce, page 128 (optional)

1. Prepare the marinade: Place the

garlic, ginger, scallion, cilantro, brown sugar, coriander, and pepper in a food processor and finely chop. Add the coconut milk, soy sauce, and lime juice and pulse to mix. Taste for seasoning, adding soy sauce or lime juice to taste.

> **TIPS:** *Coconut milk and fresh lemongrass are available at Asian markets and, very possibly, at your local supermarket. Choose long fragrant stalks of lemongrass. If you can't find it fresh, use bamboo skewers that you've soaked in lemon juice for 8 minutes and rubbed with a strip of lemon zest.*

2. Trim the lemongrass

stalks, removing and discarding the flexible dark green leaves. Cut off the roots and strip off any blemished outside leaves. You should be left with a core that's about 6 inches long. Cut any thick stalks in half lengthwise; leave slender ones whole. You'll need a dozen 6-inch pieces in all.

3. Rinse the swordfish steaks under

cold running water and then blot dry with paper towels. Cut the swordfish steaks into strips about 4 inches long and 1 inch wide. Using a metal skewer, make a tunnel lengthwise through each strip. Insert a piece of lemongrass through each tunnel. Pour the marinade in a nonreactive baking dish and place the skewered fish on top of it, turning to coat all sides. Let marinate in the refrigerator for 1 hour, turning the skewered fish after 30 minutes to marinate evenly.

4. Set up the grill for

direct grilling (see page 8 for both charcoal and gas) and preheat to high.

5. When ready to

cook, brush and oil the grill grate. Arrange the fish sticks on the grate at a diagonal to the bars. Grill until cooked through, about 30 seconds per side (2 minutes in all), basting with melted butter, if desired. Transfer the fish sticks to a platter. Sprinkle with the chopped peanuts and cilantro and serve at once with peanut sauce, if desired.

MAKES 12 fish sticks, SERVES 4

DIRECT GRILLING

RUNNING AMOK

Any dish with the name *amok*

demands to be served at a barbecue. Even if the traditional Cambodian recipe calls for the fish to be steamed, not grilled, in a banana leaf. People have been wrapping foods in leaves and cooking them in the fire for a long time. Why not try it for *amok*? The dish features a rich coconut gravy, fragrant with ginger, garlic, chiles, cilantro, and scallions. I've taken a few liberties with the traditional version: Cambodians wouldn't caramelize the shallots and garlic, and I've omitted the eggs. I think you'll find the dish exceedingly tasty. Not only do the leaf packages produce moist, explosively flavorful fish, they keep it from sticking to the grill grate—always a challenge when grilling fish.

There are lots of choices for the fish in this recipe. Cambodians would use a white river fish. Here in Miami, I use catfish or grouper. You could also use swordfish, sea bass, hake, or salmon.

TIP: *The traditional wrapping for amok is a banana leaf. If you live in Florida or Hawaii, you may be able to find these fresh. Hispanic and Asian grocery stores sell frozen banana leaves. Fresh and frozen work equally well. If you can't find a banana leaf, wrap the fish in aluminum foil, after first lightly spraying the inside with oil.*

2 tablespoons vegetable oil

3 cloves garlic, chopped

2 to 4 shallots, finely chopped (about ½ cup)

2 scallions, trimmed, both white and green
parts finely chopped

2 tablespoons chopped fresh cilantro

1 tablespoon chopped peeled fresh ginger

2 Thai chiles or 1 jalapeño pepper, seeded and
chopped

1 tablespoon chopped fresh lemongrass,
or 1½ teaspoons freshly grated lemon zest

¾ cup unsweetened coconut milk

2 tablespoons Asian fish sauce or soy sauce

1 teaspoon ground coriander

½ teaspoon ground turmeric

½ teaspoon freshly ground black pepper

4 pieces boneless, skinless catfish fillets
(6 ounces each)

Coarse salt (kosher or sea) and freshly
ground black pepper

4 sprigs fresh cilantro

YOU'LL ALSO NEED:

1 or 2 whole banana leaves (enough to make
4 pieces each 9 by 12 inches, optional)

Wooden toothpicks soaked for 1 hour in cold water to
cover, then drained, or butcher's string

1. Heat the oil in a wok or small frying pan
over medium heat. Add the garlic, shallots, scallions (reserving 2 tablespoons of greens for
garnish), cilantro, ginger, chiles, and lemongrass
and cook until a dark golden brown, 4 to 5 minutes,
stirring with a wooden spoon. Stir in the coconut
milk, fish sauce, coriander, turmeric, and pepper.
Increase the heat to high and let the mixture boil
until thick and very flavorful, about 5 minutes,
stirring with a wooden spoon. The oil will just
start to separate from the coconut milk. Transfer
the seasoning mixture to a bowl and let it cool to
room temperature.

2. Generously season the fish fillets on both sides with salt and pepper.

3. Set up the grill for direct grilling (see page 8 for both charcoal and gas) and preheat to high.

4. When ready to cook, if using fresh banana leaves, place them on the hot grate and grill until pliable, 10 to 20 seconds per side (or pass them over a hot burner on the stove for 1 to 3 minutes). Frozen banana leaves when thawed will be pliable enough to fold without grilling. Cut the banana leaves (or aluminum foil) into four 12-by-9-inch pieces and put on a work surface, dark side down. Spread some of the seasoning mixture in the center of each piece and put a fish fillet on top. Spoon on more seasoning mixture, spreading it over the fish. Place a cilantro sprig on top. Fold the long sides of the banana leaf over the fish. Fold over the top and bottom of the banana leaf to enclose the fish. Secure the flaps of the banana leaf with a toothpick or tie with butcher's string. The recipe can be prepared up to this stage several hours ahead.

5. Place the packets on the hot grate and grill until the fish is cooked through, 4 to 6 minutes per side. To test for doneness, insert a metal skewer into a packet. When the fish is fully cooked, the skewer will come out very hot to the touch after 20 seconds. Open the packets and sprinkle the reserved scallion greens over the fish. Serve the fish in the banana leaves.

SERVES 4

VARIATION: You can use glowing embers to grill fish packets. Place them directly on charcoal as it burns in the grill. This will give you richer flavor. The fish packets will take the same amount of time to cook.

PUT IT ON A PLANK

Chances are, if you've visited the Pacific Northwest you've enjoyed one of the most distinctive American ways to grill fish: on a cedar or alder plank. The process satisfies and gratifies on quite a few levels. First, the wood imparts a unique flavor all its own (a spicy, winelike flavor in the case of cedar; a woodier, smokier flavor in the case of alder). It also tends to absorb any strong fishy flavors—a plus when serving strong flavored fish, like salmon or bluefish, to people who are iffy about seafood. The plank keeps the fish from drying out and from sticking to the grill grate (a perennial problem). Last, it also eliminates the need to turn the fish over (a task which bedevils even experienced grill masters).

Planked fish originated with the Native Americans of the Pacific Northwest, who roasted the local salmon in special cedar holders over blazing embers. Inspired by the method (and the resulting flavor), chefs adopted the method, cooking the fish directly on a plank. Fish can be grilled on a plank using either the direct or indirect method. The former generates more smoke, but you have to work carefully and fast lest the plank itself catch on fire. Indirect grilling eliminates this risk and will probably allow you to reuse the plank several times.

The typical plank for grilling fish is about 12 to 14 inches long and roughly 6 to 8 inches wide, with a thickness of between ½ and ¾ inch. Cedar and alder planks are available at gourmet shops or you can order them by mail (see page 312). Of course, you can always go to your local lumberyard and have planks cut to size for you. Just be sure to ask for untreated cedar, alder, or oak. Get plenty of extras: Once you try grilling on wood, you'll want to cook all your fish that way.

INDIRECT GRILLING

FISH GRILLED ON A BOARD

Simplicity itself, this is one of the best ways I know to cook salmon. Grilling it on a plank imparts all sorts of intriguing spice flavors to the fish. The mustard cuts the oily taste, while the brown sugar accentuates the sweetness. Plus, you're looking at about 3 minutes of preparation time. I call for the fish to be grilled indirectly in this recipe—this eliminates the risk of setting the plank on fire. Brave hearts can try the direct method, following the instructions at the end of the recipe.

> **TIP:** Be sure to allow yourself a couple of hours for soaking the plank before you plan to grill. This keeps the wood from catching fire, and the resulting steam moisturizes and flavors the fish. Many cooks in the Pacific Northwest soak planks in seawater to take advantage of the extra flavor from the salt. To achieve the same effect if you don't live near the ocean, add 3 tablespoons of salt for each quart of water and stir until dissolved.

1 or 2 pieces salmon fillet
    (1½ pounds total)
Plenty of coarse salt (kosher or
    sea) and freshly ground black
    pepper
6 tablespoons Dijon (smooth) or Meaux (grainy) mustard
6 tablespoons brown sugar

YOU'LL ALSO NEED:
1 cedar plank (6 by 14 inches), soaked in salted
    water for 2 hours, then drained

1. Remove the salmon skin or have your fishmonger do this for you. Run your fingers over the fish, feeling for bones. Pull out any you find with needle-nose pliers or tweezers. Rinse the salmon under cold running water and then blot dry with paper towels. Very generously season the salmon on both sides with salt and pepper. Lay the salmon on the soaked plank and carefully spread the mustard over the top and sides. Place the brown sugar in a bowl and crumble it between your fingers. When powdery, sprinkle it over the mustard.

2. Set up the grill for indirect grilling (see page 9 for both charcoal and gas) and preheat to medium-high.

3. When ready to cook, place the salmon and plank in the center of the hot grate, away from the heat. Cover the grill and cook the fish until cooked through, 20 to 30 minutes. To test for doneness, insert an instant-read meat thermometer through the side: The internal temperature should be about 135°F. Or insert a slender metal skewer through the side; it should come out very hot to the touch after 20 seconds. Transfer the salmon and plank to a platter and serve right off the plank.

SERVES 4

VARIATION: You can use the direct method to grill the salmon. Soak the plank well. Spread the mustard and sugar on the salmon, but do not put the fish on the plank. Set up the grill for direct grilling over a three-zone fire (see page 8 for both charcoal and gas), and preheat to medium-high. When ready to cook, place the plank on the hot grate and leave it there until you smell smoke, 3 to 4 minutes. Immediately turn the plank over and place the fish on top. Cover the grill and grill the fish until cooked through, 10 to 15 minutes. Check the plank from time to time: If the edges start to catch fire, squirt them with a water pistol or mister or move the plank to a cooler part of the grill.

WHOLE FISH IN A SALT CRUST

Less is more, goes the saying. Case in point, fish grilled in a crust of salt, one of the most spectacular dishes in Italy, made with just two ingredients—the fish and the salt. We're talking major theatrics here—first, imagine a whole fish buried in salt, roasting away atop your grill, then the thrill of showing it off at the table. But there's more to this than just looks: The salt crust allows the smoke flavor to penetrate the fish, while sealing in the moistness. So the next time you want to spend a mere 10 minutes preparing dinner and wind up with a masterpiece, grill a whole fish in salt.

1 large whole fish (3 to 4 pounds; see Note)
**8 to 12 cups coarse salt (kosher or sea), or more
   as needed**
Salsa Verde (recipe follows)

YOU'LL ALSO NEED:
   **2 cups wood chips or chunks
      (preferably oak or apple),
      soaked for 1 hour in water
      to cover, then drained
   Aluminum foil roasting pan just
      large enough to hold the fish**

1. Trim the fins off the fish using kitchen shears. Rinse the fish, inside and out, under cold running water, and then blot dry, inside and out, with paper towels. Spread salt $\frac{1}{4}$ to $\frac{1}{2}$ inch deep in an aluminum foil pan so that it covers an area slightly larger than the fish. Place the fish on top, pressing it into the salt. Spread enough salt over the fish to completely cover it. Pat the salt to make it compact.

2. Set up the grill for indirect grilling (see page 9 for both charcoal and gas) and preheat to high. If using a gas grill, place all the wood chips or chunks in the smoker box or in a smoker pouch (see page 12); you will be ready to grill when you see smoke.

3. When ready to cook, if using a charcoal grill, toss all of the wood chips or chunks on the coals. Place the pan with the fish in the center of the hot grate, away from the heat. Smoke-roast the fish until cooked through, 30 to 40 minutes. To test for doneness, insert an instant-read thermometer in the thickest part of the fish through the side: The internal temperature should be about 135°F. Or insert a slender metal skewer into the thickest part of the fish through the side. It should come out very hot to the touch after 20 seconds.

4. To serve, present the fish in its salt crust to your guests at the table. Using 2 large spoons, remove the top portion of the salt crust. Lift the dish off the bottom crust and transfer to a platter. Remove and discard the skin (this eliminates all the excess salt). Remove the top fillet and discard the bones. Serve the fish with Salsa Verde on the side.

SERVES 4

NOTE: Snapper or red fish would be a good choice. You can also grill small fish for individual servings, in which case you'll need four weighing about $1\frac{1}{2}$ pounds each. Black bass and porgies will work well.

Salsa Verde

Italians serve green sauce—*salsa verde*—with some of their most beloved preparations, such as fish baked in a salt crust or with *bollito misto.*

2 tablespoons minced fresh flat-leaf parsley

2 tablespoons minced fresh mint

2 teaspoons drained capers, finely chopped

1 clove garlic, minced

½ teaspoon grated lemon zest

2 tablespoons fresh lemon juice

¼ cup extra-virgin olive oil

2 tablespoons boiling water

Coarse salt (kosher or sea) and freshly ground black pepper

Combine the parsley, mint, capers, garlic, lemon zest and juice, olive oil, and boiling water in a non-reactive mixing bowl and whisk to mix. Season with salt and pepper to taste. The salsa is best eaten within a few hours of making.

MAKES about 1 cup

MUSSELS GRILLED WITH PINE NEEDLES

In Charente, a region on the west coast of France famed for its shellfish and brandy (it's the home of Cognac), they have a most singular way of cooking mussels. What's unique is the heat source: the Charentais grill their mussels under a blazing carpet of dry pine needles. Like many things French, there's more poetry than practicality here, for I've tried the procedure several times without success—the pine needles simply don't burn hot enough to cook the mussels. But there *is* a way to prepare mussels on the grill, and you do get an amazing, aromatic smoke flavor from the burning pine needles. The process is a bit tricky, so I've outlined several options.

4 pounds mussels

1½ sticks (12 tablespoons) salted butter

3 cloves garlic, minced

3 tablespoons finely chopped flat-leaf parsley

YOU'LL ALSO NEED:

1 bucket (3 to 4 quarts; see Note) dry pine
    needles, or 2 cups wood chips or chunks
    (preferably oak), soaked for 1 hour in water
    to cover, then drained

Heavy-duty aluminum foil or a cast-iron skillet
    (optional)

1. Beard the mussels by pinching any
clumps of threads between your thumb and forefinger and pulling hard. Alternatively, pull out the
threads with needle-nose pliers. Scrub the mussels
with a stiff brush under cold running water. Discard
any with cracked shells or with open shells that fail
to close when tapped.

2. Melt the butter in a saucepan over medium
heat. Add the garlic and parsley and cook until the
garlic loses its rawness, 2 to 3 minutes. Do not let
the garlic brown. Divide the garlic-parsley butter
among 4 small serving bowls. Have a large bowl
ready for the empty mussel shells.

3. Grill the mussels using the pine-needle
method or direct grilling method (see pages 230
to 231).

4. Serve the mussels at once. Shell them
before dipping in the garlic-parsley butter.

SERVES 4

NOTE: The best place to find pine needles is in the
woods or a park. Gather dry needles from the
ground, picking through them to remove twigs and
pinecones. If the needles are damp, spread them
out on a baking sheet to dry.

GRILLING MUSSELS

In the best of all possible worlds, you'd grill mussels in blazing pine needles. Three ways to do this are described below. Of course, not everyone has easy access to pine needles, let alone the inclination to set them ablaze on the grill. So you'll also find instructions for grilling mussels in a skillet directly over the fire, with wood chips creating the smoke. No matter which method you use, using tongs, transfer the mussels with their juices to attractive bowls to serve.

PINE-NEEDLE METHOD

The three ways to grill mussels over pine needles are the practical way, the Rube Goldberg way, and the macho way. Whichever method you use, keep in mind that the pine needles produce lots of smoke and fire. Set up your grill on an open patio or in a backyard, well away from buildings or trees. (Do not attempt this recipe on an apartment balcony or closed porch.) If you have long hair, it's a good idea to tie it back; also keep your sleeves rolled up. And, of course, any time you grill there should always be a fire extinguisher close by.

• **For the practical method,** you'll need a fish or vegetable grate (a metal plate with holes in it). Carpet it with pine needles and arrange the mussels on top. The advantage of this method is that a fish grate is a little easier to work with than aluminum foil. But you have to own a fish or vegetable grate.

• **The Rube Goldberg method** calls for you to make low-sided trays from aluminum foil. The advantage of this method is that you can have the trays ready ahead of time and simply place them on the fire. Press sheets of heavy-duty aluminum foil over an inverted rectangular baking dish, folding and crimping the sides to create trays. Remove the trays from their baking-dish molds and place them on a wire rack open side up. Using the tip of a paring knife, make ¼-inch holes at 1-inch intervals all over the bottom to allow the fire to reach the pine needles. Place a ½-inch layer of pine needles in each tray and arrange the mussels on top. Slide the trays off the wire rack onto the grill grate. When all the mussels are cooked, you can simply crumple up the trays with the ashes in them, place them in a bucket of water to extinguish any sparks, and then throw them away.

• **The macho method:** *Warning—do not attempt this unless you are extremely comfortable playing with fire.* This way is macho because it generates the most smoke and fire, but it's a little impractical because you're limited as to how many mussels you can grill at one time. To grill mussels this way, toss handfuls of pine needles directly on the grill grate and, using long-handled tongs, lay the mussels on top of them as quickly as possible. Then stand back: The needles will catch fire almost in a split second. Grill until the pine needles are burnt and the mussel shells open, 3 to 5 minutes. As the mussels open, transfer them to serving bowls, using tongs. Arrange more pine needles and mussels on the grill grate and continue until all are cooked.

NOTE: The mussels will take a few minutes longer to cook on an aluminum foil tray or fish or vegetable grate than directly over the fire.

DIRECT-GRILLING METHOD

SET UP THE GRILL for direct grilling (see page 8 for both charcoal and gas) and preheat to high. Place a large cast-iron skillet on the grill and preheat it as well. If using a gas grill, place all the wood chips or chunks in the smoker box or in a smoker pouch (see page 12) and preheat on high until you see smoke.

WHEN READY TO COOK, if using a charcoal grill, toss all the wood chips (no need to soak them) or chunks on the coals. Place the cleaned mussels in the hot skillet and cover the grill. Work in several batches if necessary—don't overcrowd the pan. Grill the mussels until the shells open, 6 to 8 minutes, stirring once or twice with a long-handled wooden spoon. Cook any remaining mussels the same way.

DIRECT GRILLING

BARBECUED CLAMS

An odd way to cook clams? Long before there were chowders or even pots for steaming, North American Indians cooked clams in campfires. Sometimes they roasted them on hot stones or right on the embers; sometimes they cooked them in seaweed on the coals. Grilling is one of the best ways to cook shellfish, for the fire imparts an unmistakable smoke flavor and the clams stew in their briny juices right in the shell. East meets West here—the Chinese are particularly adept at cooking clams. I've borrowed their secret, an electrifying sauce made with ginger, garlic, scallions, and fermented black beans.

FOR THE BARBECUE SAUCE:

8 tablespoons (1 stick) salted butter, cut into 1-tablespoon pieces

1 tablespoon fermented black beans, finely chopped (optional; see Note)

2 cloves garlic, minced

2 scallions, both white and green parts, trimmed and minced (set aside 2 tablespoons scallion greens for garnish)

1 tablespoon minced peeled fresh ginger

1/2 cup sake, Chinese rice wine, or dry sherry

2 tablespoons Sriracha or Thai sweet chile sauce (optional; see Note)

1/2 teaspoon fresh lime juice

24 clams

1. Make the barbecue sauce: Melt

2 tablespoons of the butter in a saucepan over medium heat. Add the black beans, if using, garlic, scallions, and ginger and cook until fragrant but not brown, about 3 minutes. Increase the heat to high, add the sake, and bring to a boil. Let the sake simmer briskly until reduced to about 3 tablespoons, 4 to 5 minutes. Reduce the heat to low and whisk in the remaining butter, piece by piece. Whisk in the chile sauce, if using, and lime juice. Remove the pan from the heat and place on a warm corner of the stove.

> **TIP:** *Any size clam can be grilled, from tiny littlenecks to jumbo quahogs. (For that matter, oysters can be grilled the same way.) I find that clams about 2 inches across work best—they're small enough to be tender, but large enough to give you something to eat.*

2. Scrub the clams with a

stiff brush under cold running water, discarding any with cracked shells or shells that fail to close when tapped.

3. Set up the grill for direct grilling (see

page 8 for both charcoal and gas) and preheat to high.

4. When ready to cook, arrange the clams

on the hot grate. Position the shells so the bars of the grate hold them level. Grill until the shells pop open, 4 to 6 minutes for littlenecks, 7 to 9 minutes for cherrystones, 10 to 13 minutes for larger clams. Transfer the clams to a platter, removing and discarding the top (empty) shells. Spoon the sauce over the clams and place a pinch of the reserved scallion greens on each. Serve at once.

SERVES 4 as an appetizer, 2 as a light main course

NOTE: Fermented black beans are a Chinese condiment made by salting or pickling soy beans (they are also known as salty black beans). They're sold in plastic bags or jars. Thai chile sauce comes in two forms. The Thai name for sweet chile sauce is *nuoe cham ga;* the nonsweet version is called Sriracha. Don't be put off by visions of tongue-torturing chiles; both are more like ketchup than hot sauce. All these ingredients can be found at Asian markets, at gourmet shops, and at most supermarkets. Even if you omit them, you'll get a pretty cool clam sauce.

TIP: *If you plan to grill a lot of clams, you may want to invest in a GreatGrate shellfish grill, a metal grid that holds clams and oysters flat and steady for grilling. It's available from Gourmet Gilchrist Swamper Products (see Mail-Order Sources, page 311).*

ON THE SIDE

Culinary supporting actors? Side dishes don't get their fair share of the limelight. This chapter shines the spotlight on the culinary ancillaries that make good barbecue great and great barbecue unforgettable. In the following pages, you'll get a fresh look at techniques for grilling vegetables, such as roasting them in the embers, and you'll find some recipes for vegetables not normally associated with grilling, like artichokes or horn peppers. I say it's high time to move the side dishes to center stage, and a properly fired-up grill is the perfect way to do it.

GRILLED ARTICHOKES

The high, dry heat of the grill brings out a vegetable's natural sweetness. Conventional wisdom holds that the best vegetables for grilling have a high water content, such as peppers, onions, mushrooms, zucchini, and corn. Firm, dense, low-moisture vegetables make less likely candidates. When was the last time you were offered a grilled beet or rutabaga at a barbecue? But every rule has its exception: In this case it's an edible flower you would think would be leathery and tough when grilled—the artichoke. This recipe came to me from Cagliari, Sardinia, by way of a culinarian and former Thomas J. Watson Foundation fellow, Katherine Deumling. You'll love the crackling crisp leaves and haunting smoke flavor, not to mention licking the garlic oil off your fingers as you pull the grilled artichoke apart with your hands.

> **TIP:** Selecting artichokes for grilling may run counter to your intuition: The best ones are older chokes whose leaves have started to spread open. This allows the oil—and the heat—to penetrate deep into the artichokes, giving the leaves their signature crispness. Avoid hard, tightly closed globe artichokes, which may taste great boiled or steamed, but are difficult to grill. The other ingredient you need is patience.

8 artichokes

1 lemon, cut in half

1½ to 2 cups extra-virgin olive oil

Coarse salt (kosher or sea) and freshly ground
   black pepper

4 cloves garlic, minced

3 tablespoons finely chopped flat-leaf
   parsley

1. Using a sharp knife, cut off and discard the top third of each artichoke. Then cut off the stems flush with the bottoms and discard. Using kitchen shears, cut the spiny tips off the artichoke leaves and rub all the cut edges with lemon. Using a grapefruit spoon or melon baller, scrape out the purplish inside leaves and "choke" (fibrous part) of each artichoke, creating a hollow cavity in the center. Squeeze lemon juice into this cavity. Generously brush the artichokes inside and out with some of the olive oil and season with salt and pepper.

2. Set up the grill for direct grilling (see page 8 for both charcoal and gas) and preheat to medium.

3. When ready to cook, place the artichokes on the grill, stem side up, and grill until the cut side is nicely browned, about 30 minutes. If the artichokes start to burn, move them to a cooler section of the grill, if possible.

4. Invert the artichokes, move them to a cooler part of the grill, and generously brush them inside and out with more olive oil (really slop it in), and place about ½ teaspoon chopped garlic and 1 teaspoon chopped parsley in the cavity of each. Season again with salt and pepper.

TIP: *You can't rush grilled artichokes. It takes long, slow, patient grilling over a moderate fire to achieve the proper crispness. I call for a medium fire here, but you may need to reduce the heat to medium-low to keep the artichokes from burning. Using a three-zone fire (see page 9) will give you a cooler area to move the artichokes to if they start to burn.*

SERVES 4 to 8

Move the artichokes back over the heat, cover the grill, and continue grilling them, basting with oil every 10 to 15 minutes, until very tender, 30 to 45 minutes longer, 1 to 1¼ hours in all. If the artichokes start to burn, move them to a cooler part of the grill. When fully cooked, the leaves of the artichoke should pull off easily. Drizzle with any remaining oil and serve at once, providing empty bowls for the leaves and finger bowls and napkins.

INDIRECT GRILLING

KIELBASA-BARBECUED CABBAGE

Some barbecue you love because it's so darned delicious. Some you cherish for its sheer drama. Barbecued cabbage inspires both affections. I first came across this outrageous dish at the Memphis in May World Championship Barbecue Cooking Contest and it was love at first sight and bite. I was smitten with the spectacular presentation. I relished how the cabbage absorbed the heady flavors of butter, pork, and wood smoke. The first barbecued cabbage I tasted was flavored with bacon, and that's the version you'll find in my book *How to Grill*. But I soon discovered you could add wonderful shadings of garlic and spices by using diced kielbasa instead. Either way, you have the magnificence of a whole cabbage, smoked-scented and handsomely browned, with a rich smoky filling.

> **TIP:** *Some pit masters wrap their cabbage in aluminum foil before grilling. This gives you a softer, juicier cabbage, but you won't get as much smoke flavor. Cook it unwrapped, as I do here, or roast it wrapped in foil for 30 minutes, discard the foil, and then let the cabbage finish grilling exposed to the smoke.*

1 medium-size green cabbage (about 2 pounds)

3 tablespoons unsalted butter

1 small onion, finely chopped

2 cloves garlic, minced

3 ounces kielbasa (about 3 inches), cut into
   1/4-inch dice

1/4 cup of your favorite barbecue sauce (use any
   of the recipes in this book or your favorite
   bottled brand)

Coarse salt (kosher or sea) and freshly ground
   black pepper

YOU'LL ALSO NEED:

2 cups wood chips (preferably hickory or
   pecan), soaked for 1 hour in cold water to
   cover, then drained

1. Crumple a 12-inch-long piece of aluminum foil and shape it into a ring about 3 inches in diameter. Use this ring to hold the cabbage upright while stuffing and cooking it.

2. Set the cabbage on a cutting board on its crown. Cut out the core by angling your knife about 3 inches down toward the center of the cabbage and cutting in a circle that is about 3 inches in diameter. Pull out the core and discard it. The piece removed should look like a cone. Prop the cabbage upright on the aluminum foil ring, cavity facing up.

3. Melt 2 tablespoons of the butter in a skillet over medium heat. Brush a little melted butter (about 1/2 tablespoon) over the outside of the cabbage. Add the onion, garlic, and kielbasa to the skillet with the melted butter and cook over medium heat until lightly browned, 3 to 5 minutes. Spoon the kielbasa mixture into the cavity in the cabbage. Pour the barbecue sauce on top and top with the remaining 1 tablespoon of butter. Season the outside of the cabbage with salt and pepper.

4. Set up the grill for indirect grilling (see page 9 for both charcoal and gas) and preheat to medium. If using a charcoal grill, place a large drip pan in the center. If using a gas grill, place all the wood chips or chunks in the smoker box or in a smoker pouch (see page 12) and preheat on high until you see smoke, then reduce the heat to medium.

5. When ready to cook, if using a charcoal grill, toss all the wood chips or chunks on the coals. Place the cabbage on its aluminum foil ring in the center of the hot grate, away from the heat, and cover the grill.

6. Cook the cabbage until very tender (when done, it will be easy to pierce with a skewer), 1 to 1½ hours. If using a charcoal grill, you'll need to add 12 fresh coals per side after 1 hour, if the cabbage is not done. To serve, peel off any dried-out or charred outside leaves and discard. Present the cabbage on its ring to your guests, then cut into wedges and serve.

SERVES 8

CORN ROASTED IN THE HUSK

Husk on or husk off? This is the great debate when it comes to grilling corn, and each camp has its partisans. I generally adhere to the husk-off school—I like the smoky flavor you get when the flames brown the corn kernels. (You also get a nifty snap and crackle as the kernels roast.) The husk-on folks believe that the husk seals in flavor and moistness, but I find it tends to steam the corn, not roast it. Still I'm willing to allow for husk-on grilling in at least one instance— roasting the corn in the embers. The process is like high drama with the best of endings, from the eerie sight of the green ears lined up on the glowing coals to the aesthetic dissonance of serving what looks hopelessly burned, to scraping off the blackened husk to reveal golden, smoky, incredibly sweet kernels inside. Applause, please.

12 basil leaves (see Note)

10 tablespoons (1¼ sticks) salted butter

2 cloves garlic, minced

½ teaspoon freshly ground black pepper

8 ears of corn in the husk (the husks must completely
   cover the corn)

YOU'LL ALSO NEED:

A charcoal grill

Natural lump charcoal or wood chunks (optional)

1. Make the basil butter: Stack the basil leaves and roll them lengthwise into a tight small tube. Thinly slice the tube lengthwise with a knife or kitchen shears and fluff the resulting slices to make the thin slivers of basil that are known as a chiffonade. Melt the butter in a heavy saucepan over medium heat. Add the garlic, sliced basil, and pepper and cook until fragrant and the garlic has lost its rawness, 2 to 3 minutes. Do not let the garlic burn. Keep the basil butter warm until ready to serve.

> **TIP:** To truly roast the corn in the embers you'll need a charcoal grill lit with charcoal (the natural lump variety, please) or wood embers. If you have a gas grill, you can try roasting the corn in the husks. Work over a high heat so the husks actually blacken. If your grill doesn't get hot enough to do this, remove the husks and roast the ears directly over the fire until golden-brown, basting with basil butter.

2. Light charcoal or wood chunks in a chimney starter (see page 15). When the coals glow red, dump them into the bottom of the grill and rake them into an even layer. Let burn until the coals are just beginning to ash over, 5 to 10 minutes.

3. Lay the corn on top of the coals and cook until the husks are charred jet black on all sides, 2 to 3 minutes per side, 8 to 12 minutes in all, turning with tongs to ensure even cooking. Transfer the corn to a heatproof platter.

4. Pull the burnt husks and corn silk off the corn; wear clean, heavy-duty insulated gloves (see page 18) to do this. Alternatively, you can use a stiff-bristled brush or scraper for removing the husks. Brush each ear with basil butter and serve at once, passing any remaining butter on the side.

SERVES 4

NOTE: Of course, you can use any other herb you fancy.

GRILLING IN THE EMBERS

Forget about gleaming stainless steel supergrills that cost more than you paid for your first car in college. Forget gas grills altogether, and consider a method of grilling that's as old as mankind itself.

Back before man had invented grill grates or gridirons or even sharpened sticks for making shish kebabs, people cooked foods in the fire. Literally in the fire, or, more precisely, on the coals. They laid root vegetables or meats directly on the embers and let the radiant heat of the coals do the cooking. When the food was ready, the ashes were brushed off. Barbecue had been born.

Although I'm willing to grill just about anything in the embers (see the recipe for Dirty Steaks on page 194), the most likely candidates are root vegetables—potatoes, yams, beets, turnips—and at least one fruit, the breadfruit, which is the traditional accompaniment to jerk pork in Jamaica. But any vegetable with a protective skin or husk can be charred in the embers, from eggplants (cooked in this fashion they make a killer *baba ganoush*) to corn. When you grill in the embers, you sacrifice the skin; the blackened exterior is easy to remove with a paring knife, heatproof gloves, or a stiff-bristled brush. The charring imparts an incomparable smoke taste to the interior. Ember-charred sweet potatoes, for example, have a depth and complexity of flavor you'd have never dreamed possible.

One of the virtues of grilling in the embers, especially for fledgling cooks, is that the food not only can but

should be burnt. Vegetables should be cooked until the outsides are black as coal. When you pull a potato or pepper out of the fire, it may still be hot enough to set a paper towel or plate on fire. Use tongs to transfer hot vegetables to an aluminum foil tray or heatproof platter and let them cool slightly. Brush off any excess ash with a pastry brush.

Of course, to practice this style of grilling, you need a charcoal grill or campfire. When using the former, I prefer natural lump charcoal—the kind made from whole pieces of wood that come in jagged chunks. You can certainly use briquettes—and I have—but any fuel that contains packing pallets, furniture scraps, and coal dust, as most commercial briquettes do, seems a lot less appetizing to me than do chunks of lump charcoal.

You can also cook in the embers of a wood fire. The backyard-bound grill jockey can buy hardwood chunks (no pressure-treated lumber, please) at his or her local hardware store or grill shop and light them in a chimney starter the same way you would charcoal. Oak, hickory, and mesquite are among the many woods you can buy in chunk form. Mesquite burns the hottest and has a tendency to snap, crackle, and pop, so exercise caution when using it. Better still, if you're in the outdoors, build a campfire, letting the blazing logs die down to glowing embers. (As with any fire outdoors, take care that it doesn't spread.)

In many parts of the country, the arrival of winter puts a stop to (or at least sharply curtails) outdoor grilling. But if you are lighting a fireplace, the hearth is a splendid place to roast on the embers. It'll give you a whole new appreciation of "burnt" foods.

"CAVIAR" ON THE COALS

No, it's not real caviar, it's a gutsy eggplant dip known in Russia as *givech* (eggplant caviar; I suppose there's something soft, gooey, and caviar-like about roasted eggplant and peppers). Tradition calls for the vegetables to be baked in the oven. Some years ago, to pump up the flavor, I took to roasting the vegetables on the grill. The results were good, even excellent, but the ultimate eggplant caviar would have to wait until I discarded the one piece of equipment most people consider essential for grilling—the grill grate. The secret is to lay the vegetables on the hot coals and roast them in the embers. If you like the flavor of smoke and fire, you're going to love this eggplant caviar—even if you don't think you like eggplant.

> **TIP:** *To make caviar on the coals you'll need a charcoal grill. If you only have a gas grill, you can make a respectable rendition, charring the vegetables over a high heat on the grill grate until the skins are handsomely blackened.*

Tradition calls for the vegetables to be puréed or very finely chopped to make a sort of dip or spread. To make an ember-roasted salad instead, cut the vegetables into 1/2- or 1-inch dice.

1 cylindrical eggplant
   (1 to 1¼ pounds)
1 small red onion
1 green bell pepper
1 red or yellow bell pepper
1 large ripe red tomato
1 clove garlic, minced
3 tablespoons finely chopped
   fresh herbs, including dill, chives,
   and/or parsley
2 tablespoons red wine vinegar, or more
   to taste
1 tablespoon fresh lemon juice
4 tablespoons extra-virgin olive oil
Coarse salt (kosher or sea) and freshly
   ground black pepper
Garlic-Rubbed "Rabbit Ears" (grilled bread
   slices; recipe follows)

YOU'LL ALSO NEED:
A charcoal grill
Natural lump charcoal or wood chunks
   (optional)

1. Light charcoal or wood chunks in a chimney starter (see page 15). When the coals glow red, dump them into the bottom of the grill and rake them into an even layer. Let burn until the coals begin to ash over, 5 to 10 minutes.

2. Place the eggplant, onion, bell peppers, and tomato directly on the coals. Cook until charred black on the outside. It will take a total of 8 to 12 minutes to char the vegetables: 2 to 4 minutes per side for the eggplant and onion, which should be soft in the center when done; and 1 to 2 minutes per side for the bell peppers and tomato. Turn the vegetables with long-handled tongs to ensure even cooking. Transfer the charred vegetables to an aluminum foil pan or heatproof plate and let cool.

3. Using a paring knife, scrape the burnt skin off the vegetables. Don't worry about removing every last bit; a little burnt skin adds character. Core and seed the peppers. Chop the vegetables (coarsely or finely, as you desire; a food processor works well for this) and place in an attractive non-reactive serving bowl.

4. Stir in the garlic, herbs, vinegar, lemon juice, and olive oil. Season with salt and black pepper to taste; the eggplant caviar should be highly seasoned. You can serve the eggplant caviar right away, but it will taste better if you let it sit for an hour or two in the refrigerator to let the flavors ripen. Reseason the dip before serving, adding salt or vinegar as necessary. Serve with Garlic-Rubbed "Rabbit Ears."

MAKES about 3 cups, SERVES 4 to 6

VARIATION: To make eggplant caviar using a gas grill, preheat it to high. Place the vegetables on the hot grate and char as best you can. This will take 12 to 20 minutes in all.

Garlic-Rubbed "Rabbit Ears"

Italians call it _bruschetta._ I call it grilled bread, and nothing makes a better vehicle for a dip or spread or even just eating out of hand. The bread is grilled using the direct method. These elongated oval slices of bread look a bit like rabbit ears to me.

1 thin loaf French bread (20 to 24 inches long)

2 tablespoons extra-virgin olive oil, or more as needed

2 cloves garlic, cut in half

1. Cut the bread sharply on the diagonal into ½-inch slices. Lightly brush each side of the slices with olive oil (don't overdo it or the dripping oil will cause a fire).

2. Set up the grill for direct grilling (see page 8 for both charcoal and gas) and preheat to medium-high.

3. When ready to cook, arrange the bread slices on the hot grate and grill until nicely toasted on both sides, 1 to 3 minutes per side, turning with tongs. Don't turn your back on the grill for a minute: Grilled bread burns quickly. Transfer the toast to a platter or wire rack.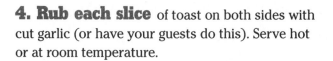

4. Rub each slice of toast on both sides with cut garlic (or have your guests do this). Serve hot or at room temperature.

MAKES 20 to 24 slices

GRILLED HORN PEPPERS

Taking their name from their slender, tapered, twisted shape, horn peppers are claimed by two of the world's greatest grill cultures: Turkey and Japan. In both countries, they are prepared in virtually the same way. A recipe that requires only one ingredient and that's beloved by barbecue buffs at opposite ends of the globe makes for pretty perfect grilling for me.

> **TIP:** Horn peppers come in both red and green, but I've only seen the green ones grilled. They lose some of their heat during grilling, but they'll still bring a sweat to your brow. Have plenty of beer or yogurt on hand for extinguishing the fire.

1 pound horn peppers (about 20)

YOU'LL ALSO NEED:
**8 small metal or bamboo skewers,
    bamboo skewers soaked for 1 hour in
    cold water to cover, then drained**

1. Lay the peppers side by side in groups of 5 or 6 and skewer them crosswise in two places with bamboo or small metal skewers (the idea is to make a sort of raft).

2. Set up the grill for direct grilling (see page 8 for both charcoal and gas) and preheat to high.

3. When ready to cook, place the skewered horn peppers on the hot grate and grill until darkly browned on both sides, 2 to 5 minutes per side (4 to 10 minutes in all). Transfer the peppers to a platter, unskewer, and serve hot or at room temperature. In Turkey, grilled horn peppers would be served with lamb or beef shish kebabs; in Japan, with yakitori or beef teriyaki.

SERVES 6 to 8

PEPPER SOUP ON THE GRILL

If you've done any grilling this summer, you've probably flame-charred steak, some burgers and hot dogs, maybe even chicken, a whole fish, and a vegetable or five. But one frontier remains to be crossed—a dish so improbable, only a flame-addled barbecue nut could conceive it. I'm talking about turning those grilled vegetables into a grilled soup. This satiny soup made from fire-charred yellow bell peppers can be served hot or chilled; the latter is particularly refreshing in the summertime. Peppers are among the few foods you can burn that will still taste great.

6 cloves garlic, peeled

1 medium onion, peeled and quartered
(leave the root end attached)

3 tablespoons extra-virgin olive oil

Coarse salt (kosher or sea) and freshly ground
black pepper

6 large yellow bell peppers

4 cups homemade chicken stock (page 52),
low-sodium canned chicken broth, or
vegetable broth

1 tablespoon balsamic vinegar, or more to taste

4 whole fresh basil leaves, plus 4 thinly slivered
basil leaves, for garnish

½ cup plain yogurt or sour cream, plus 2 tablespoons,
for garnish

1 teaspoon brown sugar, or more to taste (optional)

YOU'LL ALSO NEED:

**6 wooden toothpicks, soaked for 1 hour in
   cold water to cover, then drained**

1. Skewer the garlic cloves on toothpicks.
Brush the garlic and onion pieces with 1 tablespoon
of the olive oil and season with salt and black pepper.

2. Set up the grill for direct grilling (see page
8 for both charcoal and gas) and preheat to high.

3. When ready to cook, place the garlic,
onion, and bell peppers on the hot grate. Grill the
garlic and onions until nicely browned on all sides,
2 to 4 minutes per side (4 to 8 minutes in all) for the
garlic and 2 to 4 minutes (6 to 12 minutes in all) for
the onion (the quarters have 3 sides). Grill the bell
peppers until charred black on all sides, 4 to 6 minutes per side (16 to 24 minutes in all). Turn with
tongs to ensure even roasting.

4. Transfer the garlic and
onions to a heatproof plate to
cool. Place the bell peppers in a
large bowl, cover with plastic
wrap, and let cool; the resulting
steam helps loosen the skin.
Unskewer the garlic and trim the
roots off the onion. Scrape the
burnt skin off the bell peppers
with a paring knife (it's okay to
leave a few burnt spots). Core and seed the bell
peppers. Put the garlic, onion, and bell peppers in a
saucepan and add the stock, the remaining 2 tablespoons olive oil, and the vinegar and whole basil
leaves. Gently bring to a simmer over medium heat
and let simmer until the vegetables are soft, 5 to 10
minutes. Season with salt and black pepper.

> **TIP:** *There are two
> ways to roast the pep-
> pers for this recipe: You
> can cook them on the
> grill or, for the ultimate
> smoke flavor, char them
> on the embers, as de-
> scribed on pages 244 to
> 245.*

5. Purée the soup in a blender until a little
thicker than heavy cream. Add the yogurt and

purée in short spurts just to mix. If serving the soup cold, strain it into a bowl and let cool to room temperature, then refrigerate. If serving the soup hot, strain it back into the saucepan and heat, but do not let it boil, for 2 minutes over medium-high heat. Straining is optional, but will produce a finer texture. Taste for seasoning, adding salt, black pepper, or vinegar to taste; the soup should be highly seasoned. If a touch of sweetness is desired, add the brown sugar.

6. Ladle the soup into bowls and garnish with a dollop of yogurt. Sprinkle slivered basil over each bowl of soup and serve.

SERVES 4

VARIATION: You can ember roast the vegetables. Light charcoal or wood chunks in a chimney starter (see page 15), and when the coals glow red, dump them into the bottom of the grill. Rake the coals into an even layer and let burn until they begin to ash over, 5 to 10 minutes. Place the garlic, onion, and bell peppers directly on the coals (do not peel or oil the garlic or onion and leave the onion whole). Cook until the vegetables are charred black on all sides, 1 to 2 minutes in all for the garlic (wrap the cloves in aluminum foil before placing them on the coals), 1 to 2 minutes per side (3 to 6 minutes in all) for the onion, and 1 to 2 minutes per side (4 to 8 minutes in all) for the bell peppers. Turn the vegetables with long-handled tongs to ensure even charring. Complete the recipe, starting with Step 4. You'll need to scrape the charred skin off of the garlic and onion as well as from the bell peppers.

POTATOES IN THE EMBERS

Long before there were grills, or even ovens, people roasted root vegetables in the embers. The process requires no special equipment and it imparts a charred smoky flavor you simply can't get by baking, roasting, or grilling. This recipe will give you a whole new perspective on baked potatoes, for when you strip off the aluminum foil, you'll find an incomparably steamy, fluffy, white flesh. The bacon-chive sour cream butter rolls all the traditional garnishes into one convenient topping.

FOR THE POTATOES:

**4 jumbo baking potatoes (12 to 14 ounces each),
    scrubbed**

1½ to 2 tablespoons olive oil or melted butter

**Plenty of coarse salt (kosher or sea) and freshly
    ground black pepper**

Garlic powder

FOR THE FLAVORED BUTTER:

**4 tablespoons (¼ stick) salted butter,
    at room temperature**

2 slices bacon, cut into ¼-inch slivers

¼ cup sour cream

2 tablespoons chopped fresh chives or scallion greens

Freshly ground black pepper

YOU'LL ALSO NEED:

A charcoal grill

Natural lump charcoal or wood chunks (optional)

1. Rub the potatoes with olive oil and season generously with salt, pepper, and garlic powder. Tightly wrap each potato in several layers of aluminum foil.

2. Put the bacon in a small nonstick frying pan and cook over medium-high heat until golden brown and crisp, 3 to 4 minutes, stirring with a wooden spoon. Drain the cooked bacon in a strainer over a metal bowl (the resulting fat is great for brushing grilled potatoes or making barbecue sauce).

> **TIP:** Roasting potatoes in their skins in the embers makes the skins too charred to eat, so I like to wrap the potatoes in aluminum foil before roasting.

3. Place the butter in a mixing bowl and whisk until soft and creamy. Beat in the sour cream, chives, and bacon pieces. Season with pepper to taste. Place the flavored butter in an attractive bowl for serving.

4. Light charcoal or wood chunks in a chimney starter (see page 15). When the coals glow red, dump them into the bottom of the grill and rake them into a pile on one side of the grill. Let burn until the coals begin to ash over, 5 to 10 minutes.

5. When ready to cook, lay the potatoes next to the mound of coals. Using a small shovel, long-handled spatula, or tongs, shovel glowing embers on top of the potatoes. Let the potatoes roast under the coals until very tender, 1 to 1¼ hours, rotating them from time to time and adding fresh embers as needed. When cooked through, the potatoes will feel squeezably soft through the aluminum foil (wear heatproof gloves when you test them). Alternatively, use a metal skewer to test for doneness; it should easily pierce the potatoes. You may need to replenish the coals after 45 minutes to 1 hour. Simply place

fresh charcoal or wood chunks on top of the
mound of coals. They'll light in about 10 minutes.

6. When the spuds are cooked, remove
them from the coals using long-handled tongs
and transfer to an aluminum foil pan. Let cool
for 5 minutes. Unwrap the potatoes, cut in half
lengthwise, and serve in the skin with the bacon-
chive sour cream butter alongside.

SERVES 4

VARIATION: You can use a gas grill to cook the
potatoes. Rub them with olive oil and season with
salt, pepper, and garlic powder but do not wrap
them in aluminum foil. Lightly prick the potatoes
in a couple of places with a fork. Set up the grill
for indirect grilling (see page 9) and preheat to
medium-high. Place the potatoes on
the hot grate and grill until nicely
browned and very tender,
1 to 1¼ hours.

HASH ON THE HALF SHELL

My barbecue buddy "Oklahoma" Joe Davidson won first prize in a South Carolina hash competition with these baked stuffed potatoes. (The South Carolina contestants were not pleased with this upstart from Oklahoma.) Hash on the half shell may look like your ordinary baked stuffed potato, but the addition of chopped barbecued brisket takes it to a whole new level. If you don't have brisket, you could add chopped pulled pork, boneless ribs, crumbled bacon, or, for a vegetarian touch, even grilled mushrooms.

4 jumbo baking potatoes (12 to 14 ounces each)
2 cups diced cooked brisket or other smoked meat
1 cup sour cream
8 tablespoons (1 stick) butter, cut into ½-inch dice
2 cups coarsely grated Colby, Jack, or Cheddar cheese
Coarse salt (kosher or sea) and freshly ground black pepper
½ cup finely chopped fresh chives or scallion greens

YOU'LL ALSO NEED:

1 cup wood chips or chunks (optional; preferably hickory or pecan), soaked for 1 hour in water to cover, then drained

1. Set up the grill for indirect grilling (see page 9 for both charcoal and gas) or preheat the oven to 400°F.

2. Scrub the potatoes and prick each in several spots with a fork. Place the potatoes in the center of the hot grate, away from the heat, and grill or bake in the oven until soft, 1 hour. Transfer the potatoes to a cutting board and let cool to room temperature. The potatoes can be cooked up to 3 days ahead.

3. Cut each potato in half lengthwise. Scoop out the potato flesh with a spoon, leaving ¼ inch of flesh in the shell. Coarsely chop the potato flesh and transfer it to a mixing bowl. Stir in the brisket, sour cream, 6 tablespoons of the butter, and half of the cheese. Season with salt and pepper to taste; the potato mixture should be highly seasoned. Stuff the mixture back into the potato shells and sprinkle the tops with the remaining butter and cheese and the chives. The recipe can be prepared through this step up to a day ahead.

> **TIP:** Joe insists that you use the proper size potato—jumbo bakers that weigh in at 12 to 14 ounces. You can grill them using the indirect method or bake them in the oven. Hey, you can even smoke them in a pit (but go easy on the smoke). You could certainly cook the potatoes a day or two ahead of when you plan to serve them, which is what I do.

4. Set up the grill for indirect grilling (see page 9 for both charcoal and gas) and preheat to medium-high. If using a gas grill, place the wood chips or chunks, if using, in a smoker box or smoker pouch (see page 12) and preheat to high until you see smoke, then reduce the heat to medium-high.

5. When ready to cook, if using a charcoal grill, toss all of the wood chips or chunks on the coals. Arrange the potato halves in the center of the hot grate, away from the heat. Cover the grill and cook the potatoes until the cheese is melted and the filling is bubbling, 10 to 15 minutes. Serve at once.

SERVES 8

INDIRECT GRILLING

RED, WHITE, AND BLUE POTATO SALAD

TIP: *Of course you could boil the potatoes for your salad, and a lot of people do. But I like the additional flavor that comes from smoke roasting the potatoes, using the indirect method on the grill. I suggest doing this a day or two ahead of time, when you've fired up your grill for something else. (It takes a real grill maniac to fire up the grill just to make potato salad.) You could also use leftover baked potatoes or, if you prefer the soft waxy consistency of a boiled potato, use those instead.*

Every barbecue needs potato salad.

What better to serve at a Fourth of July bash than a patriotic potato salad made with red, white, and blue potatoes? Red and white are fairly common, of course, and I suggest using fingerling (small) potatoes with tender skins. Blue potatoes come to us by way of Peru (although they're now grown in the United States), and their bluish flesh never fails to delight. Many supermarkets carry red, white, and blue fingerling potatoes these days, but if you can't find them, everyday full-size red- or white-skinned potatoes will taste just as good.

1 or 2 slices of bacon or pancetta (optional)

3 tablespoons mayonnaise, or more if needed

1 tablespoon Dijon mustard, or more to taste

1 tablespoon tarragon vinegar or distilled white
   vinegar, or more to taste

1 tablespoon capers with their juices

2 scallions, both white and green parts,
   trimmed, finely chopped (set aside
   2 tablespoons scallion greens for garnish)

1½ pounds red, white, and Peruvian blue
   fingerling potatoes

1½ tablespoons olive oil

Plenty of coarse salt (kosher or sea) and
   freshly ground black pepper

YOU'LL ALSO NEED:

1 cup wood chips or chunks (preferably hickory
   or oak), soaked for 1 hour in water to cover,
   then drained

An aluminum foil drip pan large enough to hold
   the potatoes

1. Cut the bacon, if using, into ¼-inch slivers,
put it in a small nonstick frying pan, and cook over
medium heat until lightly browned and the fat is
rendered, 3 to 4 minutes. Using a slotted spoon,
transfer the cooked bacon to paper towels to drain.

2. Make the salad dressing: Place the
mayonnaise, mustard, vinegar, capers, scallions,
and bacon, if using, in a large nonreactive serving
bowl and whisk to mix. Set the salad dressing aside.

3. Scrub the potatoes with a brush, but
leave the skins on. Place the potatoes in an aluminum foil drip pan. Drizzle with the olive oil and
season very generously with salt and pepper. Toss
the potatoes to mix.

4. Set up the grill for indirect grilling (see
page 9 for both charcoal and gas) and preheat to

medium-high. If using a gas grill, place all the wood chips or chunks in the smoker box or in a smoker pouch (see page 12) and preheat on high until you see smoke, then reduce the heat to medium-high.

5. When ready to cook, if using a charcoal grill, toss all the wood chips or chunks on the coals. Place the pan with the potatoes in the center of the hot grate, away from the heat. Cover the grill and cook the potatoes until tender, about 40 minutes. To test for doneness, insert a metal skewer into a potato; it should pierce it easily. Remove the pan with the potatoes from the grill and let cool.

6. Cut any large potatoes in quarters; cut medium-size potatoes in half. Leave small potatoes whole. Add the potatoes to the salad dressing and toss to mix. Taste for seasoning, adding salt, mustard, or vinegar as necessary; the salad should be highly seasoned. If the salad is too dry, add a little more mayonnaise. Sprinkle with the reserved scallion greens and serve at once.

SERVES 4 to 6

YOU CAN GRILL WHAT?

Everything is fair game when it comes to barbecue. So here are some foods you may never have dreamed you could grill. Or may never have dreamed existed, for that matter. Seaweed, rumaki (made with watermelon rind and bacon), eggs or biscuits in hollowed-out orange rinds—each meets fire here. And I revisit grilled cheese, the all-American favorite, moving it from the lunch counter griddle to the flame-kissed grate of a barbecue grill. I've always believed if you can cook something on the stove or in the oven, it's probably even better on the grill. Here's proof.

DIRECT GRILLING

SESAME-GRILLED NORI

Seaweed as a snack? *Kim goo ee*—paper-thin sheets of nori crisped over an open flame—is popular in Korea. I first tasted it in Cambridge, Massachusetts, in the 1970s, prepared by my Korean friend Sekyo Nam, and I recently rediscovered it in Korea Town in Los Angeles. Nori is the black seaweed used for wrapping sushi, and it's harvested off the coast of Maine. Brushed with sesame oil, sprinkled with salt, and toasted crackling crisp over open flames, it's delicious.

12 sheets nori
1 tablespoon Asian (dark) sesame oil
Coarse salt (kosher or sea)

1. Set up the grill for direct grilling (see page 8 for both charcoal and gas) and preheat to high. Lightly brush each sheet of nori on both sides with some of the sesame oil and sprinkle each with salt.

2. When ready to cook, using tongs, lay the nori on the hot grate and grill until it becomes toasted and crinkled, 20 to 40 seconds per side.

Do not let it burn. Stack the sheets on a plate for serving.

MAKES 12 sheets,
SERVES 4 to 6

NOTE: One of the most ingenious uses for flame-toasted nori (besides for snacking) is as a wrapper for steamed rice. Place a small square of the seaweed on top of a bowl of rice. Holding chopsticks about 1 inch apart, press the seaweed down into the rice, then bring the sticks together to come away with a cork-shaped lump of rice enveloped in seaweed. Pop the whole thing into your mouth.

TIP: Nori, which is sometimes known as laver, is a pressed green-black seaweed that is sold in paper-like sheets. Look for it in Japanese markets, natural foods stores, gourmet shops, and in an increasing number of supermarkets.

DIRECT GRILLING

WACKY RUMAKI

Classic rumaki features a water chestnut and a chicken liver wrapped in bacon and grilled on a small skewer. It's associated with the Polynesian-American restaurants of the 1940s and '50s. My inventive buddies at Boss Hawg's Barbecue & Catering Co. in Topeka, Kansas, got to thinking about rumaki alternatives. This one, made with pickled watermelon rind, may sound peculiar, but it tastes great.

2 jars (10 ounces each) pickled watermelon rind, drained

10 to 12 slices bacon, cut into 3½- to 4-inch pieces

YOU'LL ALSO NEED:
About 32 small (6-inch) bamboo skewers, soaked for 1 hour in cold water to cover, then drained

1. Wrap each watermelon rind piece in a piece of bacon, securing the bacon by inserting a skewer through it into the watermelon.

2. Make an aluminum foil shield for the bamboo skewers by folding a 24-by-12-inch sheet of aluminum foil in half and half again so that it forms a 12-by-6-inch rectangle.

3. Set up the grill for direct grilling (see page 8 for both charcoal and gas) and preheat to medium-high.

4. When ready to cook, place the aluminum foil shield in the center of the grill. Arrange the rumakis on the grill so that the exposed part of the skewers are resting on the aluminum foil shield. This will keep them from burning. Grill until the bacon is crisp and brown, about 2 minutes per side (about 4 minutes in all), turning with tongs. The dripping bacon fat may cause flare-ups, so be prepared to move the rumakis. A quick squirt from a water pistol can help extinguish any flare-ups, but don't overuse this technique or you'll put out the fire.

> **TIP:** Even if it sounds just too plain weird to you, give this rumaki a chance. If you'd rather substitute something less bizarre, wrap chicken livers or scallops in the bacon. Note the use of an aluminum foil shield to help keep the bamboo skewers from burning.

5. Transfer the rumaki to a platter and serve them immediately.

MAKES about 32 rumaki, SERVES 6 to 8

PROSCIUTTO-GRILLED PRUNES

The sweet, earthy flavor of prunes makes a great counterpoint to the salty taste of ham and the fragrance of wood smoke. These, grilled with prosciutto, make a terrific hors d'oeuvre. They are equally delicious stuffed with almonds.

24 pitted prunes

2 ounces cold Roquefort, Gorgonzola, or other blue cheese cut into pieces the size of olive pits

8 paper-thin slices of prosciutto (about 6 ounces)

YOU'LL ALSO NEED:

24 wooden toothpicks, soaked for 1 hour in cold water to cover, then drained

1. Stuff each prune with a piece of cheese. Cut each prosciutto slice lengthwise in thirds. Use each third to wrap a prune, securing the prosciutto by running a toothpick through the prune.

2. Set up the grill for direct grilling (see page 8 for both charcoal and gas) and preheat to high.

3. When ready to grill, brush and oil the grill grate. Grill the prunes until the prosciutto is sizzling and lightly browned, 1 to 2 minutes per side, turning with tongs. Transfer the grilled prunes to a platter and serve at once.

MAKES 24, SERVES 6 to 8

GRILLING IN THE EMBERS

SALSA ON THE COALS

Family, love, and Mexican cooking—the movie *Tortilla Soup* has them all. If you haven't seen it, run, don't walk, to your nearest video store to rent it. The stunning food for the film was created by Susan Feniger and Mary Sue Milliken of Santa Monica's Border Grill and the *Two Hot Tamales* TV show. The film's hero is a semiretired chef whose Sunday suppers are odes—no, epic poems—to Mexico's magnificent cuisine. His passion for grilling is infectious

> **TIP:** *Mexicans would prepare the salsa using a molcajete, a lava stone mortar and pestle. You can also chop the vegetables by hand or use a food processor.*

and he's not afraid to remove the grate from the grill and roast his vegetables right on the coals. That's the inspiration for this salsa, the ingredients of which are roasted directly on the embers. The salsa looks cool as all get-out as you prepare it (your guests will be amazed to see tomatoes, onions, and jalapeños burning away on the embers) and the resulting smoke flavors are as gutsy as you could wish for. Sorry gas-grillers; for the full effect, you need charcoal for this one.

2 to 4 jalapeño peppers

4 medium-size very ripe tomatoes or large plum
tomatoes (1 to 1½ pounds total)

1 poblano pepper

1 small onion

1 clove garlic, minced

1 teaspoon coarse salt
(kosher or sea), or
more to taste

1 canned chipotle chile,
minced

⅓ cup chopped fresh cilantro

3 to 4 tablespoons fresh lime juice, or
more to taste

Tortilla chips, for serving

YOU'LL ALSO NEED:

A charcoal grill

**Natural lump charcoal or wood chunks
(optional)**

> **TIP:** *For the best results, use natural lump charcoal or even wood for your fire. If you have a gas grill, you'll have to settle for charring the vegetables on the grate. The results will be perfectly tasty, but not quite as stunning as the live coal method.*

1. Light charcoal or
wood chunks in a chimney
starter (see page 15). When the
coals glow red, dump them into
the bottom of the grill and rake
them into an even layer. Let burn
until the coals begin to ash over,
5 to 10 minutes.

2. Place the jalapeños,
tomatoes, poblano, and onion directly on the coals.
Cook until charred black on the outside, about
1 minute per side (2 to 3 minutes in all) for the
jalapeños, 1 to 2 minutes per side (3 to 6 minutes in
all) for the tomatoes and poblano, and 2 to 3 minutes per side (6 to 9 minutes in all) for the onion.
Turn the vegetables with long-handled tongs to
ensure even cooking. Transfer the charred vegetables to an aluminum foil pan or heatproof plate and
let cool.

3. Using a pastry brush, brush any ash or cinders off the vegetables. Scrape the seeds out of the jalapeños unless you want a really fiery salsa. Scrape the burnt skin off the poblano, and then seed and core it. There are three ways to chop the vegetables: You can grind them in a large *molcajete,* you can coarsely chop them by hand, or you can coarsely chop them in a food processor. If using a *molcajete* or food processor, quarter the vegetables first. I like coarsely chopped vegetables (¼-inch pieces), but you can chop them more finely if you like.

4. Place the garlic and salt in the bottom of an attractive nonreactive serving bowl and mash to a paste with the back of a spoon. Add the charred vegetables, chipotle, cilantro, and lime juice and stir to mix. Taste for seasoning, adding more salt or lime juice as necessary; the salsa should be highly seasoned. Serve with tortilla chips.

MAKES about 1½ cups, SERVES 4 to 6

DIRECT GRILLING

GRILLED PROVOLONE

Beef-eating Argentineans aren't much on side dishes when it comes to barbecue, but *provoleta asada,* a grilled provolone-like cheese, appears wherever these grill jockeys put meat to fire. They grill disk-shaped slices of *provoleta* over blazing oak embers just long enough to melt the cheese but not so long that it oozes into the fire. A light dusting of flour keeps the cheese from sticking to the grill grate.

TIP: Provoleta *is a firm, ivory-colored cow's milk cheese. The closest equivalent in North America is a hard, aged provolone. In Miami, with its large Argentinean community, you can find provolone for grilling at many supermarkets. Elsewhere in the country, you might look for it at an Argentinean or Italian market. Of course, you can cook the cheese on a gas grill, but for a truly authentic flavor, you'd grill over blazing oak embers in a charcoal grill.*

¼ **cup flour**

2 slices aged provolone cheese
    (½ inch thick; about 8 ounces each)

½ **teaspoon dried oregano**

½ **teaspoon hot red pepper flakes**

Garlic-Rubbed "Rabbit Ears" (grilled bread
    slices, page 248), for serving

YOU'LL ALSO NEED:

1 cup wood chips or chunks (optional;
    preferably oak), unsoaked (see Note)

1. Set up the grill for direct grilling (see page 8 for both charcoal and gas) and preheat to high. (Ideally, you'll be using oak chunks to grill over; see Fuels on page 12.) If using a gas grill, place all the wood chips or chunks, if using, in the smoker box or in a smoker pouch (see page 12) and preheat on high until you see smoke.

2. Spread the flour out in a shallow bowl. Dip the cheese slices in the flour on both sides, shaking off the excess.

3. When ready to cook, if grilling over charcoal, toss all of the wood chips or chunks, if using, on the coals. Brush and oil the grill grate. Place cheese slices on the hot grate. Grill until the bottoms are lightly browned and beginning to melt, 2 to 4 minutes, then, using a grill fork (place the tines between the bars of the grate to pry the cheese off), flip the cheese and grill the other side the same way.

4. Transfer the cheese to a hot plate or platter and sprinkle with the oregano and hot red pepper flakes. Serve at once with the grilled bread. Provide butter knives for spreading the melted provolone.

SERVES 4

NOTE: If you are using wood chunks as your fuel, you'll need enough to fill a chimney starter.

DIRECT GRILLING

SAGANAKI

The Greek answer to grilled cheese, *saganaki,* is splendid—sizzling slabs of salty kasseri cheese, spiced up with garlic, pepper, and lemon; doused with Greek brandy; and dramatically served flaming at the table. Most often, the cheese is "grilled" in a frying pan or under the broiler, but it's a lot more fun and flavorful to actually cook it on the grill—especially over wood. I've tinkered with the traditional recipe a little, but I think you'll be delighted with the results.

> **TIP:** *The traditional cheese used to make saganaki is kasseri, a mild, salty, smooth-textured, semifirm cheese from Greece. Like feta, kasseri is made from sheep's milk, but it lacks feta's sourish bite. You can also use an aged version of kasseri called kefalotyri.*

4 tablespoons extra-virgin olive oil

2 tablespoons minced fresh flat-leaf parsley

2 cloves garlic, minced

½ teaspoon cracked or coarsely ground black
   peppercorns

¼ cup flour

4 slices kasseri cheese (½ inch thick;
   3 to 4 ounces each)

⅓ cup brandy, preferably a Greek brandy,
   such as Metaxa

Crusty bread, for serving

1 lemon, cut into wedges, for serving

YOU'LL ALSO NEED:

1 cup wood chunks (optional; preferably oak),
   unsoaked (see Note)

1. Put the olive oil, parsley, garlic, and peppercorns in a small bowl and stir to mix. You'll use this mixture for basting the cheese.

2. Set up the grill for direct grilling (see page 8 for both charcoal and gas) and preheat to high. (Ideally, you'll be using oak chunks to grill over; see Fuels on page 12.) If using a gas grill, place all the wood chips or chunks, if using, in the smoker box or in a smoker pouch (see page 12) and preheat on high until you see smoke.

3. Spread the flour out in a shallow bowl. Dip the cheese slice in the flour on both sides, shaking off the excess.

4. When ready to cook, if grilling over the charcoal, toss all of the wood chips or chunks, if using, on the coals. Brush and oil the grill grate. Place the floured cheese slices on the hot grate. Grill until the bottoms are lightly browned and beginning to melt, 2 to 4 minutes, basting the tops with the garlic-flavored oil. Using tongs, turn the cheese and grill the other side the same way. Put the brandy in a small saucepan and place it at the edge of the grill to warm, but do not let the brandy boil.

5. Transfer the cheese to heatproof plates or a platter. Pour any remaining garlic oil over it. Remove the saucepan from the grill and, working away from anything flammable and making sure that your sleeves are rolled up and your hair is tied back, ignite the brandy with a long kitchen match. Pour the flaming brandy over the cheese. Serve at once with crusty bread and lemon wedges for squeezing over the cheese.

SERVES 4

NOTE: If you are using wood chunks as your fuel, you'll need enough to fill a chimney starter.

INDIRECT GRILLING

CAMEMBERT ON A PLANK

It takes a wacky guy to write a book about beer-can chicken. There's a grill meister living in Canada who's almost as eccentric as I am—Ted Reader—and the stimulating *The Sticks & Stones Cookbook* he and Kathleen Sloan wrote is chock-full of offbeat grilling techniques, including using vines, stones, and boards when cooking on the grill. Grilling Camembert on a cedar plank was inspired by Ted's maple-planked Brie with roasted garlic. My recipe calls for a homemade chutney, but you could certainly use a good commercial brand. I think you'll find the contrast of the smoky, buttery, melting cheese and tart, gingery chutney to be unbeatable.

> **TIP:** *You can order grilling planks by mail from Chinook Planks (see Mail-Order Sources, page 311). Or go to your local lumberyard and ask for an untreated cedar or alder plank that's about 6 inches wide, 14 inches long, and ¹/₂ to 1 inch thick. Don't use pressure-treated lumber. Remember to leave yourself a couple of hours to soak the plank. (If you don't have a baking dish large enough to soak the plank, use a clean sink or bathtub.)*

2 Camembert cheeses (8 ounces each)

About 1 cup Peach Chutney (recipe follows) or
another flavored chutney, homemade or
commercial

¼ cup chopped toasted pecans or walnuts
(see Tip)

2 tablespoons melted butter

Garlic-Rubbed "Rabbit Ears" (grilled bread
slices, page 248), or crackers, for serving

YOU'LL ALSO NEED
1 cedar plank, soaked for 2 hours, in cold water
to cover, then drained

1. Carefully cut the rind

off the top of each cheese (take
only a paper-thin layer) and discard it. Spread half of the chutney over the top of each cheese,
mounding it in the center. Sprinkle each cheese with half of the
nuts and drizzle with 1 tablespoon of melted butter.

> **TIP:** *To toast pecans
> or walnuts, place them
> in a dry skillet over
> medium heat. Cook
> until they are fragrant
> and just beginning to
> brown, 4 to 6 minutes.
> Transfer the pecans to
> a bowl to cool.*

2. Set up the grill for indirect grilling (see
page 9 for both charcoal and gas) and preheat to
medium-high.

3. When ready to cook, place the soaked
cedar plank directly over the fire. Grill until the
edges just begin to smoke, 3 to 5 minutes. Invert
the plank and move it to the center of the grill,
away from the heat. Arrange the cheeses on top.
Cover the grill and cook the cheeses until the sides
are lightly browned, the cheese starts to melt, and
the topping is bubbling, 12 to 20 minutes. Transfer
the plank to a heatproof platter and serve at once,
spreading the chutney-topped cheese on grilled
bread slices or crackers.

SERVES 8 to 10

Peach Chutney

Chutney originated in India (the word comes from the Hindi *chatni*). But no Bombay pit master ever saw the likes of this one. Fresh Georgia peaches stand in for the traditional green mango. Now, mango has been called the peach of the tropics, so the substitution makes perfect sense. One thing's for sure—the honeyed, musky, sweet-sour flavor of peach makes for an irresistible chutney—especially when paired with the smoky flavor of barbecue. Really ripe peaches are so fragrant that you can smell them when you walk into a room. Nothing less will do for this chutney. If perfect peaches are not available, you can use apricots, nectarines, or mangoes.

Serve this tangy chutney with all manner of grilled or barbecued chicken, turkey, pork—as well as with the grilled Camembert.

2 pounds fresh ripe peaches

½ cup diced red onion

½ cup diced red bell pepper

¼ cup raisins

1 jalapeño pepper, seeded and diced (for a hotter chutney, leave the seeds in)

2 slices (¼ inch thick) fresh or candied ginger, finely chopped

2 tablespoons seeded diced lemon, including the rind

3 tablespoons cider vinegar, or more to taste

3 tablespoons brown sugar, or more to taste

½ teaspoon ground cinnamon

⅛ teaspoon ground allspice

⅛ teaspoon ground cloves

1. Rinse the peaches and peel, if desired.

Cut the peaches into 1-inch pieces, discarding the pits. Put the peach pieces, onion, bell pepper, raisins, jalapeño, ginger, lemon, vinegar, brown sugar, cinnamon, allspice, and cloves in a heavy saucepan over medium heat. Let simmer until the peaches are soft, 10 to 15 minutes.

2. Taste for seasoning, adding vinegar or

brown sugar as necessary. The chutney should be a little sweet and a little sour. Transfer the chutney to a bowl and let cool to room temperature. The chutney can be refrigerated, covered, for several months. Let return to room temperature before serving.

MAKES about 1½ cups

D I R E C T   G R I L L I N G

MOZZARELLA "S'MORES"

You remember s'mores—flame-roasted marshmallows and pieces of chocolate bar sandwiched between graham crackers. The marshmallows melted the chocolate, creating a gooey mess that was so irresistible, you just had to eat some more. My hors d'oeuvre version features flame-roasted mozzarella cheese, sun-dried tomatoes, and basil squeezed between grilled bread slices or crackers. Everyone still winds up with an irresistibly gooey mess—great party fare.

> **TIP:** *To make these s'mores, use fresh mozzarella, or even tangy buffalo milk mozzarella, not the kind sold in a vacuum-sealed plastic wrapper. You'll find fresh mozzarella at Italian markets and gourmet shops. It is becoming increasingly common in supermarkets.*

16 sun-dried tomato halves (see Note)

2 to 3 tablespoons extra-virgin olive oil,
   if needed

1 ball of fresh mozzarella (8 to 10 ounces), cut
   into 16 pieces (cut the cheese into 4 thick
   slices, then cut each slice in quarters), or
   16 bocconcini (bite-size mozzarella balls)

16 fresh basil leaves

16 slices Garlic-Rubbed "Rabbit Ears"
   (grilled bread slices, page 248) or 32 crackers

YOU'LL ALSO NEED:

2 to 6 long barbecue forks or skewers

1. Place the tomatoes in an attractive serving bowl.

2. Arrange the mozzarella, basil leaves, and grilled bread or crackers in bowls or on a platter.

3. Set up the grill for direct grilling (see page 8 for both charcoal and gas) and preheat to high. In the best of all worlds, you'd use a charcoal grill, raking the embers into a pile at the bottom of the grill and leaving off the grill grate. If using a gas grill, preheat it superhot.

4. Skewer a cube of mozzarella. Roast it over the fire, turning the skewer to evenly melt the cheese. If using a gas grill, you'll need to bring it as close as possible to the fire without touching the grate. When the mozzarella begins to melt and brown, after 1 to 2 minutes over charcoal, a little longer over gas, use a knife or fork to scrape the cheese off the skewer onto a piece of grilled bread. Never attempt to eat the melted cheese directly off the hot skewer—you'll burn your lips. Top the cheese with a basil leaf and a piece of sun-dried tomato and place a second piece of grilled bread on top. Eat at once.

MAKES 16 pieces; SERVES 4 to 6 as an appetizer, 2 as a light lunch

NOTE: Sun-dried tomatoes come in two forms: oil-packed and dried. Oil-packed tomatoes just need to be drained before you use them. The dried kind need to be soaked in water and marinated in olive oil. To reconstitute the tomatoes, place them in a heatproof bowl and add boiling water to cover. Let soak for 1 hour. Drain the tomatoes well and blot dry. Toss with the olive oil.

GRILLED EGGS

Never underestimate the power of astonishment. Even though you've recovered from the shock of seeing a chicken barbecuing upright on a beer can, or an ear of corn or an eggplant roasting nestled in the embers, there's one dish you'll probably find unfathomable: grilled eggs. An egg calls for a skillet or a saucepan, you'll argue. Who ever heard of grilling an egg? Well, visit Southeast Asia and you'll find eggs that are roasted in their shells over blazing coconut shells and served wrapped in lettuce leaves with fresh herbs and chiles. The notion isn't quite as foreign as it sounds—after all, deviled eggs and egg salads are classic accompaniments to American barbecue. One thing's for sure: The mere sight of whole eggs roasting away on your barbecue grill will firmly assure your reputation as a maestro who knows no limits.

TIP: *There are really only two tricks to grilling an egg. First, prick the end with a needle to release the steam (this keeps the eggshell from cracking). Second, work over a moderate heat, so the egg roasts slowly.*

1 head Boston or Bibb lettuce, broken into
  leaves, washed, and spun dry
1 bunch fresh basil, preferably Thai basil,
  washed, dried, and torn into sprigs
1 bunch fresh cilantro, washed, dried, and
  torn into sprigs
1 bunch fresh mint, washed, dried, and torn
  into sprigs
2 cups mung bean sprouts
  (see Note)
2 to 4 serrano or jalapeño peppers,
  thinly sliced
Chile-Lime Dipping Sauce (recipe follows;
  see Note)
4 large eggs

YOU'LL ALSO NEED:
A needle or pin

1. Arrange the lettuce leaves, basil, cilantro,
mint, bean sprouts, and peppers in attractive piles
on a platter. Pour the dipping sauce into 4 small
bowls.

2. Using a pin or needle, gently prick the large
end of each egg to make a tiny hole.

3. Set up the grill for direct grilling (see
page 8 for both charcoal and gas) and preheat to
medium.

4. When ready to cook, place the eggs on
the hot grate. Roast until the shells are lightly
browned and the eggs are cooked through, 2½ to 3
minutes per side (10 to 12 minutes in all), turning
them 4 times with tongs so all sides are grilled. To
test for doneness, place one of the eggs on a table
and give it a spin. If it turns quickly and easily for a
long time, it's cooked through. If it doesn't, continue
grilling the eggs and check again after 30 seconds.

5. Transfer the eggs to a plate and set aside until cool enough to handle. Shell each egg and cut it lengthwise in quarters or have your guests do this.

6. To eat, place an egg quarter on a lettuce leaf, add basil, cilantro, mint, bean sprouts, and slices of pepper. Roll up the lettuce leaf to make a tight bundle. Dip it in the sauce and enjoy!

SERVES 4

NOTE: Mung beans are the long, crisp white sprouts frequently used in Thai and Chinese cooking. They are available at many supermarkets and Asian markets.

Tradition calls for the eggs to be served with a thin soy sauce-based dipping sauce, like the chile-lime one here. You could also serve the eggs with the Thai-style peanut sauces on pages 75 and 128.

Chile-Lime Dipping Sauce

An explosive accompaniment to all sorts of grilled fare, from eggs to grilled fish to satés, versions of this dipping sauce abound in Southeast Asia. It's usually made with white pepper, but you can substitute black if that's what you have on hand.

¼ cup sugar, or more to taste

3 cloves garlic, minced

½ teaspoon freshly ground white pepper

6 tablespoons soy sauce, or more to taste

6 tablespoons fresh lime juice (see Note), or
more to taste

2 scallions, both white and green parts,
trimmed and thinly sliced

1 to 2 serrano or jalapeño pepper(s), seeded
and thinly sliced (for a hotter dipping sauce,
leave the seeds in)

¼ cup finely chopped dry-roasted peanuts

1. Place the sugar, garlic, and white pepper in a nonreactive mixing bowl and mash to a paste with the back of a wooden spoon. Add the soy sauce, lime juice, and 6 tablespoons of water and stir until the sugar is dissolved. Taste for seasoning, adding soy sauce or lime juice as necessary.

2. Stir in the scallions, serrano pepper(s), and peanuts just before serving. Pour the sauce into 4 small bowls for dipping.

MAKES about 1¼ cups

NOTE: To get 6 tablespoons of lime juice, you will need to squeeze 3 or 4 limes.

DIRECT GRILLING

GRILL MASTER'S BREAKFAST

"Barbecue . . . it's not just for breakfast anymore" may be the motto of the Kansas City Barbecue Society, but this *is* for breakfast, and while it no doubt originated over a campfire, it's easy to do on a backyard grill. The basic procedure goes something like this: You squeeze two fresh oranges and drink the juice, then use the hollow rinds to cook in—one orange for biscuits or muffins, the other for scrambled eggs. They look great and taste even better. Besides, it gives you an excuse to fire up your grill before breakfast!

> **TIP:** *You can cook your breakfast using either the direct or indirect method. I like the edgy, seared orange flavors that arise from direct grilling, but with indirect grilling, your breakfast is less likely to burn.*

2 large oranges (2½ to 3 inches in diameter)

FOR THE BISCUITS:
1 cup Bisquick or other biscuit mix
½ cup grated Cheddar cheese
1 scallion, both white and green parts, trimmed
and finely chopped
⅓ cup milk, or more as needed

FOR THE EGGS:
2 large eggs
2 tablespoons milk or heavy (whipping) cream
1 scallion, both white and green parts, trimmed
and finely chopped
¼ cup grated Cheddar cheese
Coarse salt (kosher or sea) and freshly ground
black pepper

1. Cut aluminum foil into 4 strips, each 12 by 2 inches. Crumple the foil strips and shape them into 4 rings, each 2 inches in diameter.

> **TIP:** *I've added one high-tech element here—aluminum foil rings to help hold the orange rinds upright.*

2. Cut each orange in half crosswise and squeeze out the juice (this is most easily done with a juicer). Put the juice in a glass. Using a spoon (a grapefruit spoon works well), scrape the inside of each orange rind clean, taking care not to puncture the shell.

3. Make the biscuit batter: Place the Bisquick, Cheddar, and scallion in a bowl and stir to mix. Stir in the milk. If the batter seems a bit dry, add a little more milk. Set 2 orange rind halves upright on 2 aluminum foil rings and divide the biscuit mixture between them.

4. Make the scrambled eggs: Break the eggs into a bowl, add the milk, and beat with a fork until smooth. Beat in the scallion and Cheddar, and

season with salt and pepper. Set the remaining
2 orange rind halves upright on the remaining
2 aluminum foil rings and divide the egg mixture
between them.

5. Set up the grill for direct grilling (see
page 8 for both charcoal and gas) and preheat to
medium-high.

6. When ready to cook, place the orange
rind halves on their rings on the hot grate and cook
until the biscuits are puffed and browned and the
eggs are set, 12 to 15 minutes. The biscuits and
scrambled eggs can be eaten right out of the
orange rinds. Serve with the orange juice.

SERVES 1; can be multiplied, as desired

VARIATION: You can use the indirect method
to grill the biscuits and scrambled eggs. Set up the
grill for indirect grilling (see page 9 for both charcoal and gas) and preheat to medium-high. When
ready to cook, place the filled orange rinds in the
center of the hot grate, away from the heat, and
cover the grill. Cook until the biscuits are puffed
and browned and the eggs are set, 20 to 25
minutes.

ROTISSERIE-GRILLED GARLIC ROLLS

Nothing sets the mood for a barbecue like a well-laden, slow-turning rotisserie. And if you really want to grab attention, try grilling garlic bread on the rotisserie. I first tasted this unusual bread at the Mercado del Puerto in Montevideo, Uruguay, where it was served as an accompaniment to the local plate-burying steaks and sausages. It's equally good enjoyed at home.

> **TIP:** *If you don't have a rotisserie (or you do and it's otherwise engaged), you can grill the garlic rolls using the indirect method, following the directions in the Variation on the following page.*

12 tablespoons (1½ sticks) salted butter,
   at room temperature

3 cloves garlic, minced

3 tablespoons chopped fresh flat-leaf parsley

6 rolls (each 3 to 4 inches long and
   2 to 3 inches wide; see Tip, page 290)

YOU'LL ALSO NEED:
A grill with a rotisserie

1. Put the butter, garlic, and parsley in a bowl and stir to mix. Using a serrated knife, make 3 slashes in each roll, 2 on the diagonal on the top and 1 on the diagonal on the bottom. Using a spatula, spread some garlic butter into each slash, reserving 3 tablespoons of garlic butter for basting. Skewer the rolls lengthwise on the rotisserie spit.

2. Set up the grill for rotisserie grilling, following the manufacturer's instructions, and preheat to medium-high.

3. When ready to cook, attach the spit to the rotisserie mechanism of the grill and turn on the motor. Grill the rolls until crusty and golden brown, 10 to 15 minutes, brushing the outsides with the remaining garlic butter. Unskewer the rolls and serve at once.

TIP: *One good roll for spit roasting is a hard-crusted, soft-crumbed French roll (sort of a miniature baguette).*

MAKES 6 rolls

VARIATION: You can use the indirect method to grill the rolls. Set up the grill for indirect grilling (see page 9 for both charcoal and gas) and preheat to medium-high. Make the garlic butter, as described above. Make several deep slashes in the top of each roll and spread garlic butter in each, using a spatula. Spread more butter on the outside of the rolls, using a spatula or pastry brush. When ready to cook, place the rolls in the center of the hot grate, away from the heat. Cover the grill and cook the rolls until crusty and golden brown, 10 to 15 minutes, basting with any remaining garlic butter. Serve at once.

INDIRECT GRILLING

BARBECUED TOFU

There are 5 million or so vegetarians in the United States and they, too, have the inalienable right to gather round the grill. Eating tofu has been shown to offer a host of health benefits, from lowering blood pressure and cholesterol to reducing the risk of cancer. The following barbecued tofu has all the spice and smoke flavors any 'que head could wish for.

ADVANCE PREPARATION: 2 to 4 hours for the tofu to absorb the rub

> **TIP:** *Tofu comes in a variety of grades and textures; extra-firm or firm tofu holds up best on the grill. No, you don't have to visit a health food store to find it—tofu is routinely stocked in the produce section of most supermarkets.*

2 tablespoons vegetable oil

2 cloves garlic, minced

3 tablespoons All-Purpose Barbecue Rub
    (page 37) or your favorite rub,
    plus 1 teaspoon for basting

2 blocks of tofu (1 pound each)

1 cup of your favorite barbecue sauce, or one
    of the sauces in this book

Hamburger buns (optional), for serving

YOU'LL ALSO NEED:

1 cup wood chips or chunks (preferably hickory
    or oak), soaked for 1 hour in cold water to
    cover, then drained

1. Put the oil and garlic and 1 teaspoon barbecue rub in a small bowl and stir to mix. Set the oil aside.

2. Cut each block of tofu in half through the short side to obtain 4 broad thin "steaks." Blot the tofu pieces dry with paper towels and arrange in a baking dish. Sprinkle the remaining rub over the tofu on both sides, gently patting it on with your fingertips. Don't forget to apply a little rub to the sides. Refrigerate the tofu for 2 to 4 hours.

3. Set up the grill for indirect grilling (see page 9 for both charcoal and gas) and preheat to medium. If using a gas grill, place the wood chips in the smoker box or in a smoker pouch (see page 12) and preheat on high until you see smoke, then reduce the heat to medium.

4. When ready to cook, if using a charcoal grill, toss all the wood chips or chunks on the coals. Brush and oil the grill grate. Place the tofu slices on the center of the hot grate, away from the heat. Cover the grill and let the tofu smoke for 15 minutes.

5. Brush each piece of tofu on both sides with the garlic oil. Slide the tofu pieces directly over the fire and cook until nicely browned on both sides, 3 to 5 minutes per side. During the last

2 minutes of grilling, brush the tofu on both sides with some of the barbecue sauce and let both sides sizzle over the fire as well. Transfer the barbecued tofu to a platter and serve at once, with the remaining barbecue sauce on the side. If you like, serve the tofu on hamburger buns.

SERVES 4

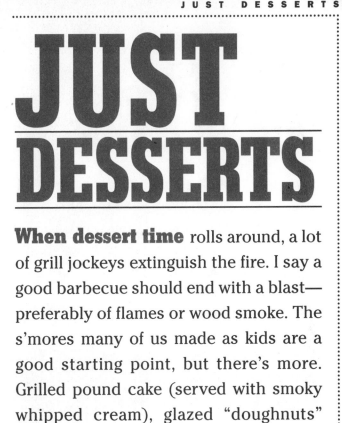

JUST DESSERTS

When dessert time rolls around, a lot of grill jockeys extinguish the fire. I say a good barbecue should end with a blast—preferably of flames or wood smoke. The s'mores many of us made as kids are a good starting point, but there's more. Grilled pound cake (served with smoky whipped cream), glazed "doughnuts" (grilled doughnut peaches), and flame-roasted coconut custards are just a few of the desserts you can serve at a cutting-edge barbecue. In fact, about the only thing you can't grill is ice cream. Or can you? In this chapter, you'll even find a baked Hawaii (my version

of baked Alaska) and a refreshing grilled nectarine smoothie. When it comes to dessert, the barbecue is just beginning.

GRILLED POUND CAKE

I've always been fond of toasted pound cake, and the grill's a natural for toasting. Smoke and sugar often work in mysterious and complementary ways—think of barbecue sauce and grilled chicken or crème brûlée. Here they work their magic on whipped cream. If you think regular pound cake is good, just wait until you taste it hot off the grill.

4 cups mixed berries, such as
    blueberries, raspberries, and
    strawberries
2 to 3 tablespoons sugar
2 teaspoons fresh lemon juice
1½ cups heavy (whipping) cream,
    well chilled
3 to 4 tablespoons confectioners' sugar, or
    more to taste
1 tablespoon Laphroaig or other smoky
    single-malt scotch, or 1 tablespoon
    blended whiskey
1 to 2 drops liquid smoke (optional)
8 slices pound cake (about ¾ inch
    thick each)
8 sprigs fresh mint

1. Rinse the berries, removing any stems or leaves. If using strawberries, cap them and cut any large berries in half or in quarters. Place the berries in a nonreactive bowl with the sugar and lemon juice. Not more than an hour before serving, gently toss the berries with the sugar and lemon juice to mix.

2. Prepare the whipped cream: Chill the bowl of an
electric mixer or a metal bowl in the freezer. When cold, add the cream and, using an electric mixer, beat until soft peaks form, 5 to 7 minutes. Add the confectioners' sugar and scotch (or whiskey and liquid smoke) and continue beating the whipped cream until stiff peaks form, 1 to 2 minutes more. Don't overbeat or you'll get whiskey-flavored butter. Keep the whipped cream chilled until you are ready to serve.

TIP: *There are two ways to make whipped cream smoke-scented. The first is to flavor the cream with a smoky single-malt scotch, like Laphroaig (which owes its pungent smoke flavor to the peat fires that are used to roast the barley). Laphroaig isn't cheap, but the stuff is so spectacular, everyone—grill jockey or not—should own a bottle. The other option is to flavor the whipped cream with a more commonplace whiskey, adding a drop or two of liquid smoke for flavor. Be sparing with the liquid smoke—a little goes a long way.*

3. Set up the grill for direct grilling (see
page 8 for both charcoal and gas) and preheat to medium-high.

4. When ready to cook, brush and oil the
grill grate. Grill the pound cake slices until toasted on both sides, 1 to 2 minutes per side. Transfer the toasted pound cake to plates and top with the sweetened berries and dollops of smoky whipped cream. Garnish each serving with a mint sprig and serve at once.

SERVES 8

DIRECT GRILLING

"GLAZED DOUGHNUTS"

Doughnut peaches burst on the food scene in the United States in the 1990s. It was love at first bite. We loved the steam-rollered look of these flat peaches with their indented centers (they really do resemble doughnuts). We loved their musky sweetness and their high ratio of flesh to pit. What most of us didn't appreciate at the time is just how well suited the flat shape of a doughnut peach is to grilling. Then again, a decade ago, most Americans didn't realize you could grill fruit. Here, smokily grilled doughnut peaches are glazed with bourbon, butter, and brown sugar, and I doubt there's a tastier "doughnut" in existence.

TIP: *For about a month and a half during the summer, doughnut peaches are available at gourmet green-grocers, natural foods stores, and at an increasing number of supermarkets. To find an outlet near you, contact the California-based exotic produce supplier, Frieda's (www.friedas.com), which introduced the doughnut peach to North America. Ripe doughnut peaches are very fragrant and gently yielding when squeezed. Let the peaches ripen at room temperature. If you can't find doughnut peaches, you can use ripe regular peach halves instead.*

½ cup bourbon

½ cup firmly packed light brown sugar

8 tablespoons (1 stick) unsalted butter

½ teaspoon ground cinnamon

¼ teaspoon ground cloves

Pinch of coarse salt (kosher or sea)

4 large or 8 small ripe doughnut peaches, stems
   removed

Vanilla ice cream (optional), for serving

Sprigs of fresh mint, for garnish

YOU'LL ALSO NEED:
1 cup wood chips (optional; preferably hickory),
   soaked for 1 hour in water to cover, then drained

1. Combine the bourbon, brown sugar, butter,
cinnamon, cloves, and salt in a heavy saucepan and
bring to a boil over high heat. Let the glaze simmer
briskly until thick, 4 to 6 minutes. Remove the pan
from the heat.

2. Rinse the peaches and pat dry.

3. Set up the grill for direct grilling (see
page 8 for both charcoal and gas) and preheat to
high. If using a gas grill, place all the wood chips, if
using, in the smoker box or in a smoker pouch (see
page 12) and preheat on high until you see smoke.

4. When ready to cook,
if using a charcoal grill, toss all of
the wood chips, if using, on the
coals. Place the peaches on the
top grate and grill until nicely

TIP: *I've made the
ice cream optional, but
it sure goes well with
grilled peaches.*

browned on both sides, 2 to 4 minutes per side,
basting each side with the glaze twice. Transfer the
peaches to plates or a platter and top with ice
cream, if desired. Spoon any remaining glaze over
the peaches. Garnish with mint sprigs and serve at
once, warning your guests to watch for the tiny pits.

SERVES 4

PEACHES 'N' CREAM

Americans have a soft spot for peaches and cream—and with good reason. There's nothing like the contrast of a brassily acidic ripe summer peach with the lip-smacking richness of whipped cream—especially when that cream is spiced with cinnamon and spiked with rum. It will melt into fragrant puddles the moment it hits the hot fruit.

TIP: *Like all fruit recipes, this one lives or dies by the ripeness of the peaches. Use ones that are squeezably soft and that are so fragrant you can smell them when you step into the kitchen (let them ripen at room temperature to this stage). Freestone peaches have stones (pits) that separate easily from their flesh. You could also use doughnut peaches, nectarines, apricots, or plums (you'll need eight apricots or plums).*

1 cup heavy
   (whipping) cream
3 tablespoons confectioners'
   sugar, or more to taste
½ teaspoon ground cinnamon
1 tablespoon light rum
4 large ripe freestone peaches
3 tablespoons melted butter
3 tablespoons granulated sugar
8 fresh mint leaves, for garnish

1. Prepare the whipped cream: Chill the bowl of an electric mixer or a metal bowl in the freezer. When cold, add the cream and, using an electric mixer, beat until soft peaks form, 5 to 7 minutes. Add the confectioners' sugar, cinnamon, and rum and beat briefly. Taste the whipped cream and add more sugar if necessary. Continue beating the whipped cream until stiff peaks form, 1 to 2 minutes more. Keep the whipped cream chilled until you are ready to serve.

2. Rinse the peaches and pat dry with paper towels. Cut each in half along the crease and twist the halves in opposite directions to separate them. Using a spoon, remove and discard the pit from each. Brush each peach half with some of the melted butter and sprinkle with some of the granulated sugar.

3. Set up the grill for direct grilling (see page 8 for both charcoal and gas) and preheat to high.

4. When ready to cook, brush and oil the grill grate. Place the peaches on the grill cut side down. Grill until golden brown on both sides, 2 to 4 minutes per side. Transfer the peaches to a platter or plates, arranging them cut side up, and place a dollop of the flavored whipped cream on top. Garnish each peach half with a mint leaf. Serve any remaining whipped cream on the side.

SERVES 4

COCONUT CUSTARD IN COCONUT SHELLS

Cool, creamy coconut custard— is there anything more delicious? How about a coconut custard grilled in a coconut shell? I often use coconut shells as serving bowls for desserts, but in this recipe, the custard is actually grilled in coconut shells. These must have functioned as pots in early culinary history, I reasoned, so why not use them as baking dishes? Sure, the shell might burn, but the crisp coconut flesh ought to keep the custard safe from the flames. Not only did the idea work, the resulting dessert, with its golden custard and flame-darkened shell, is a guaranteed showstopper. There's another advantage to cooking a custard in this manner: As

TIP: There are two ways to grill the custards. The safest is to use the indirect method on a gas or charcoal grill. You'll get a little more charring on the shell if you use the direct method, but you have to take care not to overcook the custards, or they will curdle. If the custards start to bubble and boil, they have gone too far.

the shell roasts, it imparts a delicate smoke flavor to the custard.

2 ripe (brown-shelled) coconuts
2 large eggs
Yolks of 4 large eggs
4 tablespoons sugar, or more to taste
¾ cup unsweetened coconut milk
¾ cup heavy (whipping) cream
1 tablespoon light rum
1 teaspoon vanilla extract
1 teaspoon finely grated lemon zest
½ teaspoon ground cinnamon

1. Crack each coconut in half around its circumference. The easiest way to do this is to tap the shell repeatedly with the dull spine (not the sharp edge) of a cleaver along an imaginary line going around the middle. Work over a bowl with a strainer to collect the coconut water. After about 10 gentle taps, the shell will begin to crack. Continue tapping the shell and the crack will get larger. You will be able to drain the coconut water into the bowl and pull the halves of the coconut apart easily. Save the coconut water to use for making drinks.

2. Cut aluminum foil into 4 strips, each 12 by 3 inches. Crumple the foil strips and shape them into 4 rings, each about 2 inches in diameter. Set a coconut half upright on one of each.

3. Place the eggs, yolks, and sugar in a mixing bowl and whisk just to combine. Shake the coconut milk well before opening the can. Whisk the coconut milk, cream, rum, vanilla, lemon zest, and cinnamon into the egg mixture. Taste for seasoning; if a sweeter custard is desired, add sugar. Fill each coconut half with custard mixture.

4. Set up the grill for indirect grilling (see page 9 for both charcoal and gas) and preheat to medium. When ready to cook, arrange the filled coconut halves on their aluminum foil rings in the center of the hot grate, away from the heat. Cover the grill and cook the custards until the tops are golden and the custard is set, 20 to 30 minutes. The shells will brown at their cut edges. To test for doneness, shake a shell with tongs: The custard will wiggle, not ripple, when cooked through. Another way to test for doneness is to insert a bamboo skewer or toothpick into a custard. It will come out clean when the custard is cooked.

> **TIP:** *When buying coconuts, you'll want to be sure you pick ones that are fresh. Hold a nut to your ear and shake: You should hear liquid sloshing around inside the shell. A dry coconut is apt to be rancid.*

5. Remove the coconut halves and aluminum foil rings from the grill, using tongs and a spatula, and set on a baking sheet or wire rack on a heatproof surface. (Use the tongs to steady a coconut half as you slide the spatula under the aluminum foil ring.) Let cool to room temperature, then refrigerate until serving.

6. Serve the coconut custards in the shells. If you're feeling fancy, put the shells in shallow bowls filled with crushed ice. Otherwise, serve them on the aluminum foil rings to keep them upright.

SERVES 4

VARIATION: You can use the direct method to grill the custards. Set up the grill for direct grilling , (see page 9 for both charcoal and gas) and pre-heat to medium. When ready to cook, arrange the filled coconut halves on their aluminum foil rings on the hot grate directly over the fire. Grill until the custards are cooked, 15 to 20 minutes. The shells may darken, which is fine. Let the custards cool, then refrigerate until serving.

BAKED HAWAII

When I was growing up, baked Alaska was a restaurant theatric reserved for special occasions, like your birthday or graduation from junior high school. Festooned with rococo swirls of meringue, it was ceremoniously flambéed at the tableside, and you weren't really sure if you should eat it or just look at it. Of course, nothing would seem less suited for grilling than a dish in which the main ingredient is ice cream. But by using the indirect grilling method, you can turn out a dessert that's icy on the inside and smoking on the outside—just as tradition dictates. So what's with the baked Hawaii? It's my update of the American classic, using fresh pineapple instead of cake.

1 ripe pineapple with leaves attached
1 pint your favorite-flavor ice cream or frozen
   yogurt (I like cherry), slightly softened
2 tablespoons 151-proof or light rum,
   plus ¼ cup for flambéing (optional)

FOR THE MERINGUE:
Whites of 4 large eggs, at room temperature
½ teaspoon cream of tartar
¾ cup confectioners' or superfine sugar
   (see Note)
1 teaspoon vanilla extract

1. Lay the pineapple on its side with the leafy crown away from you (don't cut off the leaves; they're part of the presentation). Using a

long, sharp knife, cut the pineapple in half lengthwise, starting at the bottom and cutting through
the leaves as well as the fruit. Working on one half
of the pineapple at a time, remove the core by
making 2 cuts into the flesh, angling the knife blade
down along the core to cut out a V-shape wedge
the length of the fruit. Repeat with the other half.
Discard the core, then remove the flesh from the
pineapple, cutting within ½ inch of the rind and
following its contours (a grapefruit knife works well
for this). It is easier to cut out the flesh if you make
a few cuts that run the length of the fruit but be
careful not to pierce the rind.

TIP: It's important to
preheat your grill as hot
as it will go, so you can
brown the meringue
quickly without melting
the ice cream.

2. Cut the pineapple flesh
into ¾-inch pieces and transfer
to a mixing bowl. Scoop in the
ice cream, add 2 tablespoons
rum, if using, and stir to com-
bine. Pack the pineapple mixture back into the
pineapple shells, mounding it up slightly. Wrap
each pineapple half in plastic wrap and place in the
freezer.

3. Make the meringue: Place the egg
whites and cream of tartar in the bowl of an electric mixer. Start beating at low speed until frothy.
Gradually increase the speed to medium, then
medium-high, and beat until the whites stiffen to
soft peaks (they'll look like soft ice cream), about
8 minutes. Increase the mixer speed to high and
beat in the sugar, followed by the vanilla. Continue
beating until the mixture is glossy and firm, but not
dry, 1 to 2 minutes. Do not overbeat or the
meringue will collapse.

4. Transfer the meringue to a pastry bag
fitted with a large star tip. Remove the pineapple
halves from the freezer. The filling should be frozen
hard. Pipe decorative swirls of meringue over the

ice cream mixture, covering it completely and extending just a little over its edge. If you don't have a piping bag, spread the meringue over the fruit with a spatula or a spoon. Place the meringue-covered pineapple halves in the freezer, uncovered, for at least 15 minutes to firm up the ice cream. The meringue-covered pineapple can be frozen for up to a day.

TIP: *In order to get the full effect of this dish, use a pastry bag fitted with a star-shaped piping tip to squirt ridged swirls of meringue over the pineapple. A pastry bag is nothing more than a conical nylon bag. A piping tip is a conical, toothed metal nozzle. Both are available at cookware shops (ask the vendor to instruct you in their use). If this sounds too complicated, simply spread the meringue over the pineapple. Your baked Hawaii will still look stunning.*

5. Set up the grill for indirect grilling (see page 9 for both charcoal and gas) and pre-heat to high.

6. When ready to cook, place the pineapple halves on the hot grate, away from the heat. Cover the grill and cook until the meringue is hand-somely browned, 3 to 6 minutes. Transfer the baked Hawaii to a heatproof platter. If you choose to flambé the dessert, warm ¼ cup of rum in a small saucepan but do not let it boil. Remove the rum from the heat and, working away from anything flammable and making sure that your sleeves are rolled up and your hair is tied back, ignite it with a long kitchen match. Pour the flaming rum over the baked Hawaii. Serve at once.

SERVES 8

NOTE: I've had some trouble finding superfine sugar, but if you can find it, it dissolves more quickly. If it's not with the baking supplies, look in the section of the supermarket that has the cock-tail mixes.

DIRECT GRILLING

GRILLED FRUIT SMOOTHIE

How about a refreshing summer smoothie made with, you guessed it, grilled fruit? The accents of smoke and fire add depth to this popular summer libation. The resulting smoothie is rich enough to double as a light dessert. In this recipe, the smoothie is flavored with nectarines, but you could certainly use grilled peaches, apricots, bananas, or pineapple instead.

> **TIP:** *This recipe is only as good as the fruit is ripe. Try to buy intensely fragrant, squeezably soft fruit. If you can't, let hard fruit ripen at room temperature.*

2 large or 3
   medium-size
   very ripe nectarines
¾ cup sugar
1 tablespoon ground cinnamon,
   or more to taste and for
   garnishing the smoothies
1½ cups frozen vanilla yogurt or
   ice cream
2 cups soy milk (see Note)
2 tablespoons maple syrup, or more to taste

1. Rinse the nectarines and pat dry with paper towels. Cut each nectarine in half along the crease and twist the halves in opposite directions to separate them. Cut each nectarine half in half and lift off and discard the pit.

2. Set up the grill for direct grilling (see page 8 for both charcoal and gas) and preheat to high.

3. When ready to cook, brush and oil the grill grate. Combine the sugar and 1 tablespoon of cinnamon in a shallow bowl and stir to mix. Dip each nectarine quarter in the sugar mixture, shaking off the excess. Save any extra sugar for future grilling. Arrange the nectarines on the hot grate and grill until nicely browned on all sides, 2 to 3 minutes per side (6 to 9 minutes in all). Transfer the nectarines to a platter and let cool. Cut one quarter lengthwise into 2 thin wedges (skinning the fruit is optional). Cut the remaining nectarine quarters into large dice. The grilled nectarines can be refrigerated in a covered bowl for up to 3 days.

> **TIP:** It seems silly to fire up the grill simply to make a smoothie, so I like to grill the fruit a day or two ahead of time when I'm grilling something else.

4. Place the diced nectarines, frozen yogurt, soy milk, and maple syrup in a blender, and working in batches if necessary, blend until smooth. Taste for seasoning, adding maple syrup and/or cinnamon to taste. Pour the smoothies into 2 tall glasses and garnish each with a nectarine wedge (press it over the edge of the glass). Lightly dust the smoothies with cinnamon and serve at once.

SERVES 2

NOTE: I've been drinking a lot of soy milk lately. I love its nutty flavor, and it's healthy as all get out. Of course, you could always substitute whole or skim cow's milk in the smoothies.

MAIL-ORDER SOURCES

GRILLING EQUIPMENT AND ACCESSORIES

Charcoal Companion
401 Roland Way #250
Oakland, California 94621
(800) 521-0505
www.companion-group.com
Accessories

Gourmet Gilchrist
    Swamper Products
P.O. Box 663
Charleston, Rhode Island
    02813
(877) 768-5766 or
    (401) 364-9657
www.greatgrate.com
Shellfish griller

Grill Lover's Catalog
P.O. Box 1300
Columbus, Georgia 31902
(800) 241-8981
www.grilllovers.com
Charcoal and gas grills;
    accessories

Grilla Gear, a division of
    World Kitchen
P.O. Box 1555
Elmira, New York 14902-1555
(800) 545-4411
www.grillagear.com
Accessories

Weber-Stephen Products
    Company
200 East Daniels Road
Palatine, Illinois 60067
(800) 446-1071
www.weber.com
Charcoal and
    gas grills;
    accessories

VERTICAL CHICKEN ROASTERS

Acquabotics, Inc.
84961 Old Highway, #8
Islamorada, Florida 33036
(800) 480-4450; dial code 00
www.beercanchickenroaster.
    com
Captain Steve's beer-can
    chicken roaster

The Barbecue Store
14601 Bellaire, #260
Houston, Texas 77083
(888) 789-0650
www.barbecue-store.com
Willie's Chicken Sitter

Buster's Drunk Chicken
    Roost
107 Enterprise Lane
Cleveland, Georgia 30528
(706) 865-9855
www.drunkchicken.com
Buster's Drunk Chicken
    Roost

The Holland Grill Company,
    Inc.
600 Irving Parkway
Hollysprings, North Carolina
    27540
(919) 557-2001
www.hollandgrill.com
Brad's Roastin' Post

Papa Jeabert's Inc.
530 C West Pinhook Road
Lafayette, Louisiana 70503
(877) 267-4468
www.chickenup.com
Papa Jeabert's Chicken Up!

Uncle Joe's True Value
P.O. Box 400
Dover, Tennessee 37058
(866) 868-6253
www.unclejoes.com
Brad's Roastin' Post

CHARCOAL AND WOOD

BBQr's Delight
P.O. Box 8727
Pine Bluff, Arkansas 71611
(877) 275-9591
www.BBQrsDelight.com
Wood grill pellets

Chinook Planks
P.O. Box 27469
Seattle, Washington 98125
(800) 765-4408
www.chinookplanks.com
Wood planks for grilling

Nature's Own and Peoples
    Woods
75 Mill Street
Cumberland, Rhode Island
    02864
(800) 729-5800
www.peopleswoods.com
Natural lump charcoal and
    smoking woods

W W Wood, Inc
P.O. Box 398
Pleasanton, Texas 78064
(830) 569-2501
Smoking and grilling woods

INGREDIENTS

General

American Spoon Foods
1668 Clarion Avenue
Petoskey, Michigan
    49770-0566
(888) 735-6700
www.spoon.com
Dried fruits, barbecue sauces,
    chutney, and condiments

Aphrodisia Products
62 Kent Street
Brooklyn, New York 11222
(877) 274-3677
www.aphrodisiaproducts.com
Herbs and spices

Brugger Brothers
3868 NE 169th Street,
    Suite 401
North Miami Beach, Florida
    33160
(800) 949-2264
www.talamancapepper.com
Talamanca peppercorns

The Chile Shop
109 East Water Street
Sante Fe, New Mexico 87501
(505) 983-6080
www.thechileshop.com
Dried chiles, salsas, and
    sauces

Coyote Cafe General Store
132 West Water Street
Santa Fe, New Mexico 87501
(800) 866-4695
www.coyote-cafe.com
Dried chiles, salsas, and
    sauces

D'Artagnan
280 Wilson Avenue
Newark, New Jersey 07105
(800) 327-8246
www.dartagnan.com
Game birds, including
    partridge

Dean & Deluca
2526 East 36th Street,
    North Circle
Wichita, Kansas 67219
(877) 826-7246
www.dean-deluca.com
Oils, vinegars, spices,
    condiments, hot sauces,
    and the like

El Paso Chile Company
909 Texas Avenue
El Paso, Texas 79901
(888) 472-5727
www.elpasochile.com
Texan and Southwestern
    ingredients

Frieda's
4465 Corporate Center Drive
Los Alamitos, California
    90720
(800) 241-1771
www.friedas.com
Exotic produce

Legal Sea Foods
33 Everett Street
Boston, Massachusetts
    02134-1993
(800) 343-5804
www.sendlegal.com
Seafood

Marché aux Delices
P.O. Box 1164
New York, New York 10028
(888) 547-5471
www.auxdelices.com
Truffles and exotic
    mushrooms

Melissa's
P.O. Box 21127
Los Angeles, California
90021
(800) 588-0151
www.melissas.com
Exotic produce

Mo Hotta-Mo Betta
P.O. Box 4136
San Luis Obispo, California
93403
(800) 462-3220
www.mohotta.com
Hot sauces and spicy
ingredients

Nueske's Hillcrest Farm
Rural Route #2, P.O. Box D
Wittenberg, Wisconsin
54499
(800) 392-2266
www.nueske.com
Bacon, ham, other meats,
and poultry

Pendery's
1221 Manufacturing Street
Dallas, Texas 75027
(800) 533-1870
www.penderys.com
Chiles and spices

Penzeys Spices
P.O. Box 933
Muskego, Wisconsin
53150
(800) 741-7787
www.penzeys.com
Spices

Peppers
4453 Highway 1
Rehoboth, Delaware
19971
(800) 998-3473
www.peppers.com
Hot and spicy ingredients

The Spice House
1031 North Old World Third
Street
Milwaukee, Wisconsin
53203
(414) 272-0977
www.thespicehouse.com
Spices

Vann's Spices
6105 Oakleaf Avenue
Baltimore, Maryland 21215
(800) 583-1693
Spices

Ethnic

Anzen Japanese Foods and
Imports
736 Northeast Martin Luther
King, Jr. Boulevard
Portland, Oregon 97232
(503) 233-5111
Japanese ingredients

Haji Baba Middle Eastern
Food
1513 East Apache Boulevard
Tempe, Arizona 85281
(480) 894-1905
Middle and Near Eastern
ingredients

India Spice and Gift Shop
3295 Fairfield Avenue
Bridgeport, Connecticut
    06605
(203) 384-0666
Indian ingredients

Jamaica Groceries &
    Spices
9587 S.W. 160th Street
Miami, Florida 33157
(305) 252-1197
West Indian ingredients

The Oriental Pantry
423 Great Road
Acton, Massachusetts
    01720
(978) 264-4576
www.orientalpantry.com
Asian ingredients

Oriental Pastry and Grocery
170 Atlantic Avenue
Brooklyn, New York
    11201
(718) 875-7687
Asian ingredients

Patel Brothers
18636 South Pioneer
    Boulevard
Artesia, California 90701
(562) 402-2953
Indian ingredients

Yekta Middle Eastern
    Grocery
1488 Rockville Pike
Rockville, Maryland 20852
(301) 984-1190
Middle and Near Eastern
    ingredients

CONVERSION TABLES

WEIGHT CONVERSIONS

U.S.	METRIC	U.S.	METRIC
1/2 oz	15 g	7 oz	200 g
1 oz	30 g	8 oz	250 g
1 1/2 oz	45 g	9 oz	275 g
2 oz	60 g	10 oz	300 g
2 1/2 oz	75 g	11 oz	325 g
3 oz	90 g	12 oz	350 g
3 1/2 oz	100 g	13 oz	375 g
4 oz	125 g	14 oz	400 g
5 oz	150 g	15 oz	450 g
6 oz	175 g	1 lb	500 g

APPROXIMATE EQUIVALENTS

1 STICK BUTTER = 8 tbs = 4 oz = 1/2 cup

1 CUP ALL-PURPOSE PRESIFTED FLOUR OR DRIED BREAD CRUMBS = 5 oz

1 CUP GRANULATED SUGAR = 8 oz

1 CUP (PACKED) BROWN SUGAR = 6 oz

1 CUP CONFECTIONERS' SUGAR = 4 1/2 oz

1 CUP HONEY OR SYRUP = 12 oz

1 CUP GRATED CHEESE = 4 oz

1 CUP DRIED BEANS = 6 oz

1 LARGE EGG = about 2 oz = about 3 tbs

1 EGG YOLK = about 1 tbs

1 EGG WHITE = about 2 tbs

Please note that all conversions are approximate but close enough to be useful when converting from one system to another.

LIQUID CONVERSIONS

U.S.	IMPERIAL	METRIC
2 tbs	1 fl oz	30 ml
3 tbs	1½ fl oz	45 ml
¼ cup	2 fl oz	60 ml
⅓ cup	2½ fl oz	75 ml
⅓ cup + 1 tbs	3 fl oz	90 ml
⅓ cup + 2 tbs	3½ fl oz	100 ml
½ cup	4 fl oz	125 ml
⅔ cup	5 fl oz	150 ml
¾ cup	6 fl oz	175 ml
¾ cup + 2 tbs	7 fl oz	200 ml
1 cup	8 fl oz	250 ml
1 cup + 2 tbs	9 fl oz	275 ml
1¼ cups	10 fl oz	300 ml
1⅓ cups	11 fl oz	325 ml
1½ cups	12 fl oz	350 ml
1⅔ cups	13 fl oz	375 ml
1¾ cups	14 fl oz	400 ml
1¾ cups + 2 tbs	15 fl oz	450 ml
2 cups (1 pint)	16 fl oz	500 ml
2½ cups	20 fl oz (1 pint)	600 ml
3¾ cups	1½ pints	900 ml
4 cups	1¾ pints	1 liter

OVEN TEMPERATURES

FAHRENHEIT	GAS MARK	CELSIUS	FAHRENHEIT	GAS MARK	CELSIUS
250	½	120	400	6	200
275	1	140	425	7	220
300	2	150	450	8	230
325	3	160	475	9	240
350	4	180	500	10	260
375	5	190			

Note: Reduce the temperature by 20°C (68°F) for fan-assisted ovens.

INDEX